BLESS ME FATHER

BLESS ME FATHER

A life story

KEVIN ROWLAND

EBURY
SPOTLIGHT

EBURY SPOTLIGHT

UK | USA | Canada | Ireland | Australia
India | New Zealand | South Africa

Ebury Spotlight is part of the Penguin Random House group of companies
whose addresses can be found at global.penguinrandomhouse.com

Penguin Random House UK
One Embassy Gardens, 8 Viaduct Gardens, London SW11 7BW

penguin.co.uk
global.penguinrandomhouse.com

First published by Ebury Spotlight in 2025

1

Typeset by seagulls.net

Printed and bound in Great Britain by Clays Ltd, Elcograf S.p.A.

The authorised representative in the EEA is Penguin Random House Ireland,
Morrison Chambers, 32 Nassau Street, Dublin D02 YH68.

A CIP catalogue record for this book is available from the British Library

ISBN 9781529958720

Penguin Random House is committed to a sustainable future
for our business, our readers and our planet. This book is
made from Forest Stewardship Council® certified paper.

I've changed a few names, other than that,
this is it – warts and all, mainly my own.

Contents

PART ONE

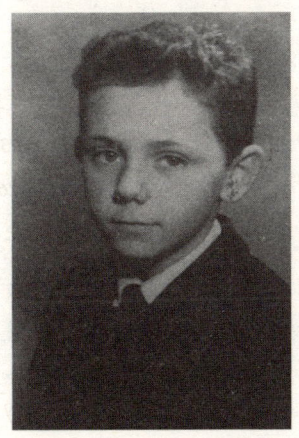

What was different about me?

I stood in wonder across the road from the cinema and watched the teenagers queue up to see the new Elvis film. The boys wore tight trousers, pointed shoes and leather jackets. Their hair was greased into quiffs, or James Dean-style.

The girls wore fantastic colourful, sometimes polka-dot dresses, over thick hoop petticoats. They had beehive, heavily lacquered hair-styles and sexy, dark eye make-up.

In those days, to me, Wolverhampton was a place of magic. This was 1961. I was born in '53.

Elvis sang: *You've gotta follow that dream wherever that dream may lead.*

I bet they're having a great time in there, smoking cigarettes, looking good, kissing their beautiful girlfriends, eating sweets, watching Elvis singing, kissing, dancing, and fighting. Everybody cheered when Elvis fought. And *these teenagers* looked great – rebellious, relaxed and cool.

Elvis sang about the man who can sing, regardless of what he has or hasn't got, being king of the world. That sentiment, and the way Elvis sang it, made perfect sense to me.

But there was a different reality for me at home.

One evening, when I was eight, we sat in the living room after dinner (tea, as we called it). Dad was sitting in his armchair when my older sister, Sarah, started a conversation.

'What do you think I'll be when I grow up, Dad?'

'You'll be a teacher,' Dad said to Sarah.

She looked happy.

'What about me, Dad?' asked my oldest brother, Pat.

'You'll be a businessman,' he said.

Pat seemed content with that answer.

I don't remember what was said to Grainne (my younger sister) or Joe (my older brother), or if they even asked the question. But I know that I did.

'What do you think I'll be, Dad?'

He paused for a few moments, became suddenly very serious, and said, 'You'll be married with a kid when you're 17.'

I didn't say anything. I pretended not to know what he meant – but I *did* know (my brother Pat had already told me how babies are made). In those days, the early sixties, when a girl got pregnant, the boy married her. Plus, Dad had a younger brother, Paddy, who had got married at 16 under those circumstances.

Was I bad, weak? What was different about me compared to the others? *There must be something wrong with me.* I felt he could see right into me.

Dad's outlook was the one that dominated our household. He was very strict and he perceived stuff like Elvis lyrics to be over-sentimental. To be clear, Dad *did* think music and singing were things to be enjoyed, but only in their place – like on birthdays, or later when we had a car and would go on a holiday. Music was not to be confused with work. That was serious. From the youngest age, my dad told me that my interests in music and clothes were wrong.

This book isn't some rock'n'roll story of how a kid with a disapproving father rebels, eventually finds his own tribe and becomes a pop singer. This is a story of someone who took what his dad said very seriously, believed it and internalised it, so that it became his reality.

I've stolen from the sweet shop

Now I'm ten years old. I'm standing in Sister Pauline's office. She's the head nun at my junior school, and I'm crying, begging her not to tell my mother that I've been caught stealing for the second time in a few weeks. The first occasion was from other kids' coat pockets in the cloakroom, and now I've stolen from the sweet shop nearest the school. I had popped in before school and a boy in another class had seen me steal a penny chew.

As we stood in line in the freezing-cold playground, waiting to go into our classrooms, Rubuski quickly put his hand up and proudly shouted, 'Please, sir. Kevin Rowland stole a penny chew from the shop!'

My heart sank as he said it. Blood rushed to my head.

'Oh no!' My world came crashing down on me.

Now I'm in trouble.

'Rowland? We'll deal with you later,' said the form teacher.

The teacher informed the head nun, and I was summoned to see her. I'd previously promised her that I wouldn't steal any more, but I couldn't seem to *not* do it.

And now they're going to tell my mum. It will break her heart. She thinks I'm good. I'm supposed to be going to boarding college to be a priest next year.

I begged her. 'Please, Sister, don't tell my mum!'

An hour earlier, the head nun had told me that I would be let off with a caning. But now she's called me back again to tell me that she's changed her mind – she's going to tell my mum, after all.

'Please, please, Sister. Please, Sister, don't tell my mum.'

The church was sacrosanct

I had started stealing at the age of seven.

I pleaded with my mum, on that lovely warm summer evening, to let me go out with 'the boys' – my older brothers Pat, aged 13, and Joe, 11, plus all of their mates – Pat's gang. Mum stood on the front doorstep, while Pat and the boys were congregating outside the front gate. More boys seemed to arrive every minute, until there were about ten of them, mostly aged between 11 and 13.

Mum had curly black hair, soft tanned skin and kind, blue eyes. I had been pestering and begging her, but to no avail. Pat was joining in. 'Come on, Mum. Let him come with us.' She kept saying, 'No, he's too young!'

I went back inside the house and looked in the mirror. I saw that I looked scruffy. I washed my face, brushed my hair, came back out and tried again: 'Mum, please let me go!' This time, she smiled and said, 'OK.'

I don't know if Mum was touched because she'd noticed I had smartened myself up, or if she just had a change of heart, but I was allowed to go.

As we walked down the hill of the old terraced houses on Park Street South, I felt a wave of freedom come over me. I was out with 'the boys'!

All the local kids respected and looked up to my brothers. They brought excitement wherever they went. And Pat Rowland was the leader. He was like Elvis – good-looking, charming, bright-eyed, with the warmest smile. I didn't just look up to him. I worshipped him!

We passed through what everyone called 'the old buildings' – derelict houses due for demolition. Joe, older brother number two, ran into a house that was already half falling down. A minute later, he emerged barefoot, wearing a battered straw hat, a check shirt and scruffy trousers rolled up to his calves. He had a tobacco pipe in his mouth. I watched in awe as one of the boys lit it for him.

'Call me Huck!' Joe shouted to everyone (after Huckleberry Finn). Pat, and some of the other boys, were now lighting up cigarettes.

Wow! This was exciting!

We were walking with purpose now, and Pat was giving instructions on which shops should be targeted and the strategy we should employ. Before long, we stopped outside a small corner shop on the Dudley Road.

'Mahoney and Mac, you two keep 'em talking,' Pat said. 'The rest of ya, grab anything. It don't matter what it is, just fucking grab it! OK?'

'OK, Pat,' we all said.

We piled in. The boys split up, moving into different alcoves and corners of the shop. I noticed a big display of Pal, a popular dog food at the time, so I grabbed a small tin and just about managed to squeeze it into the front pocket of my summer shorts, though the shape of the tin was visible behind the fabric. Almost immediately, I heard a voice from behind the counter.

'Cum 'ere, yow!'

I walked towards her. She was a fat middle-aged lady. Her thin husband stood dutifully beside her.

'Empty out yur pockits!'

I took out the tin.

'Pur' it on tha countah!'

I did.

'Where do yow live?'

'127 Park Street South.' My mother had just taught me to memorise my address, in case I got lost.

'Roight, I'll be round to see yower mutha tonoight.'

We trailed out. Pat's mates all started chastising me.

'You stoopid bastard! Watcha give her the right address for?'

It hadn't even occurred to me to give a false one.

6

'And watcha nick dog meat for?' Pat said. 'We haven't even got a fuckin' dog!'

'You said, grab *anything*!'

Mercifully, the shopkeeper didn't visit our house.

Empty-handed, we made for the boys' den. It was way into the derelict buildings, and very difficult for any outsiders to find. It was packed with the proceeds of previous endeavours. The boys didn't just have *packets* of crisps; they had cardboard *boxes* full of crisps. They didn't just have *bottles* of sweet fizzy pop; they had *crates* of it!

I soon came to understand that Joe was by far the most fearless of the gang. As the rest of us gorged ourselves on crisps and pop, he stood up, looked around at us all, and with an air of authority said, 'This is kids' stuff. When I grow up, I'm gonna rob banks!'

Wow. That sounded great! Robbing banks, just like the cowboys in the films.

. . .

Joe was the type of boy who would do anything. And I mean *anything*. At the end of the school day, he would often take me home. One night, as we walked through Snow Hill, a busy street in the centre of Wolverhampton, he decided he needed a piss. He saw no need to find anywhere quiet to relieve himself, or to return to the school, which was only a hundred yards away. He didn't even see the need to stop walking. He just took out his cock and pointed it upwards so that the urine shot high up into the air like a fountain, and pissed as he walked.

A middle-aged lady sneered as she walked past us. 'You dirty dog!'

'Ah fuck off, you old cow!' Joe shouted at her.

On another occasion, he insisted we both stood outside a newsagent's for what seemed to me like eternity. I didn't understand what was going on. Then I realised Joe was waiting for the owner to go into the living area at the rear. As soon as she had, he got down on his knees and reached his hand up to the door handle. Ever so quietly and slowly, he opened the door without fully engaging the noisy bell that was attached to the top of the door. He then crawled across the shop floor over to the counter, reached up and calmly took down a John Wayne cowboy annual he'd been coveting since a previous recce. Just as silently, he crawled back across the floor and out of the shop.

The book would have cost seven shillings and sixpence, a lot of money to us in those days. Joe loved John Wayne and he happily studied the pictures as we walked home.

. . .

Older brother number one, Pat, was a kind boy. My dad worked long hours and Mum had lots to do with running a house for five kids, so in the school holidays and weekends, Pat was like a guardian to us.

He loved musical films and took Joe and me to see *Carousel*, *Oklahoma!* and *Calamity Jane*, among others. Pat's passion for 1940s and 50s musicals was unusual for a boy of his age at that time. Some of his mates would tease him, attempting the dance moves as they mocked, saying, 'One minute they're talking to each other, the next minute they're singing and dancing!'

'Fuck off!' Pat said. He liked what he liked and wasn't easily swayed by others.

He took me to a funfair one time. Mum had given him two shillings, enough for four or five rides between us. He kept paying for me to go on rides but didn't go on any himself. After a while, I spoke up. 'Pat, why don't *you* go on any?'

With a big smile on his face, he said, 'I'm just really enjoying watching you going on them.' He was like that.

Pat and one or two of his mates would occasionally take me into the town centre and send me up to women. I'd tell them, through fake tears, that I'd lost my bus fare home and that I lived in Bridgnorth, a good few miles from Wolverhampton. Pat and his mates kept the money. I didn't mind. I enjoyed being with them.

. . .

At around seven o' clock every evening, Dad would walk down the hill from the bus stop, his khaki sackcloth sandwich bag over his shoulder, smiling and happy to be coming home. He was a carpenter. The bag smelled of sandwiches and he smelled of sawdust. My sister Sarah, two years older than me, would usually run up to meet him.

My dad seemed an incredibly strong and powerful man. I can remember him smiling and laughing much more in those days. I was still getting to know him at that time – when I was between the ages of one and four, Mum and the rest of us had been in Ireland, while Dad worked in England. The family had previously been living in Coventry, where my three older siblings were born, and Dad had started his own building business shortly before my birth. But he was inexperienced, and when he lost everything, including our house, Mum, Pat, Joe, Sarah and myself, aged one, moved over to Ireland to stay at my dad's family's small farm near Crossmolina in County Mayo, where my younger sister Grainne was born. Dad, meanwhile, stayed in England – working and sending money home to Mum, which she saved for a deposit on a house. Arrangements like this were not uncommon among the Irish at the time.

Dad was in England on his own for three years, mostly staying at Mum's brother Mick's house. The last two of those three years, we spent in a small council house on the outskirts of Crossmolina. Dad would visit us from England. They were difficult times for Mum and Dad, but as children, we didn't notice any hardship. We had everything we needed.

A couple of months before my fifth birthday, we moved back to Wolverhampton and into our house on Park Street South, Blakenhall. It was dark, dense and industrial and very different to the fields around Crossmolina. When he first arrived, from Ireland, Dad had started off as a labourer, lining up outside building sites, hoping to be picked for a day's work. But now, he was a carpenter for a big building company – Tarmac.

In those days, I can remember doing maths homework and telling Dad, 'Four and four is nine, right?'

'Not when *I* went to school,' he said.

I thought that was hilarious.

. . .

There was a wealthy area close to where we lived called Goldthorn Hill. The houses were big and the streets were wide, tree-lined and well cared for. Joe suggested he and I go up there and 'get a bike'.

It was a lovely summer's day as we walked up the hill, past the beautifully manicured gardens, until we spotted two kids' bikes strewn across the drive of a big expensive-looking house.

'OK, Kev, let's go.' Joe picked up the bigger of the two bikes. 'Quick! Get on the crossbar!'

As we rode off, Joe said he thought someone from inside the house might have seen us. We sped down the hill like crazy, singing at the top of our voices.

I wah, wah, wah, wah, wonder, why, she ran away, my little runaway

A speeding car overtook us and pulled up directly in our path. We had to stop. Two boys jumped out, then the father. He was a bald posh guy.

'Right, let's have the bicycle,' he said.

We got off it and the man put it into the back of his estate car.

The older of the two boys started angrily shouting at Joe. 'If you want a bike, you should jolly well ask your father to buy you one!'

Joe shouted back. 'We're poor. We're not like you. Our dad can't afford bikes like your dad can!'

'Come on,' the man said to his boys quietly, ushering them into the car.

I loved Joe's passionate honesty and sense of justice, but I had never thought of us as poor. I thought poor meant starving. But Joe saw the stealing in Robin Hood terms – taking from the rich.

Dad was putting a lot pressure on Joe to pass his 11-plus, the grammar school entrance exam. It seemed to be *the* constant theme in the house. Education was Dad's number-one obsession.

At my age, seven, the word 'exam' just sounded funny: 'egg-zam'. I thought of it in terms of a giant egg that Joe had to get past.

Dad had been shouting at Joe about the importance of passing. Afterwards, Joe left the room. I followed him to the front of the house, where he was standing alone. As I walked through the door, I said jokingly, 'Joe, haven't you walked past that giant egg yet?'

But Joe wasn't laughing – he was upset. His hand was up to his mouth. He was breathing very quickly and frowning. I hadn't seen anything like that before and I felt bad for having made the joke. Joe didn't pass the 11-plus.

. . .

Our family were strict Catholics and I'd started serving on the altar, assisting the priests in performing Mass, from the unusually young age of seven. I'd begged Mum and the priests to let me get involved. Soon I was with Joe and the other altar boys for a weekly training session, and within a few weeks, I was wearing all the gear – a black, full-length cassock, a dress-like garment with buttons from top to bottom, and a white cotta, a cotton and lace raglan-sleeved overshirt – and serving regularly on the altar. With the pleasant smells of incense and burning candle wax, coupled with the genuine feeling of spirituality I sometimes experienced, I liked it. But the thing I loved most was the fact that my mum was sitting in the congregation, watching and feeling proud of me.

I believed wholeheartedly in God, and I felt sorry for non-Catholics, which was how I had been taught in school.

When the news came that I would soon be making my First Holy Communion, I was excited; God was to enter my soul. But first, it needed to be cleansed. The priest stressed that the process of confession was sacred – whatever was said between a priest and penitent in confession must remain secret and could not be repeated by the priest under any circumstances, even if the penitent had confessed to a murder. I loved the seriousness and importance of it. And I was so happy that I would be absolved of all my sins.

My first confession was with Father Burke. He was a close friend of the family, in that he was my Uncle Anthony's pal through their priest college years and beyond; Uncle Anthony was my mum's brother and also a priest. Father Burke was young and friendly, and I quite liked him, but I was disturbed by the way he shouted at Joe during altar practice.

I told Father Burke all the sins I could think of. The one I remember most is, 'I stole biscuits from the tin at home.' I left feeling cleansed and pure.

In those days it was commonplace for the local priest to call around to the parishioners' homes unannounced. It was considered a privilege. Father Burke called round one evening and he sat in the living room, chatting with my parents and siblings after I went up to bed.

The next morning when I came down for breakfast, Mum said to me in a jokey tone, 'We had a good laugh last night. Father Burke was telling us how you confessed to stealing the biscuits out of the tin.'

'What? He told you what I said in confession? I thought it was supposed to be secret?'

'Ah, it was only a few biscuits,' Mum said.

Obviously, the biscuits weren't the point! I was confused. I had thought this stuff was deadly serious. But I was far too young, at seven, to have a debate with anyone, or even a discussion about the rights and wrongs of the Catholic Church. It was a closed door, and holding on to any doubts about Father Burke or the church, or thinking that they were at fault in some way, was a non-starter in our house. The church was sacrosanct and beyond any kind of criticism or even questioning.

I ignored my experience and pushed it to the back of my mind. Ignoring my truths would be something I'd have a lot of practice at.

· · ·

Punishment-wise, Dad would hit the boy children, but not the girls. It was called 'the belt'.

My first experience of it came shortly after my eighth birthday. I had accidentally broken a banister on the stairs while we were playing.

12

'You're gonna get the belt tonight,' one of my siblings said. And I did.

My brother Joe was aggrieved that I'd been hit so soon after my birthday. 'He shouldn'ta hit you two days after your birthday, Kev!' Joe said in his Irish accent. Personally, I was mostly upset because the belting on my legs had damaged the paper trousers of my birthday present: a Davy Crockett outfit.

That night, Joe said we should run away. I wasn't sure if I wanted to, or if Joe was serious, but I agreed. Very early the next morning, Joe woke me. We quietly got dressed – Joe in his grey shirt, multi-coloured V-neck slipover and grey shorts, with his big mop of blond curly hair; me with my blue sweatshirt, blue shorts and brown sandals. We gently sneaked out of the house and made our way to the centre of Wolverhampton. It was early morning, maybe 5am. The streets were deserted as we hit the usually busy Snow Hill. Through the early-morning mist, Joe saw a policeman walking towards us.

'Come on, Kev – run!'

'Hang on, Joe, I just wanna see if he's got a 'tache,' I said, for some unknown reason.

'What? Come on, Kev. Run!'

'Hang on, Joe. Just let me see if he's got a 'tache.'

I guess, deep down, I must have been too scared to run away.

The policeman came up and asked us what we were doing out so early. Joe told him we were on a 'cross-country run'. Naturally, the copper didn't believe it; we were marched down to a police box at the bottom of the street, where he called for transport. A squad car appeared a few minutes later, and we were driven home by two policemen.

'I found these two wandering around town,' one of them said to our mum.

'We went for a run, Mum,' Joe said.

Now as I recall this, I wish I hadn't stopped to see if the copper had a 'tache. I wish I'd gone with Joe. I don't think we would have got very far, but I think if Mum and Dad had known that we'd actually ran away, they would have been shocked and it might have induced some reflection on their part about how strict Dad was, which may have meant a softening that could have been beneficial to Joe and me.

. . .

Sam Cooke was singing about Cupid drawing back his bow. He was singing about another world. One that clearly existed, somewhere far, far away. It sounded romantic, exciting and beautiful.

Pat had a little transistor radio. I would lie under the blankets after my dad had turned out the light on a Sunday night, holding the radio close to my ear, listening to Radio Luxembourg, eagerly awaiting the week's new releases. I'd try to memorise the melodies and lyrics. Then all I had to do was keep awake till Pat came in from the youth club, so I could sing them to him.

As well as music, Pat loved boxing.

'You're gonna be the heavyweight boxing champion of the world,' he told me. He would buy *The Ring* magazine, and we would look at pictures of Floyd Patterson and Sonny Liston. Mum and Dad bought me a punchball for Christmas, and we trained hard. Pat would arrange informal fights for me with the local kids. He put a chart on my wall, ticking off whenever I beat a new opponent. The chart was all ticks. I had beaten all the other eight-year-olds in the street, as well as a nine-year-old.

Then one Saturday morning, as we walked home from weekly confession, we passed through the old buildings and saw an Indian kid coming towards us. The Indians and Afro-Caribbeans had recently arrived in the area and there were some tensions. We decided this Indian boy would be my next opponent. He was bigger and clearly older. That didn't bother me; bolstered by Pat's encouragement, I felt invincible.

''Ow old am ya, mate?' I said.

'Eleven,' he replied.

Great, I thought. *I'm going to do an 11-year-old.*

'Wanna foight?'

'Yeah, all right.'

I wasn't invincible. The boy gave me a proper pasting, and I went home with a bloody nose.

. . .

I loved the run-down terraced houses of Wolverhampton, the dark, decrepit, derelict buildings, the cheap posters on the walls advertising bands, the old cinema on the Dudley Road that had closed but still had the remains of a *Zorro* poster on its wall. I wondered what the film was like and if I'd ever see it.

I liked to watch the teenage boys sporting their quiffs and tight trousers, fags hanging out of their mouths. And I loved their neatly combed hair.

Dad had what I believe was a neurotic obsession with steering us away or *protecting* us – particularly me – from these things. He told me that I combed my hair too often.

As well as my own hair, I was also interested in other people's. I would stand behind Dad's armchair and comb his hair, which I think he just about tolerated. I got the impression that Dad thought my interests were sissy-ish. That caused confusion and later turmoil in me.

In 2010, during a relaxed conversation, I asked Dad why he told me that my interest in music and clothes was wrong. He said those were the things factory boys were interested in, and he was concerned I would become one. My intuition also told me that he had a concern about my sexuality. But I can't be sure.

. . .

Mum rarely dressed up – but when she did, boy!

She was a hard worker, taking care of five kids without such conveniences as washing machines or dishwashers, and she was houseproud and would hardly ever stop and rest. In those days she smoked cigarettes and would often have an un-tipped Senior Service hanging from her mouth as she ironed our clothes. I loved the smell of those fags.

Although she *owned* nice clothes, she would only wear her very oldest stuff for 'around the house', as she called it, and of course she always seemed to be 'around the house'.

The same philosophy was applied to her crockery, or 'Delft', as she called it. She had three sets: one that we would use every day, then a better set that would be brought out when visitors came, and also a third set (the very best) that was given pride of place in the cabinet but never used.

On the rare occasions she did go out, she would wear lovely tailored tweed skirt suits, with a white lace blouse that would highlight all her natural colouring. One of my mates said, 'Your mum is so pretty!' He was right – she had the kindest, brightest eyes. If we were in town and my face got dirty, she would pull out a clean hanky, wet it with her tongue and clean my face. I loved that.

My sisters and I went into my mum's wardrobe one day and put on some of Mum's clothes. We all came down to show her. I was wearing one of Mum's dresses, which was of course way too big for me, as well as one of her hats. Mum didn't object to my sisters wearing her clothes, but she clearly wasn't happy that I was wearing them too. I don't remember her exact words but I got the strong impression from Mum that she disapproved.

· · ·

I couldn't seem to second-guess my parents over what would be allowed and what wouldn't. Nor was I skilled in asking for their permission at the right time and in the right way, like some of my siblings were. I seemed to always pick the wrong moment.

A friend and I bunked in to see a film, *The Quiet Man*. I'd told Mum I was going to the park. When we came out of the cinema, it was dark. My parents quizzed me on my return.

'Where have you been?'

'To the park.'

'No, you haven't. It's been dark for an hour. Where have you been?'

'To the park!'

'Come on. The truth.'

After much toing and froing, finally I said, 'OK, I went to the pictures.'

'What to see?'

'*The Quiet Man.*'

'Well, why didn't you tell us? We'd have let you go and see *that* film!' I couldn't work them out. *The Quiet Man* was a film that was set in the west of Ireland close to where my parents were from and held sentimental value for them.

A singing priest

Now it's my last year of junior school, and some big changes are happening. Over a very short period of time, maybe three months, my brother Joe loses pretty much all of his confidence. He goes from being the most daring and wild boy in the school, to being the most shy, stuttering and withdrawn. He begins to walk with his head down and no longer speaks to anybody unless they first speak to him. It isn't that he doesn't want to speak to people, he just thinks they won't want to speak to *him*. As to why that happened, I don't know.

The other thing that happened was that it became my turn to get the pressure from Dad about the impending 11-plus exam. The pressure seemed even more intense than what Joe had gone through a few years earlier. It was an unceasing bombardment.

Dad would go on and on at me, raising his voice and ranting about how I *must* pass this exam. He was accusing me of being lazy, but I was doing all the work the teachers set. I didn't know what I could do differently. I was good at English and OK at other subjects. There didn't seem any way of getting Dad off my back. This exam was presented as a matter of life-or-death importance. If I didn't get into the grammar school, it was the end of the world as far as Dad was concerned. From my point of view, the secondary modern school where most of my mates would be going, and where Pat and Joe went, looked attractive and relaxed.

There was no encouragement in Dad's approach. It was all pressure. And it was far too much for me. In desperation one day, I said, 'OK, I'll pass it!'

Of course, I had no idea if I *could*.

Dad didn't believe me, and sneered, '*You're* not going to pass it!' I felt that I just couldn't win.

I don't doubt that it's possible I had a problem with concentration before Dad started applying this pressure, but I know for sure it got way worse after that. Schoolwork didn't feel like it was even remotely for me; it was all about what Dad wanted. Any joy I had felt from learning disappeared. I had no interest whatsoever in passing the 11-plus, except to get Dad off my back.

I couldn't seem to make my writing neat or keep my page clean, like a lot of the other kids could. It would start off neat, but I didn't seem to be able to keep it that way. Another reason for my scruffy handwriting was that I had started off writing with my left hand, but was discouraged from doing so by the teacher, and ended up writing uncomfortably with my right hand, which has continued to this day.

When the teacher started talking about long division, I had absolutely no idea what she was talking about. I pretended that I did. From the age of ten onwards, I didn't progress at maths at all. I would just sit in the classes, hoping not to be singled out. To this day, I have no idea how to do long division, long multiplication or most other mathematic equations.

· · ·

Dad bought a car, and on summer Sunday afternoons, we would all go to Cannock Chase, an area of natural beauty on the outskirts of Wolverhampton. There were lots of families and couples there, and most would have their transistor radios tuned to the BBC Light Programme, the forerunner of Radio 1. We'd listen to *Pick of the Pops*, the weekly chart show hosted by Alan Freeman. I loved to hear all the hits and watch the young couples lying down and snogging.

'Diamonds' by Jet Harris and Tony Meehan would ring out of every transistor radio, sounding full of mystery and romance.

There was a Welsh kid in my class at school, called Nathan. He was only there for about three months, but I loved every moment with him. He was almost a year older than me, and he was music mad and knew the words to all the hit songs. He had a lovely voice. At every opportunity, Nathan and I and maybe another kid would sit together and sing songs in the corner of the playground or in an alleyway. Then, if the teacher called for a performance during class, no problem – I'd comb my hair, walk up to the front of the class and happily sing any current chart hits or songs from musicals I'd seen with Pat and Joe. Singing was effortless and a joy to me. I couldn't understand why some people found it difficult.

My plan at that time was to be like Pat and Joe – a teenager – and do all the exciting things they did. Then later I would be a pop singer or a guitarist. That plan seemed perfectly achievable.

I would look fondly at the musical instruments in the shop across the road. That Christmas, when I was ten, Mum finally bought me a guitar. I was delighted. I'd been pestering her for ages. It was an acoustic, with four strings.

She sent me for lessons to a man about a mile away from where we lived. His name was Honer Johnson. I'd walk there on Sunday afternoons, where there would be about half a dozen teenage boys, all playing away. The Beatles were just becoming massively popular and there was a big upsurge in people wanting to learn guitar and join bands. Every now and then, Honer would give one of us a scale or a chord sequence to learn. We would go into a corner of the room and practise it, making sure we understood the part before leaving. I was by far the youngest there and loved the feeling of being around the cool-looking teenage boys.

The lessons were very informal. Each of us might be there for as long as two hours, and then just before we left, we would give Honer our six shillings, which was a lot of money.

Honer said my four-stringed guitar wasn't really suitable, and suggested I got a new one. He taught me to play the melody of 'An English Country Garden'. And I just about learned a couple of scales, but I didn't pick up any more. By this time, the guitar had become like maths – a mountain to climb – and I found I couldn't focus long enough to learn. If the condition had been understood in those days, I know that I would have been diagnosed with attention-deficit disorder.

. . .

The church was a big part of our lives and it wasn't unusual for me to serve two Masses on a Sunday, often at different churches. Joe and I would finish serving at St Teresa's in Parkfields (our parish church) and then walk or get a bus a couple of miles into the centre of Wolverhampton to serve a Mass at St Mary and St John's. We would also quite often serve a couple of Masses during the week before school.

At one Sunday Mass, they passed around leaflets that talked about a 'vocation'. It was referred to as 'the calling'. Every boy was directed to ask himself if he had 'the calling' from God to be a priest.

I asked Mum what happens if you want to be a priest.

'Well, at 11, you go off to Cotton College. It's a boarding school,' she said.

That sounded exciting! My Uncle Anthony and Father Burke had gone there. I knelt in prayer and convinced myself that I was being 'called'.

I told my parents that I had the calling. Mum arranged for me to go and see the parish priest. He started to give me Latin lessons every Saturday morning at his house, in preparation for my years at Cotton College. Mum and I were also summoned to Birmingham to meet the bishop and to sit my entrance exam. It seemed to have gone well.

Of course, I'd already long decided I wanted to be a musician. And though I truly *did* enjoy the feeling of spirituality that I got sometimes from serving on the altar, or praying in church, I was aware that priests were celibate, and I knew even at that pre-pubescent age that I liked the warmth of girls and didn't want to cut myself off from them. Also, a male schoolfriend and I would sometimes kiss in the playground, much to the amusement of the other kids.

But at ten years old, the thought that I'd have to be a priest at the end of the college years seemed like an eternity away, and the boarding school itself seemed like fun, whereas our house felt like a pressure cooker.

There was a record in the charts at the time called 'Dominique', by the Singing Nun. I asked my mum if I could be a singing priest.

I *was* genuinely torn. But the fact that Mum was proud of her 'religious' son was a massive factor in my decision, too. I wanted to make her happy. Sometimes when I would hear her coming up the stairs in the morning, I'd quickly kneel so that when she walked in, she would see me praying.

But I was leading a double life. At home, I was a trainee priest and a good, prayerful altar boy. Elsewhere, I was compulsively thieving, lying, fighting, flirting with the girls and causing trouble. I was using the 'fuck' and 'cunt' words all the time with my mates. I was aware of my swearing and had tried to stop it, but was unable to. I was getting in a lot of trouble at school, and had a reputation as the naughtiest kid in the class, or at least in the top three.

Anybody who misbehaved would have to report to Mr Potts' room after school for a caning. I seemed to end up there every single evening. I talked incessantly during lessons, played tricks, told jokes, talked about music, distracted other kids, passed love letters, or hummed, much to the annoyance of the teachers.

There was a tune in the charts called 'Just like Eddie', by Heinz. It was a great song and had a catchy hummed hook line: 'Mm mm mm mm mm mm mm mm mmmmm.'

A couple of us would sit at the back of the class, and every time the teacher turned her head to face the blackboard, we'd start humming the tune, very softly, just loud enough that she could only vaguely hear it. At first, she would wonder if she was imagining it, turning her ear to listen.

To me, this situation was hilarious, and I couldn't control my laughter. She soon realised who the culprits were, and we were in line for another caning.

Mr Potts (the cane king) was a big man and had an air of military-style, superior contentment about him. Prior to dishing out his punishment, he'd pace up and down the room, John Wayne-like, holding the cane horizontally across his chest, and bending it into an upside-down U shape to gain more flexibility. Simultaneously, he would be speaking to us about our wrongdoings in loud, slow and pronounced statements. 'Rowland, Rossi, O'Brien, Atkins' – the usual culprits – 'you are in trouble, again!' He seemed to relish the build-up as much as the caning itself.

My sister Grainne, 20 months my junior, was in a different class at the same junior school and it was my responsibility to take her home each day. As she was younger, her class was let out slightly earlier than mine, so she would come to my classroom and wait outside for me. One day, with no intention of humour or irony, she said to me, 'Instead of coming to your classroom at the end of the day, I should go to Mr Potts' room, because that's where you always seem to be.'

'He'll always be a thief'

But now my two worlds are colliding and I have to tell Mum that the head nun wants her to go up to the school. The next 48 hours are a blur, but I remember the feeling of dread and horror. I also recall it was a Friday when Mum was summoned up to the school to be told by the head nun about my stealing. Instead of telling Mum the truth about why the nun wanted to see her, I just said:

'Sister Pauline wants to see you.'

'What for?'

'I don't know.'

I was trying to buy time.

My form teacher, another nun, Sister Mary Austin, had sobbed inconsolably, while looking at me with a mixture of scorn and terrible disappointment.

I was *bad*, and I was going to Hell.

When I got home that night, Mum too was very tearful and upset. She relayed to me that the head nun had told her, 'He'll never be any good – he'll always be a thief.'

I suspect because I was going to a Cubs' event the next day, Saturday, in my short trousers, I didn't get dealt with by Dad that evening.

The Saturday-night family meal was sausages and mash. Normally, I would have enjoyed that dinner, but not that evening. I knew I was *for* it. I'd been pretending to myself that everything was OK and even tried to keep the jovial vibe going throughout the dinner. As we finished the food, the talk turned to my theft. Dad got angry.

'You're no more of a priest than my arse,' he said.

He was right.

'The rest of you, go out of the room. You wait here, Kevin.' I got it.

It was decided between the school and my parents that I would go back into the shop I had stolen the penny chew from, and tell them what I'd done – own up and give them the penny back.

That Monday morning, I walked into the shop, almost sick with fear. I planned to go up to the woman and tell her that I'd stolen the chew and was here to pay for it. But somehow, I couldn't do it.

I secretly dropped a penny in the tray where the chews were kept and walked out of the shop.

When I was asked about it afterwards by my parents and the head nun, I told them I had apologised and given the shopkeeper the penny. They asked what she said. I told them she said, OK. I don't know if they checked up, but I wasn't challenged about it.

I think it would have been good for me to have spoken honestly to the shopkeeper. Mainly because there was way too much secrecy and lies going on in this ten-year-old boy's head.

After having a serious talk with Mum, I resolved that I would be good, so that I wouldn't end up in Hell like some of my mates.

When I would see them doing things that would likely land them in trouble, I started to walk away, just like my mum had told me. It was hard, because my old friends (the 'bad boys') were critical of my new stance, and although I was trying to not do what they were doing, we were still half hanging around together. I didn't have any new friends. I was in no-man's land.

They didn't seem to trust me. I *wanted* to be mates with them and do all the exciting stuff, but the fear of breaking my mother's heart and going to Hell was the dominant force. It was a lot of stress.

Myself and three of the other 'bad boys' found our way into the school storeroom one lunchtime. We came across a big box of ink powder (in those days ink was delivered in powder, for the caretakers to mix with water). Giuseppe Rossi started splashing the powder around. I could see immediately that this was going to lead to big trouble and I bolted in a panic.

An hour later, one of the girls reported to Mr Potts that she had been walking through the corridor, when a gust of ink powder descended on her, soiling her nice summer dress. The ink had been thrown at her from above.

That afternoon, Mr Potts strode into our classroom and bellowed sarcastically, '*Some* boys have stolen ink powder from the storeroom and have ruined Madelaine Fielding's dress!'

Then, with a weary air of resignation, he half sighed and half shouted, 'Rowland … Rossi … O'Brien … Atkins, step this way, gentlemen!'

The other three got up and walked towards him. I stayed where I was.

'Rowland!' he said again loudly, looking away expectantly and confidently.

'No, sir,' I said.

'No, sir, what?' he shouted sarcastically.

'I wasn't there, sir.'

I felt a vague sense of pride.

A few days later, during lunch hour, the same guys (Rossi, O'Brien, Atkins and myself) wandered into the big church next door to the school. We weren't supposed to leave the playground. A brand-new public-address system had just been installed to amplify the priest's sermons. It was the first time the church had used electronic equipment, and a big deal. We went up into the pulpit. I was fascinated by the microphone. This was the closest I'd been to one. Rossi hit the switch. The red 'On' light lit up, and a big boom sounded out, letting us know that the system was ready for use. Immediately, Giuseppe started singing:

Close your eyes and I'll kiss you, tomorrow I'll miss you.

Total panic came over me, with an intensity that I hadn't ever before experienced. This was sacrilege! A pop song sung down the priest's microphone, in church! That would surely mean Hell. And I knew that my mother and the nuns would be absolutely horrified. I ran out of the church as fast as I could.

After that the lads, particularly Rossi and O'Brien, started blanking me and taking the piss out of me. I either mentioned it to my mum, though I don't remember it, or perhaps my sister told her, because shortly after, as the other kids and I were walking down from the school to the bus stop, I was surprised to see Mum walking towards us. She went straight up to O' Brien, Rossi and the others.

'I'm disappointed in you all,' she said. 'The rats desert a sinking ship!'

They tried to walk away, so as not to hear her. But she kept walking fast too.

I cringed with embarrassment at the time, but I'm touched by it now.

Shortly after, I had a disagreement with Rossi in the classroom, and it was decided that we would have a fight after school.

I had previously been pretty sure I could beat him – whenever we'd had mock fights, I always came out on top, overpowering him in some way, or punching harder, as I did with the vast majority of the kids in my class. Up to that point, I had probably been the best fighter in the gang. But now I was nervous.

As my little sister Grainne stood watching the fight, I lost, badly.

The strange thing is, six months earlier, I *know* I would have beaten him. But now, as I look back, I think the stress was making me physically as well as mentally weaker.

I started to not want to go to school. I was no longer popular and felt quite alone. I started to fake illness. My acting succeeded once or twice, but eventually my mum got wise. I remember walking out of the house one morning, getting as far as the bus stop, then thinking, *Fuck it. I can't go to school today.*

I turned back home. My mum wasn't happy when I walked back into the kitchen and pronounced myself ill. She knew I was swinging the lead and sent me back out to the bus stop.

· · ·

The way I found out that I hadn't been accepted to the priest college was odd and unpleasant.

I served Mass on the Saturday morning as usual, with my friend Graham. He had also applied to go to the college. Graham was late for Mass that day and joined Father Burke and me at the altar after the service had started. After the Mass, as we took off our cassocks and cottas, Graham happily told Father Burke that he had received his acceptance letter that morning.

Father Burke smiled and said, 'I know you have. Well done.'

'Have you heard anything about me getting in, Father?' I asked excitedly.

'No, I haven't. Why don't you go home? Maybe the letter is waiting there for you.'

I ran home. Mum was in the kitchen (the scullery, as she called it).

'Mum, did you get the letter from Cotton College about me getting in?'

'No, we haven't had a letter.'

'Ah, damn. Graham Southall got his, and he's got in!'

'Well, maybe it'll be here on Monday,' she said.

A few days later, Mum took me aside and told me I hadn't got in. I was down about it, and confused. My exam results weren't terrible at this point – only just below Graham's. And I was pretty good at spelling, better than most of the kids in the class. Also, I knew that there was a desperate shortage of priests.

I didn't put it together at the time that it must have been the stealing at school that was the deciding factor. The authorities at Cotton College would surely have written to Sister Pauline for a reference. She had told my mother that I would never be any good. Why would she tell the college anything different?

I spoke to my mum about this in the early 2000s and she said that she too was surprised that I didn't get in. But both Mum and Dad also told me that they hadn't taken my priest vocation too seriously, quite correctly, of course.

I can also now recall Father Bullen (the parish priest) getting exasperated at me for not grasping the Latin that he was trying to teach me in the Saturday-morning lessons. Graham was much better at it. So maybe I failed the exam. I was finding it harder and harder to concentrate and take in new information.

Graham went on to study at Cotton College, where he got a good education until he was 16. To my knowledge, though, he never became a priest. I ended up failing the 11-plus.

I learned Cockney very quickly

There was already talk of our family moving to London. My dad was so highly thought of at his work that in 1964 the company said they wanted to move him and the rest of us to London, to a much bigger contract, and to promote him to a site agent. It sounded exciting, but I was doubtful that it would happen. I couldn't imagine it. I'd heard Cockneys speaking on TV – they sounded funny, but good. Sister Mary Austin, my form teacher, had told us it was an awful place, that the children there never saw a blade of grass. *What's so special about seeing blades of grass?* I wondered.

That summer, 1964, we went on a family holiday to County Mayo in Ireland, where Mum and Dad were from. It was the first time we had been back to Ireland since we came over when I was four. We rented a cottage in Enniscrone, on the Sligo / Mayo border.

On the way over, we stopped off in Dublin. For some reason, just myself and my mother went to the post office in O'Connell Street, on a lovely sunny day. Mum looked pretty and brown on that day, as she always did in the summer. She showed me the bullet holes in the wall where the 1916 rebels had boarded themselves in, proclaiming an Irish Republic and an end to British rule. I was touched by it, and I could see Mum was proud of our history.

It was my first real knowledge of Ireland's past, apart from a night at a church 'social' in Wolverhampton, where my Uncle Mick and other relatives had come over from the other side of town. I remember looking around the smoke-filled, beer-bottle-strewn hall, at the many dark, sad Irish faces. There was something different about them.

The song 'Kevin Barry' came on and everyone sang along. Mum hugged me and told me, ' We're not allowed this song in England.'

'Why, Mum?'

'Because it's about what the English did to the Irish.'

I was shocked that a song could be banned. And I was excited that we were all locked away in this smoky church hall, secretly singing a rebel song.

. . .

It was a scorching-hot day in late August 1964 when all seven of us squeezed into dad's MG Magnette for the journey to north-west London. As we approached Watford, 'Things We Said Today' by the Beatles came on the radio.

Someday when we're dreaming, deep in love, not a lot to say
Then we will remember, things we said today.

It was barely audible through the interference, but the minor-sounding melody and deadpan vocal delivery seemed to perfectly fit the late-afternoon mood.

'Are we in London yet?' (I'd never been before.)

'Yeah,' Pat said, 'on the outskirts.'

I didn't believe him. It didn't look any different to Wolverhampton. I thought London would be all big buildings, but these were normal houses, with front gardens, and grass! Plenty of it!

And besides, I'd just seen a kid walking down the street wearing an orange Wolves shirt. I was convinced we were still in Wolverhampton. I found out later that we were in Watford and, at that time, Watford FC's shirt was almost identical to the Wolves top.

In five days I was due to start secondary school. I had just turned 11.

St Gregory's was a big step up from St Mary and St John's, my Wolverhampton junior school. The standard of education was higher. There were hardly any scruffy kids, and the few that *were* got hell from the others. Fortunately, Mum made sure we were always immaculately turned out, but I soon started to cop it, for other reasons.

It started in a drama class (I'd never even heard of drama previously), a few days after I'd arrived. A general election was about to

31

take place. The teacher got each of us up onto the school stage to pretend to be politicians and to give a short speech. When it was my turn, I got up and said, 'I'm the leader of the Labour Party and I will be voting Labour.'

I saw two boys sniggering and whispering to each other and I immediately realised that the Labour leader doesn't introduce himself as a Labour *voter*; he was the *leader*. The young, dark-haired, arty teacher smiled broadly at me as I progressed with the speech. I could tell that she was quite charmed by me and my accent. Just as I was finishing and about to walk off the stage, she said: 'Now, say your name and where you come from.'

I knew no other way of speaking than in my broad Wolverhampton accent: 'Moy naime is Kevin Rowland and oi' cum from Woolvuramptunn.'

The class exploded into uproar. I didn't know why. To me, it still doesn't sound funny. The teacher got angry and tried to restrain the kids, but she wasn't the disciplinarian type. They were roaring with laughter.

That sentence became a catchphrase for the whole class in the days and weeks to come. Kids would regularly walk up to me and say, 'My name is Kevin Rowland and I come from Wolverhampton,' always getting the accent completely wrong.

I should have stood up to them, but I was overwhelmed. I hadn't really experienced anything like this before. I didn't tell anyone at home about it, but I learned Cockney very quickly. I had arrived in Wolverhampton from Ireland at four years old with a broad Irish accent and had to learn Wolvo' speak. Now, within a couple of weeks of arriving in London, I had a passable London accent.

Prior to that drama-class incident, in fact only a couple of days after I'd started at the school, a nice-looking girl, possibly the prettiest and certainly the most developed in the class, sat herself next to me and made it clear she was interested in me. I was too nervous to take her up on it. As I walked away from the school that night, one of her friends ran up to me and shouted, 'Meet Mary outside St Joseph's Church at two o'clock on Saturday!'

I didn't say anything. I didn't even know where St Joseph's Church was. I had been living in London for only six days and I only knew my tube and bus journey to and from school. The rest of Wembley and Harrow and its surrounds were a mystery to me.

I'd had little girlfriends in junior school and I'd enjoyed the warmth of the romance, but at home I was still attempting to keep up the pretence of becoming a priest, certainly where my parents were concerned, and I knew that girlfriends were off limits. Plus, I'd got the clear message from Dad that any interest in girls was, along with clothes and music, frivolous and not good.

I wish now I'd had the courage to take Mary up on her offer. It might have been something positive for me.

A few months later, Mary considered me not even good enough to speak to. She had by now become the main female rebel of the class. One day when she was kicking up, the teacher pulled her from the back of the class and ordered her to sit next to me (I was sitting at the front, trying to be a good boy). She made a big, loud, vocal ordeal about having to sit next to a boy she 'didn't even like'. At the time, I felt that it was because she could see the real me – weak and undesirable. As I think about it now, standing her up on our first potential date wasn't the best of starts.

. . .

Some of my low status at school had to do with the fact that I had started people-pleasing and letting other kids shove me around. Not having long trousers was also a factor , certainly as to how I felt about myself. Towards the end of that school year, I was the only one within the four streams still wearing short trousers. Which meant that, as ours was the first year, I was the only kid in the whole *school* still wearing them. Possibly because, then as now, I was such a clothes and style lover, it was hell. It just seemed to be another example of me being different. I'd asked my parents for a pair, but it wasn't happening, and Dad didn't appreciate being asked for things too many times. My strong desire for long trousers was perceived as all part of my attraction to things that were wrong.

One of the coolest boys in the class would leave the school at lunch-time and go to the local shops and steal sweets. What he was doing seemed incredibly exciting compared with my life. He would walk into school, pockets bulging with various sweets. I was trying hard to be good, and would last for a while, but often I weakened.

It's difficult for me now to convey how serious and intense the struggle to be good felt. I saw it as life or death. I really thought a few of the boys who were stealing were going to Hell and that their mothers' hearts would be broken! I would try my best to keep away from them, just as I'd been told, but sometimes the pull was too strong. I prayed for guidance when tempted, as Mum suggested, but I didn't have the power to resist. It was like a drug. Other times I'd hang around with the good boys, hoping their ways would rub off on me – oscillating between the two groups.

One day a kind of neutral kid – neither a goody-goody nor hardened bad boy – said to me, 'I don't understand you, Rowland. One minute you're hanging around with all the hard nuts, the next minute you're with the weeds.' What he didn't understand is that I was fighting a battle within myself.

There were four streams for each year at St Gregory's Secondary Modern School. Dad, who was friendly with the school chaplain, an Irish priest (I think Dad had done some building work for his church), got me into the highest stream. It was too much for me. I was just about able to keep my head above water for the first few months (not finishing bottom of the class) but, after a while, I found it impossible to keep up with the other kids.

. . .

In early 1965, Joe was admitted into a grey, depressing, backward, mental ward at University College Hospital. He was 16 years old and his confidence hadn't returned since losing it at 14. Joe was there for about six weeks. The whole family went to visit him one Saturday afternoon.

I'll never forget what he said. 'Mum, Mum, take me out of this place!' he pleaded. 'They're putting wires on my head, and it's hurting me! Mum! Please – I'm not like these people! Please take me home, Mum. I'm not like these people, Mum! Take me home.'

The hospital had been giving Joe electric-shock treatment. That's what they did with acutely nervous people in those days. Joe came home about a week later. The shock treatment hadn't helped him at all. If anything, it had knocked his confidence and sense of wellbeing further.

As well as the massive effect on Joe himself, I believe his situation had a big effect on everyone in the family, though it was something we didn't speak about. Roles had clearly shifted. Certainly in mine and Joe's case. When we were in Wolverhampton, Joe had looked after *me* and took me to places. Now it was the opposite. When I was going over the park to play with my friends, Mum or Dad would say, 'Kevin, take Joe with ya.'

Joe was the size of a grown man, and I was a small 11-year-old. To my eternal shame, I sometimes felt awkward about that.

The other thing that's clear to me, with the benefit of hindsight, is that I lost an ally, a protector. Joe was the one who suggested we run away, after Dad had given me a belting he felt I didn't deserve. He had been looking out for me. Now there was no real barrier between Dad and me.

Sometimes Joe and I would go up to the West End on the tube, for a look around. London was new to us. One morning we got what was called a Red Rover – a one-day bus ticket that permitted travel to any part of London. As we stood in Trafalgar Square, I noticed a bus with the word 'Catford' on the front of it. I was fascinated by the names of the different areas in London. 'Joe, I wonder what Catford's like? Shall we go there?'

'OK,' Joe said.

It took ages to get to Catford and when we finally arrived, it was no different to anywhere else.

Often, we would go to football matches. On one occasion we very nearly lost each other. We were on the platform of a busy underground station, trying to board a train. It was one of those days when the train carriages were packed like sardines.

The train doors opened. Everybody pushed hard into each other's backs to try and cram their way into the carriage. Joe and I were holding hands. I got in first, pushing hard to make a space for Joe, but other people had got in front of him, meaning we had lost our hand grip. I looked around but couldn't even see him. And I couldn't get out of the train before the doors shut. I was jammed in. I quickly forced my way towards the door, and caught a glimpse of my lovely brother Joe's worried face. He was pacing on the spot. He frantically waved to me as the train pulled away.

Joe got on the next train in the same direction, and I was waiting on the platform of the next station in exactly the same spot as I had boarded. We had both figured out the right thing to do. Such a relief.

Joe has remained quiet and withdrawn, with low self-esteem.

. . .

The St Gregory's way of announcing exam results was for the teacher of each subject to read out the results directly to the whole class, starting with the top scorers and working downwards. On one particular day, the geography exam results were being read out. I had already come bottom of the class in a few other subjects that term. A pattern was emerging and the other 32 kids in the class knew it. I was hoping I hadn't done as badly in this subject.

As the teacher worked down the names from the top, the kids whose names had already been read out happily acknowledged themselves. As it got to the 22nd name, a boy, Parrot, started up a loud chant.

'ROW-LAND, ROW-LAND, ROW-LAND, ROW-LAND …'

He was quickly joined by a couple of other kids sitting nearby. The teacher continued reading out the results. Then a lot more of them joined in, until by the time the teacher got to number 28 and my name still hadn't been called, the whole class, girls and all, were shouting. It was deafening and horrible. The teacher tried to stop them, but he couldn't. He was a nice man, but he didn't have the respect of the kids. The faces of everybody in the class were all turned on me. 'ROW-LAND, ROW-LAND.' I felt the blood rushing to my head. I managed somehow to hold back the tears.

I didn't tell anyone at home about this. I believed I would just be blamed for it.

I used to fantasise about how my life would be if I were in a lower stream and not living under this stress. The kids in the lower classes looked cool and relaxed and a lot of them wore nice clothes.

During a conversation with Dad in the late 1990s, I learned from him that both the headmaster and my class teacher very much wanted to transfer me down from the top class to a lower stream, but the chaplain, at the behest of my dad, had persuaded them to keep me in the top class. This conversation was the first I'd heard of it.

Dad told me in a way that made it clear he felt he had done me a favour, putting himself out under difficult circumstances for this no-hoper: 'If it wasn't for me you'd have been in a lower stream! They wanted you in a lower class but I insisted you stay in the top class and the priest helped me.'

Shit! My school life could have been so much easier! I felt so frustrated, knowing that it didn't have to be that way.

In the same conversation, Dad told me that I didn't do well at school because I was lazy. That was rubbish. I wasn't lazy. I was overwhelmed, stifled and demotivated.

· · ·

I'd heard about Margaret Helen before I'd seen her. All the kids in the local park had talked about her. Her family's garden backed onto the park. Her younger brother Paul and I played football together. We'd call him 'the Yank' because although the family were Irish, they had spent a couple of years in America. I'd stopped one of the bigger boys from hitting him. She saw me from her garden, before I'd seen *her*, and she'd told one of the other kids that she liked me, and that she would be waiting at the bottom of her garden.

As I walked towards her, I realised they hadn't exaggerated. She was stunningly beautiful, with pure, unblemished white skin and shiny eyes that seemed to hold more depth than I'd ever seen. Her body screamed sex to me, even at that pre-pubescent age. We were like magnets. Staring at each other. Neither of us averting our gaze. All the other kids gathered around to watch. We looked at each other for a few moments and then I kissed her. The other kids applauded.

It was signed, sealed, delivered. She was my girl.

'Concrete and Clay' by Unit 4 + 2 was on the radio at the time; it exactly captured how I felt.

You to me, are sweet as roses in the morning,
And you to me, are soft as summer rain at dawn.

We talked and kissed a few more times at the bottom of her garden, then suddenly she disappeared. She didn't seem to be around any more. I would see her in the park occasionally, but she wasn't as friendly. The more elusive she became, the more nervous and desperate I got. She had told me from the off about another boy from her school, Brian. But she didn't really make it clear that he was a boyfriend.

She suggested I come to the swimming pool where they would be. The thought of meeting him hadn't bothered me. I was quite intrigued. I'd heard her and others mention him, and was kind of keen to meet him. I didn't take this guy too seriously, probably because I felt that she and I were meant to be.

She was with Brian when I arrived at Harrow's open-air swimming baths. Margaret was sitting on the edge of the pool, with her feet dangling in the water. Brian was standing *in* the pool, facing her legs. I jumped in the pool, directly to the side of her.

'This is Brian,' she said.

'Oh, hello,' I said, in a friendly way. I didn't think it was any big deal. His mood was different. He barely looked at me. He grabbed her legs seductively and pulled her into the pool close to him. I just wandered off sheepishly.

After that, I'd sometimes walk alone in Harrow Rec. The park was a sad, lonely place without her. Occasionally I'd call round for her or to see her brother Paul. On one or two occasions, we had a kiss and a cuddle. And although it felt great to me, she didn't seem to be as enthusiastic. I couldn't make her mine. Maybe she wanted me to fight for her that day in the pool. Or maybe she just preferred Brian.

The sad but beautiful 'Out of Time' was in the charts, where Chris Farlowe sings about his baby being out of time.

I didn't tell anyone at home what was happening.

I cherished the idea that she was the one, until at 15 she laughed cruelly at me from the inside of her much older boyfriend's car, after he'd almost run me over on a zebra crossing.

· · ·

If I made any kind of mistake or something bad happened to me, for example Margaret going off me, I would try to keep it secret, because I felt I would be seen as responsible for it. From the age of about 11, I rarely told my parents anything significant about my life. On the very rare occasions that I *did* mention any outside difficulties, I made sure I had a very good case against the other person. I would witness my siblings telling the family about some difficult issue they were facing, and I would think, *Wow, you don't even know anything about my problems. I wouldn't even know where to start in telling you. There are too many to face.* I just kept up the act.

Also, I made up stories. I *would* talk about what went on at school, but it was often lies, certainly with regard to what was happening with myself.

· · ·

Cigarettes looked really cool. I would draw pictures of teenagers with quiffs, Mod or Beatle haircuts, and complete the sketch with a fag in the trap.

Nearly all of the bad-boy smokers at school wore fashionable clothes. They would stand in the corner of the playground ('Smokers' Corner'), secretly puffing away at every breaktime – hand cupped around the fag to conceal it from the playground-duty teacher. Every now and again, a teacher would head towards Smokers' Corner, and the boys would hastily extinguish and hide their fags.

'Take it dahn', mate,' the boy said.

I inhaled deeply.

'The cunt's about to fall over!' he said to his mates.

Cigarettes made me feel sick at first. I tried not to let the bigger kids see that I was going dizzy and nearly falling over after one of them gave me my first drag on his snout.

The dizziness lasted a few weeks and then I got used to it. Smoking was something that I had very mixed feelings about. On the one hand, it was cool, it seemed to *give* me something – an exciting, secret new world – and it looked good. On the other hand, Pat didn't agree with smoking, and he didn't like the idea of me doing it. I didn't tell him.

I would hide the fags well away from the house, usually under planks of wood at the side of the local garages, although sometimes the rain would get at them, and I'd pick them up in the morning on my way to school.

Pretty soon, I lost the power of choice. I couldn't stop. My mother would give me money each morning for a school dinner, which was the same price as a packet of five cigarettes. Fags would be the priority.

One day I tried to stop. I threw away the remaining three I had in my packet. I only lasted half a day – I was down and miserable and empty without nicotine. I went back to the place I'd thrown them, but they were gone. I found a few dog-ends (almost-finished cigarettes) in the street and smoked them instead. I was 13 and I had a nicotine habit. Fags weren't even fun any more. They were a necessity. I *had* to get money every day to buy them. I stole from Pat, from Joe, and from anywhere I could, for cigarettes.

On one occasion, I took coins that had been left on the kitchen windowsill. That evening, as we all sat in the front room, Mum said, 'Right. I want a word with everyone. Some money's gone missing …'

'Ooh, I've got a pain in my side,' I said.

'Are you OK?' Mum said with concern.

'Yeah, I'm fine, but I think I'd better go to bed.'

I got up and walked out of the room. For some reason, it wasn't brought up again. I've no idea why. It was obvious who had stolen the money.

. . .

There was a boy I will call Prezza in school who was two years older than me and a lot bigger – pretty much the size of a fully grown man, whereas I was small for my age. He was dark – around my complexion – and like me, he could easily have passed for Spanish or something similar. He would regularly bully me, mentally and physically, by dragging me behind one of the playground buildings, away from everyone else, and saying: 'You're black, Rowland … You're a wog.'

'No, I'm not,' I'd say.

He'd hit me.

'Yeah, you are, you cunt. You're a wog, Rowland.'

He'd repeat that over and over while he overpowered me. The more I disagreed, the more he'd hit me.

I said 'Yes, I am' a few times, to appease him.

I didn't tell anyone about it, but one day a kid in my class, Brian O'Houlihan, walked past us and saw Prezza holding me by my tie, forcing me to stand on tiptoe up against a wall, with his clenched fist pushed tight under my chin, almost lifting me off the ground. Afterwards, O'Houlihan said, 'Why don't you tell Collins? He'll fuckin' murder him!' (Collins was the cane-happy deputy head that everyone was afraid of.)

'Nah, I can't do that,' I said.

'Fuckin' tell him. That'll stop the cunt!'

I did. Prezza got the cane, and it stopped.

I learned recently from one of Prezza's classmates that his father was Indian and that he had a complex about it. I wish I'd known that at the time. I also learned from the same guy that, in adult life, Prezza got a life sentence for murder.

. . .

There were music lessons at St Greg's. We were all lent a violin. I thought of it more as a guitar. I tried to write a song.

Over the hills – over the hills.
Far away – far away
Is where I'm going – where I'm going,
This – ve-ry day!

Then I realised it was pretty much the same melody as 'Do You Love Me' by Brian Poole and the Tremeloes.

. . .

Scouts was somewhere I *was* allowed to go. It was considered healthy and our troop was Catholic.

On a two-week summer Boy Scouts camping trip, three of us – Chris Barking, Chris Dillon and myself – were given a tent, a map, some food and cooking supplies, and sent off into the Lake District for the night, a few miles from the rest of the troop, as part of an assignment to earn a badge.

The difference between me and these two smoking peers was that for them it was a bit of fun – mischief. They would smoke occasionally, when the time was right, or when an opportunity presented itself. For me, there was no choice. I *had* to have nicotine. I lived in fear of not having enough cigarettes or running out of matches.

After we had spent the night in the tent, the two Chrises got out and started preparing our breakfast. I made an excuse and stayed in the tent. I had smoked the last of my fags the previous day but I knew Chris Barking had some. I went into his bag, found his four remaining cigarettes and a box of matches. I took two cigarettes and a few matches, and I also tore off a bit of 'strike' from the side of the matchbox. Of course, now the 'strike' section on the side of the box had a chunk missing from it. Any shame I felt when I was doing it barely registered. The compulsion to smoke was far stronger. I told the two Chrises I needed to go to the toilet and went away quietly and smoked one of the fags.

After breakfast, Chris Barking announced, in a slightly embarrassed but not unfriendly way, 'Someone's taken two fags, a few matches and a bit of strike from my bag.'

'It wasn't me,' I said.

Obviously, they both knew it was.

Chris Barking would have at least shared one of his cigarettes with me. In fact, after breakfast he lit one up and *did* pass it around. I was now pretending to need a drag of his fag, when really we all knew I'd stolen *two* cigarettes.

. . .

I was supposed to go to altar practice on Saturday mornings, but I was getting disillusioned. I didn't seem to connect with anyone there. Often, I'd pretend to go, but instead bunk into the Saturday-morning pictures.

It was quite easy to force open one of the cinema back doors. Once inside, I'd look around the packed auditorium at the kids sitting in there with permission from their parents. I didn't fully understand Dad's refusal to allow us such things.

The ABC had its own song that they would sing each week.

'*We're all friends together, we're minors of the ABC.*' ('ABC' was shouted.)

Going there, and particularly bunking in, connected me with the memory of Pat and Joe's younger years. They often told me how they would sneak into the Saturday-morning flicks in Wolverhampton. 'Uncle Bob' would invite the children who had a birthday that week to come up on the stage and receive a gift and have all the other kids sing 'Happy Birthday' to them. Joe would get up *every* week. After many consecutive appearances, Uncle Bob cottoned on, and said, ''Ere. Yow were up last wik, sayin' it was yower bloody birthday. It caw' be your birthday every cowin' wik. Get down, ya little bugga!'

. . .

I didn't integrate into living in London as well as I could have. I guess the problems at school were part of it, and I was very influenced by Pat's telling me that the kids in Wolverhampton were harder and more noble. I was fertile ground for Pat's indoctrination. When I mentioned that I loved to watch the Mods with their beautifully coiffured hair in Harrow, Pat said, 'Them fucking Mods wouldn't last five minutes in the centre of Wolverhampton.'

Blimey. They must be so tough, those Wolverhampton blokes, I thought. *People there must be fair-minded, stronger and kinder than these fuckers I'm dealing with now.* Not a healthy way to think. Wolverhampton people are great but, in my experience, no more noble or tough than anyone else.

I would long for the days when Wolves came to play in London. I'd only actually seen them play twice when we lived in Wolverhampton and I wasn't in any way emotionally bonded to them when we arrived down south. I had planned to support a London team, but after the piss-taking about my accent, I decided to support Wolves. It was a small gesture of defiance.

I loved to hear those Wolverhampton accents and feel the safety and togetherness of that football crowd. It wasn't about the game for me. I would barely watch it. It was all about the crowd. I'd study the fans – their clothes, their accents, the songs they sang, their expressions, the togetherness they seemed to feel, the way they related to each other. To this day, I can't understand people who just go to a football match and sit in a neutral position. To me it's always been about the singing. I'm still fascinated by how those songs actually emerge. Somebody writes those lyrics and puts them to music! But I've never yet met anyone who has claimed authorship of a Wolves song or that of any other club.

. . .

One of my classmates at school was called Tony. Both of us had heard the expression 'tossing off'. We knew it was something sexual but didn't know what it meant. We tried to enact what we thought it was. We would take turns sitting on each other's laps, and the one underneath would literally bounce (toss) the seated one off them. It felt vaguely arousing – we were pre-pubescent, but things were stirring.

We would sit next to each other, at the back of the class, and sometimes put our hands under the desk and onto each other's cocks (over the fabric of the trousers). It felt warm and good. Occasionally, I would have one hand on Tony's cock while raising the other hand and asking the teacher a question. I loved the audacity of that and found it hard to stifle my laughter.

I think many in the class knew – and I didn't see any reason to hide it. We didn't really think of it as properly sexual, more fun and rebellious. But one kid in particular, Murphy, took offence, and waited for me as I walked up to the bus stop after school. He quickly came towards me.

'Wha' you doin' touchin' each other's cocks, Rowland? That's fuckin' disgustin'! You dirty cunt. Wha' you fuckin' doin'? I saw ya, you cunt!'

He started thumping me.

I didn't fight back. He punched me until I fell to the ground then he walked away in disgust.

I had many yarn-spinning sessions with my brother Pat, where I would tell him who I'd beaten up, what I'd stolen, etc. While I often *did* steal and fight, I also made up stories. I don't know if Pat believed me, but he never once challenged me on the authenticity of the tales. Looking back now, I wish that I hadn't felt that I needed to live up to a real or imagined idea of how I should be. I wish I was just able to be as I was.

On this occasion, I laughingly mentioned that while I had my left hand up, asking the teacher a question, my right hand was under the desk and on my mate Tony's cock. I wanted Pat to see how I was taking the piss out of the teacher. But Pat's expression completely changed. I don't remember exactly what he said, but he let me know that he didn't approve. This was just before homosexuality became legal and it was still very much taboo in our circles.

· · ·

A family trip to the hallowed Wolverhampton and a visit to my relatives yielded a couple of little rhymes that my cousin Tim had seen written on the toilet wall at his school, St Joseph's, where I would have gone if we'd stayed in Wolverhampton.

As coincidence would have it, on my return to St Greg's, the boys' internal first-floor toilets had just been re-plastered and beautifully painted in a high-quality sky-blue eggshell finish. I'd recently stolen a new heavy-duty black magic marker pen. The nib was more than a quarter of an inch in width. I was pleased with the marker and keen to find a good opportunity to use it.

I asked to be excused from a lesson, saying I was bursting to go to the toilet. I knew during class time the corridors would usually be deserted. I went into the newly painted toilets.

In massive letters, I wrote, 'THE PAINTER'S WORK WAS ALL IN VAIN. THE PISS-HOUSE POET STRIKES AGAIN.'

I had been debating on two variations of the ditty, so I decided to write the other version on the opposite wall.

'THE PAINTER'S WORK WAS ALL IN VAIN. THE SHIT-HOUSE PHANTOM STRIKES AGAIN.'

I quietly left the toilet and was fortunate that nobody saw me coming out. I was buzzing with excitement, as if electricity was running through me.

There was hell to pay! The headmaster called a special assembly of all 300 boys. He told us how he was disgusted at the filthy language used. He made it very clear that he would find the perpetrator at all costs.

'I will find you. Your mind is filthy. You are sick. You think you have got away with this. You haven't. Somebody will give you up. I will keep the whole school in detention until you give yourself up.'

Christ, why did I do it? I thought. Now all the excitement was gone. Only fear remained.

I didn't tell anyone, but I must have looked nervous during the head's address, because the boy standing next to me (Murphy – the same guy who was repulsed by my touching Tony's cock) guessed that I was the culprit.

'It was you, wasn't it, Rowland?' Murphy said.

'No.'

'Yeah, it was. I can tell.'

'Nah, it wasn't.'

The toilet walls were painted over almost immediately. I was disappointed that my work hadn't been seen by a larger audience. Mercifully the head didn't put all the boys in detention and the whole thing blew over.

I also wrote 'I hate Jews' in the phone box at the end of our street. I didn't hate Jews. I hadn't even knowingly met any. I'd just picked it up at school, where there was a big anti-Jewish feeling, and in Harrow generally. I had never heard anyone mention Jews in Wolverhampton, but as soon as I got to London, I heard boys talking about how mean Jews were.

A kid my age living down the road from me who I was quite friendly with, David Green, one day told me he was Jewish. I hadn't even known.

'You don't like Jews, do you?' David said.

'What? Of course I do.'

'You wrote, "I hate Jews" in the phone box.' Someone in the street had told him.

I denied it profusely, but I could see he didn't believe me. I liked him and felt ashamed.

· · ·

'Eh, eh, England, eh, eh, England, we'll support you ever more! We'll support you ever more,' to the tune of the Protestant hymn, 'Bread of Heaven', echoed around the tunnel of Wembley Park tube station, sung by hundreds of England football fans on a warm night in July 1966. We were all making our way to Wembley Stadium for the opening game of the 1966 World Cup Finals: England v Uruguay.

The singing fans were mostly middle-aged men wearing old-fashioned, 1950s-style clothes: beige gabardine raincoats and windcheaters. Their hair was dressed back, and they were tough. I didn't know any of them, but there was a great atmosphere and I was happy to be singing and walking with them.

'Eh, eh, England, eh, eh, England, we'll support you ever more! We'll support you ever more.'

They had tickets. I didn't. I'd been told by a kid at school that the World Cup was starting that night. I hadn't even known. Mum was usually OK with me going to a football match and gave me permission.

I paced up and down outside the stadium, wondering how I could get in. The crowd inside were singing and shouting – the game had begun.

A policeman walked up to me.

'Son. Have you got a ticket?'

I thought, *Shit, he's gonna tell me to go home and stop hanging around if I tell him the truth.* But for some reason, I had an attack of honesty. 'No, I haven't.'

'Here y'are, son.'

He handed me a ticket. It had 'England v Uruguay' written on it.

'Are you sure?'

'Yeah. Go on, son. Get yourself in!'

I couldn't believe it. 'Ah, thanks!'

In I went.

A few weeks later, England got to the final. On the day of the game, Dad was driving the family home from a week-long caravan holiday in Selsey Bill on the south coast. I really wanted to go to the game.

'Can I go to the match at Wembley, please, Dad?' I asked. We lived about two miles from the stadium.

'How will ya get in?'

'I'll find a way in!' I pleaded.

Dad was softening, but Mum was concerned.

'He hasn't got a ticket! He'll be arrested!'

'Ah, they'll only throw him out,' Dad said, much to my surprise.

The last bit of the journey through north-west London was torture for me, until finally Dad pulled up the MG Magnette at the bottom of Wembley Way. The game had already started. I raced up the big, deserted boulevard. I was so excited. It was ten past three. The game had kicked off at 3pm.

Once again, I paced up and down outside the ground without a ticket, but this time there was no copper to give me one.

Shit. Now it's half-time and I still can't find a way in.

Then: 'Oi, mate. You tryna' geh in?'

There were three of them – boys about my age. The kid who spoke was blond, slightly bigger than the others, and wearing sky-blue jeans. I guessed they were from nearby Stonebridge.

Before I could answer, one of the boys, looking towards the stadium, shouted 'It's Cassius Clay!'

He was by now called Muhammad Ali, but he was Cassius to us. He was coming down the steps, leaving the stadium. He was over in London to fight Henry Cooper.

We ran towards him. 'Cassius, Cassius!'

Muhammad wasn't particularly friendly. I was surprised; it seemed his blarney was just for the media. He quickly got in the back of a chauffer-driven Rolls Royce, but waved to us as they pulled away. We were delighted. We'd seen Cassius Clay, the heavyweight champion of the world!

'Come on, mate! You wanna fackin' get in, or what?' the blond boy said to me.

'Yeah, course I fackin' do!' I said.

'Right. The gate on entrance G is loose. If enough of us pull it, we can make a gap big enough to squeeze in, one at a time.'

We ran as fast as we could.

'Cam' un. The game's nearly over!'

The boys showed me the place where the mesh metal was looser than the other gates and, with sufficient pull, we would be able to squeeze through. We were all skinny; it would just be a case of getting our heads through. But there was a problem – the stewards (men, dressed in black military-style uniforms with white caps) were patrolling the inner, circular corridor.

'Keep calm. Pretend we're just chattin',' Blondie said.

We waited. After about ten minutes, the stewards could stand it no longer – they went in to watch the game, leaving the corridors un-patrolled.

'Now! Come on,' one of the boys said.

We all grouped at one end of the entrance and pulled the mesh for all we were worth. The smallest boy stood where the biggest gap was. He put a leg through, sideways, then his head, then hauled the rest of himself through. He was in. Now inside, he went to the end and started pulling with us.

A slightly bigger boy tried it next. He was struggling to get his head through.

'Cam' un', you cunts! Pull!' said Blondie.

We pulled for all we were worth. The boy got in.

'Let the geezer in the blue jacket go next,' Blondie said. That was me.

I was worried about getting my head stuck in the metal and hurting myself. Just then, a man of about 40 appeared from nowhere. We were sure he was going to tell us off. Instead, he said, 'Goo' un, sahn. If you can get your 'ead froo, you're in.' He was much stronger than us and helped us pull the mesh gate open more widely.

It was that kind of day – magical. A grown, respectable-looking man, ably assisting and encouraging young lads to bunk into Wembley Stadium. My dad, a strict disciplinarian and a staunch Irish republican, dropping me off at Wembley Way, knowing I was planning to bunk into the World Cup final to support England. It was like a positive spell had taken over London.

I tried my head for size, to see if it would fit through. It did. I pulled my head out and put my right leg through sideways, then my right shoulder, then my head, then the other leg. I was in!

Now it was Blondie's turn. The three of us now on the inside and the man on the outside pulling the mesh open. Blondie was bigger than the rest of us, and his head wasn't going through easily, but there was no way were we going to let him down.

'Cam' un! We can fackin' do it!'

Blondie got in. He had marks on his forehead where the metal had rubbed on him, but no one cared about that.

Now what? The stewards were standing just inside the entrances to all the lower tiers.

'Let's try and bolt past 'em?' I said.

'Fuck that!' Blondie said. 'They'll nab a couple of us. We'll go on the upper tier. Split into twos. If they see us mob-'anded, they'll know we've bunked in.'

I paired up with one of the smaller boys, while Blondie and the other kid went off together. We ran like crazy to the upper tier, feeling electrified.

The game was still going on as we arrived in the gods. It was beyond packed, and with us being so small, we couldn't see a thing, only the backs of the spectators.

Suddenly: 'Come on, son.'

A couple of men motioned to us and lifted us up onto the six-foot-high wall at the very back of the stand. We sat there and had a panoramic view of the pitch. Here was a warmth, a spirit of togetherness like I had never experienced!

'*Eh, eh, England, eh, eh, England, we'll support you ever more. We'll support you ever more.*'

The pitch seemed tiny and a long way off, but we could see all the action perfectly. England were 2–1 up. They were wearing red shirts and looked fantastic.

There were minutes to go. Then the Germans equalised. As I looked down on the pitch, I saw a blond man in a sports jacket, obviously German, dancing with delight on the dog track. He tried to get on the pitch, but was stopped by the stewards.

'Shit! Extra time!' someone said.

It wasn't 'shit' as far as I was concerned. I was going to see another 30 minutes of play and experience another 30 minutes of this amazing atmosphere!

England scored again, and again. It was over. All of us were deliriously happy.

When I got home, the whole family were happy. Pat was away on holiday and had watched it on the telly. When he returned, he was really pleased I'd got in.

'What was it like, Kev?'

'It was fucking great, Pat!'

Usually guilty of something or other

Willesden School of Building was an absolute dump. It *wasn't* a 'building school'. It may have been once but, when I started there in 1966 at 13 years old, it was nothing but a backward school.

During my last term at St Greg's, the teacher had passed out sheets of paper giving details about the school for us to pass on to our parents. 'It's a school for boys who want to go into the building trade,' it said. 'Some of the previous pupils went on to be surveyors.' I'd heard my dad use the word 'surveyor' as something positive, though I didn't know or care much what it meant.

Without thinking about it, I took the sheet home and gave it to my parents. My dad initially got angry at the suggestion that I should leave St Greg's. I wasn't intending to leave, just passing on the sheet as instructed.

A few weeks later, I was walking to Scouts with Brian O'Houlihan, who was in my class, when he said warmly, 'Me and Pee'ah Green are goin' t' the building school in Willesden and I was finkin', if you went as well, that'd be free of us frum Sunt Greg's and it'd be easier for us t' settle in.'

It seemed like a good idea. I started to think differently about the school. It could be a new start, something different.

Though my dad had been initially riled by my bringing home the sheet of paper, one day, right out of the blue, he brought the subject up again, this time enthusiastically. (I suspect he may have driven past the big, modern, Willesden Technical College, which was directly across the road from the dilapidated old building school, and mistaken it for the building school.) In any event, he seemed keen on me going there.

As well as coming full circle on the school idea, Dad was also now talking about me going into the building trade with him, after I left school. He had recently started his own company. This time, he was more successful than his first attempt ... It was a small building firm, but it was highly respected for doing first-rate work, and later converting Victorian houses in Notting Hill into flats. Although Dad wanted to earn money, it was never his primary concern. He was more interested in doing a good job. He was a perfectionist. Pat had always been quite keen to go into the business with him, but Dad didn't want that for Pat.

'Do you like the building game?' Dad said to me, enthusiastically, that summer.

'Yeah,' I lied. How could I tell my dad I hated the thing that he spent most of his time doing to feed us?

On Saturdays or Sundays, I would work for Dad along with Pat and Joe, often scraping old wallpaper off walls or the like.

'What is it you like about the trade?' Dad continued.

I was, by then, taking on Dad's viewpoint that the things I was interested in were wrong. I was doing my best to second-guess what he would want to hear at every turn. Also, Pat had said to me, 'If you get a job as an apprentice carpenter when you're 15, in two or three years' time, you'll be coming out with me and Joe on Saturday nights!' That sounded great.

I was trying to come up with something to answer Dad's question, but I couldn't think of a single thing I liked about the building game.

Is he trying to catch me out? I thought.

'Eh ...'

Finally, Dad said enthusiastically, '*I* like to see buildings going up; it makes me feel good.'

That made total sense. It was positive.

'Yeah, me too,' I said.

When he talked to me about one day taking over his building firm, I froze with embarrassment. I couldn't believe that he was considering trusting me with it. I wasn't worthy of it, quite apart from the fact that I wasn't interested in it.

Bizarrely, I didn't really associate going to this school with a life in the building trade. I was 13, and employment seemed a lifetime away. I was finding it so hard at St Greg's and just wanted a new start.

Even at that point, a part of me was conscious that I was running away – that it would have been better for me to stay at St Greg's and tough it out. I probably would have been relegated to a lower stream anyway, which would have made things much easier.

I did, however, make up my mind that in my last term at St Greg's, I wasn't going to come bottom of the class. I wanted that for *me*, not for Dad or anyone else! I wanted to show those fuckers who had chanted my name that I wasn't stupid.

I ended up coming about 27th or 28th out of 32 or 33 in most subjects. That was the very best I could do, in a stream that I shouldn't even have been in.

· · ·

Brian O'Houlihan and I should have known something was amiss with the building school when Peter Green didn't get into it and *we* did (Peter was in our class and way ahead of Brian and me in terms of grades).

There was no proper physical education, no drama, no French and no music of any kind. It was just the basics: maths, physics, English, geography and something that passed for PE. There were classes called plumbing and carpentry, but really they were just the same as the metalwork and woodwork lessons at St Greg's, except not as good. And there were no girls at this school. There was only the vaguest school uniform. The school had no respect for itself. It may have been good once, but now it was on its last legs. It closed a few years later, in 1970.

It called itself Church of England, but all that meant was they said the Lord's Prayer every morning. The fact that it wasn't Catholic meant that there were hardly any Irish kids there, so culturally it was different from what I was used to. The boys were mainly local Willesden, English. Mostly good kids, but different.

The headmaster was insane: when one of the boys broke into the always-locked storeroom and found loads of brand-new, expensive PE equipment still in its wrappers, we realised the head had hidden it from us for his own bizarre reasons. He was also an intense disciplinarian.

My new start didn't really work out the way I'd hoped; I couldn't do the work that I was being asked to do by the teachers. Maths and physics particularly were just a complete mystery. I'd sit there, pretending I knew what they were talking about. I kept my head down and tried to be invisible. I felt exactly the same as I had at St Greg's, and it was a darker school – there was very little light there, no music, no colour, no girls, only drudgery – and I had got too far behind to ever catch up academically.

There was *one* good thing about the school – a fantastic young English teacher by the name of Peter Kent-Baguley. He was kind and inspiring, always positive, and he appeared to like me. He would get us to write essays and encourage us to let our imaginations fly. He was, I think, from an upper-middle-class background and didn't seem to have any of the prejudices that some of the other (mostly ex-grammar schoolboy) teachers were burdened with. And in the way of the best of well-educated people, he was completely fair and open-minded. Everybody was treated as an individual and with patience.

I loved doing English with him. In the end-of-term exam, I wrote an essay on a football match I'd been to. He loved it. He said he felt like he was *at* the game. I got the highest marks in the class that term. To me that was a massive deal. I'd never come top of a class in anything! I was still a nonstarter at maths and the sciences and I'd always had a flair for essays, but with this guy, I soared.

Mr Kent-Baguley was stylish in a traditional English kind of way (corduroy suits and nice brogues). I would look forward to going into school in the morning to see him.

I had a good friend in my class called Stephen Godfrey. We both loved clothes and music and would constantly talk about our interests. We were both the shortest kids in the class but, for some reason, I called him Little G. Peter Kent-Baguley seemed to like him too. It felt as if he'd picked the two of us out. But maybe all the kids felt like that with him.

We had been instructed to wear only *white* plimsolls for PE. I'd got a new pair and was breaking them in around the house. I was home alone on a Saturday afternoon when Dad for some reason didn't have his key and knocked on the front door. I answered wearing the plimsolls. He didn't look happy and, once inside, exploded in rage, convinced that I had deliberately bought them in white because I favoured them over a black pair. I was so flustered that I was unable to get my explanation out – that the school had insisted on white!

On another occasion, he saw me trying to convert a plain-collar shirt into a button-down, by sewing buttons onto the collar. He exploded again. On this occasion, Mum came to my aid.

'Ah, he's only doin' up an owl' shirt for himself.'

I wondered if Dad was concerned about my sexuality. Or maybe he was pissed off because it was clear my interest in the building trade was a sham.

Dad would say things like, 'Look at the big man, with the cufflinks.' I wore cufflinks that I'd stolen from Woolworths.

I was so afraid of Dad that I would recognise the sound of his car pulling up outside the house. I dreaded him coming home. I didn't know what sort of mood he would be in, but it was often a bad one, certainly where I was concerned.

I was usually guilty of something or other, or wasn't doing something I was supposed to do. Homework was a big one. It seemed to be Dad's number-one obsession as far as I was concerned. He would often start raging about the fact that I wasn't doing any homework, often when the school hadn't even *set* me any. If I tried to explain, he would shout me down and say that I should be studying anyway. On a couple of occasions, I just pretended I had been given homework and then made like I was doing it.

It seemed to me that when Dad looked at me, he saw something he didn't like. I thought he could see right through me and into my soul, and that I was bad.

From about ten years old, I stopped trusting my own judgement, feelings and ambitions and instead pretended to be someone else. That's how I lived and that is how I subsequently lived a lot of my life.

I actually used to fantasise about being orphaned and adopted by another family. I thought fantasies like that were normal for children – until in adult life, I mentioned it to a friend and asked if he had the same fantasy. He laughed and said, 'No, I never thought like that.'

. . .

Because Willesden School of Building was such a backward, run-down institution, there wasn't a physical education teacher, so Mr Kent-Baguley had to double-up at PE. All of a sudden, I became good at running! I was 13 going on 14 and had never previously showed any interest or aptitude in it, but because this guy was taking the class, I became good enough to be selected to represent the school in the Brent Schoolboy Championships.

I was delighted to be picked for the race. But I let him down that day. I was very nervous and I had promised myself that I wouldn't smoke a cigarette until the contest was over. I lasted until lunchtime. Little G and O'Houlihan were also running. We were hanging around Gladstone Park at lunchtime, as we usually did. The other two were adamant that they wouldn't impair their chances of performing well by having a fag. I too wanted to not smoke, but couldn't hold out.

I lit a cigarette as the other two watched. I felt such a weakling. And I believed that's what they were thinking as they watched me.

As soon as I'd smoked the fag, that was *it*. I knew I was fucked.

Looking back now, I think it must have been psychological. No *one* cigarette could have that strong a physical effect. But as far as I was concerned, I definitely wasn't going to do any good, because I'd *had* the cigarette.

I couldn't stay anywhere close to the front-runners. It just wasn't in me.

I didn't come last, at least, but I was way, way back in the field, maybe 118th out of 165, and well behind Little G and O'Houlihan, whom I usually equalled.

Peter Kent-Baguley stood on a hill with the teachers from all the other schools, as I ran past him. I was embarrassed at how badly I was doing.

'Come on, Rowland, less of the dramatics,' he shouted.

He was right. I was pulling a face of pain, wanting him to see how hard I was trying. He had picked me and I didn't do the business. I ran far worse on that day than I usually did.

After the contest, instead of facing up to the way I felt, wretched, I went over to the boy who won the race that followed ours and made a big fuss of him (he happened to be from St Greg's). At home, I told my family that I'd done much better than I had.

My written work with Peter Kent-Baguley seemed to deteriorate after that. He had encouraged me so much, but now I began messing around in his class, often with Little G.

I had a fight in the school that didn't go well and I lost more confidence. Then Little G disappeared. No one knew what had happened to him. One of the kids said he'd gone off to work on the funfair with his dad. Losing him was a blow – he and I had sat together in every lesson. He had a Moddy-type vibe about him and he brightened the place up. Almost 50 years later when he contacted me on Facebook, I found out what had happened – his parents had separated and his dad took him out of the school and up to Soho.

It wasn't easy to forge bonds with other kids. Most had paired up by now. I was an outsider again.

Then Peter Kent-Baguley announced he would be leaving the school at the end of the term. It didn't sink in. My marks in English were way down – nearer to the bottom than the top. As he announced the end-of-year results to the class, he told me off: 'Rowland, 27th [out of 40]. And if Godfrey [Little G] had been here more, you would have done even worse.'

His exit *seemed* sudden, but it wasn't. It was just that I hadn't acknowledged that he was actually going. And when I went back the next term, bizarrely, it felt like a shock that he wasn't there.

I got a chance to thank him many years later when we made contact through social media. He was still the same – doing positive work, helping the homeless and campaigning for Fair Trade imports to be used by local councils. A really great guy.

. . .

My dad was very unhappy about my poor school results, but there was never any discussion about lowering the bar, only more pressure to do better. I knew any level-headed conversation about it was out of the question, so I just tried to block it out and dodge him as much as I could, until the inevitable confrontation.

I believe Dad was under a lot of pressure himself. His building firm had got off to a slow start and he had a mortgage and five kids. He seemed stressed out and easily annoyed a lot of the time.

When I had started school in Wolverhampton at five years old, I wasn't noticeably behind other kids in my class, but as time went on, I just seemed to drop further and further behind. The currency of value in our house, above all else, was education – and I didn't have it.

Money for fags

During the school summer holidays of 1967, I started hanging out with four or five boys over the park who were about a year older than me. A couple of them were from the Hogan family who lived in my street. I knew one of the others from St Greg's, but as he was older, we hadn't really made much contact. Another of them was called Jim – I particularly liked his company. He was mad on pop music.

Jim said, 'Without music, life wouldn't be worth living.' I knew exactly what he meant.

We would enthuse about the hits of the day together. It was great to meet someone else who liked music as much as I did. Jim made me think it was OK to be passionate about it – he was a perfectly intelligent boy. In fact, he was at grammar school. We would all just sit around the same park bench each day and talk about music and Mod clothes.

A few weeks later, I fell out with the Hogans. I went over to the park one day and Jim told me they didn't want me to hang around with them any more.

'You've argued with every *one* of us this week, Kev!' he said.

I hadn't even noticed. I certainly recalled disagreeing with Jim and one or two others, but I hadn't realised it was that serious. I thought we were just disagreeing.

I spoke about this a few years ago with my younger sister, Grainne, and she recalls me calling Jim 'Dim' repeatedly, despite him asking me to stop.

I moved myself over to the other side of the park and got friendly with some kids there. They were about a year younger than me. One of them was called Danny. He would sing as we sat in the park shelter. He had the most beautiful voice. He sang the hits of the day and knew the words to all of them, just like I used to when I was at primary school.

The other kids would say what a nice voice he had. I sometimes felt envious. I had stopped singing by this point and wasn't at all confident about my voice.

Danny sang with complete abandon.

While I'm far away from you, my baby …

A really positive development around this time was when I got an after-school and Saturday-morning job, delivering paraffin and hardware goods on a trades bike. The guy I replaced was a Moddy-looking face I'd seen around Harrow. He had turned 15 and was now leaving school, that was the leaving age at the time. Getting that job felt like a coming of age. Even the old trades bike was really cool. Although it was black, heavy and very old (probably from the 1930s or 40s), and hard to pedal, it had a kind of thuggish vibe to it – 14- and 15-year-old bad boys would often be seen riding trades bikes, delivering meat, veg and the like. It complemented the 'Peanut' clothes I was wearing – basically grown-out Mod stuff – a 'zipper' (a short MA-1 flying jacket) and Levi's 501 jeans with a very small turn-up over working boots. My hair was short and parted high.

The job meant money for fags, and although the lady who owned the shop, while very exacting, was not particularly unfair to me, it didn't stop me stealing from her. At every opportunity I would thieve, usually from her piggy bank (stuffed with notes), which she kept in her bedroom above the shop. There was a storeroom at the top of the house that I would be required to stock. That would give me the opportunity to sneak into her bedroom and relieve her piggy bank of a few pounds. Selfishly, I even stole money from the middle-aged shop assistant's purse. No one was out of bounds to me. Stealing was an addiction.

But the highlight of my busy Saturday-morning paraffin round was delivering to the O'Malleys in Devonshire Road. I knew the family from our local church. Tony O'Malley would sometimes answer the door. He was a cool-looking guy, maybe six or seven years older than me and, as everyone in the area knew, a professional musician! He looked great, had a happy, relaxed vibe about him, and always gave me a good tip.

A couple of years later, Tony O'Malley was in the charts with 'Friends', with his band, Arrival. Later still, he would be a key member of the amazing group Kokomo. I discovered the band in 1975 and, on scrutinising their first album cover, I was delighted to realise it was the same Tony O'Malley I'd delivered paraffin to! To this day, 'Anytime' by Kokomo, sung by Tony O'Malley and Dyan Birch, and written by Neil Hubbard, remains one of my all-time favourite tracks.

I met Tony a few years ago and we talked briefly about Harrow and growing up there as Irish Catholics. He told me that his sister, Mary O'Malley, had written the play *Once a Catholic* about that very subject.

That summer, 1967, I got arrested for forging a tube pass and bunking fares. I had got an old out-of-date pass and carefully doctored it. I got away with flashing the pass as I walked through the busy tube-station barriers for a while, but one inquisitive ticket collector put an end to it and, at 14, I made my first appearance at Harrow Juvenile Court.

Dad was understandably horrified and responded with a stricter regime. I was kept in for a few weeks, then, when I was finally allowed to go to the Catholic youth club again, I could only go once a fortnight and I had to be in at 9.30pm – 30 minutes before the club ended.

. . .

There was a boy called Palter in my class. I hadn't previously had any truck with him, and he didn't seem to be a naturally aggressive kid. He was quite decent, but he hung around with the hard nuts and was about my equal in the fighting ratings – somewhere around the middle, heading towards the bottom.

One day in the 'plumbing' (metalwork) class, I wrote some graffiti in ink on his white, cotton, protective apron. I don't know why, and I can't recall what I wrote, but obviously it was out of order and something he didn't find funny. Egged on by his hard mates, he decided to up the ante. He walked over to me and, with his metal cutters, snipped the tie string at the back of my apron. He and his pals found it hilarious.

I wasn't going to take that from *Palter*! It meant a fight after school. I decided this time I wasn't going to lose. *I'll use my belt.*

I'd just bought a leather belt a couple of weeks earlier. It was two inches wide.

Palter cockily walked out into the playground and took off his jacket, giving it to one of his hard mates. They were whispering instructions into his ear, like seconds to a boxer. I didn't have any seconds. He hadn't seen the belt I had wrapped around my right knuckles, hidden in my trouser pocket, just like Dad would do with me.

Palter put his fists up, I took my hands out of my pockets, unwrapped the belt and laid into him.

He put his hands up to protect himself, but he couldn't. I belted him around the head and got a couple on target. He winced in pain. It was over in a few seconds.

I had been concerned that a particularly hard and man-sized pal of Palter's would jump in and kick the shit out of me, but he didn't. On the contrary, he took my hand and raised it, and led me on a run through the playground, victorious-boxer style. I felt elated.

My pleasure and hard-boy status were short-lived. As soon as I arrived at school the next morning, two of Palter's mates who weren't at the fight accosted me in the classroom and one of them, Gardener, *did* me.

I was stupid for not expecting it and preparing for it. It should have been obvious that Palter's mates would take revenge. Oddly enough, at the time, I felt strongly that I could have beaten Gardener. He didn't hit me hard. It was token more than anything, as if he was unsure. But I didn't fight back.

I started to slouch around this time. Not intentionally. Although a lot of the young hooligans slouched, in a cool way, I would sometimes find it hard to have the energy to stand up straight.

Also, I didn't eat healthily. I had the clear impression that I was less healthy than the others. I was pale and thin and it would be commented on in the family, right through my teens and into my twenties. Belsen gone wrong, Mum would jokingly say.

I didn't like vegetables. I didn't really like meat that much either. I would eat very little at home, and get aggro for it. I loved sweets, and I would buy or steal them on the way to and from school. Mum would joke that I 'lived on fresh air'.

I literally remember thinking to myself, I'm acting now at home and in other places. I won't be able to keep this act up forever. Someday I will have to start being myself.

. . .

One day, Mum had a chat with me. The park keeper had been round to our house and told her about my writing in felt-tip pen on the park noticeboard: 'PARKY IS A BASTARD'.

Mum said, 'Kevin, it's not as if people are coming around here saying *good* things about you.'

Her words reached me. I felt moved, as she spoke. I could see for a few moments that she was right. But I almost instantly forgot about what she said and carried on.

Brian O'Houlihan noticed the bruises from Dad's belt on my legs, complete with belt-hole marks, administered for either the writing on the park noticeboard or some other incident, and said, 'Fucking hell!' as if to say, 'That's a bit strong.'

On this occasion, I was glad of Brian's attention. We were alone and it seemed like he cared. But generally, I wouldn't tell mates about anything like that. I was ashamed. I wanted to be seen as cool – grown-up, independent – and deep down, I thought that whatever happened to me was my fault.

'Kevin, you're the damnedest kid,' Dad would say to me when I was asking to go somewhere that he wouldn't allow me to go. I don't think he meant that statement scornfully. It would be more out of frustration. I was persistent when I wanted something. And I couldn't understand my parents' logic as to what *was* allowed and what *wasn't.* There didn't seem to be much science to it. It was inconsistent and had a lot to do with what mood Dad was in.

I occasionally had the vague sense that Dad's controlling was not only about him wanting to protect us by keeping us in, but it also seemed as if he didn't want us to leave him. That he wanted to keep us around. I would often feel guilty for wanting to go out, as if I was betraying him.

Many of my classmates would want to get home after school as quickly as possible. Not me. I was always looking for kids to hang around with; smoke, muck about, steal from shops and so on. But usually, I operated alone. Getting home late was a balancing act. On the one hand I was in no rush to get home, but on the other, if I was home *too* late, I'd be in trouble. The fact that the school was in Willesden, maybe five miles away, gave me a reasonably plausible excuse to be 'late-ish'.

No sex education

I discovered wanking at the age of 14. The first time it came about, I was off school, with the flu. I was lying in bed reading one of my sister's comics. There was an artist's illustration of a girl about my age. I looked at her as I held my cock. It felt pleasant, so I continued. I don't remember exactly how it happened. But I started to enjoy holding my cock more and more as I looked at the illustration. Then all of a sudden, white liquid came out of the end of my cock – it was the most lovely thing.

Of course, I had long since known about wanking. Sharing a bed with two older brothers meant it was impossible to avoid. I would lay in between them, sweating profusely and trying to sleep amid intense shaking from either side of me.

Pat had already told me how babies were made when I was seven and he was 13 (I told the other kids at school, but none of them believed me). Now I was delighted. Perhaps Pat, Joe and I would do it together. I couldn't wait to tell Pat that I had arrived. I was wanking! But when I did, he just said, 'Tsst. Well, don't fuckin' spunk on me.' We were still all three sharing a bed at this point.

I was disappointed. To me, it seemed like a big step forward. 'Why are you down on it?' I asked Pat.

'Wanking is a negative thing to do,' he said. That puzzled me, because he'd been very enthusiastic about it when he was 13 or 14. He went on to say that instead of going out and achieving things, some people just lived in fantasy, and wanked. That made sense, and I felt a little bad about my new hobby, but it didn't affect the frequency with which I did it.

Sometimes I couldn't even wait to get home from my after-school job, the urge was so strong. I'd buy a *Parade* (the semi-nude magazine of the day) and go down one of the alleyways near the hardware shop, squat down behind a fence and wank. I also started to go to bed early so that I could get on with it. After going through a period of a few months where I would sometimes do it two or three times a day, I started to enjoy it less and less. I started to feel drained and quite dirty. I don't know how much of that was the actual wanking and how much was psychological and, hence, the physical reaction.

I wish that there was someone I could have spoken to about the changes that were happening in my body. It was screaming out with desire! It was an all-consuming urge. Yet it was secret. There was no sex education at all at Willesden School of Building, not even a mention in the science class, and my parents didn't say anything about it either.

I don't know why Dad didn't tell me anything. At the time, I just thought he viewed it as bad and didn't want to encourage me, or that he didn't think I was worthy of telling. But he was actually quite stressed a lot of the time, and he may have just overlooked it.

A couple of years later when I was 16 (having already had sex by that time), in a conversation where Mum was saying how busy she was, I said, you need a home help, meaning someone to help with the house-work. Apparently, that was a term that was around in the 1950s – the government would supply 'home help' for women who had just given birth. Mum corrected me about the real meaning of a home help.

She must have said something to Dad afterwards because, that evening as I lay on my bed reading, he walked in, hands in his pock-ets, looking awkward. 'Mum said you were getting confused about a home help?'

'Oh yeah. I was, but I understand now.'

'That's for when a woman has a baby.'

'Yeah, I realise now.'

'Is there anything else you want to know, like?'

'Nah, I'm all right, thanks, Dad.' I felt excruciatingly embarrassed. I could see that he was as well. He left the room.

It's obvious now that my 'sex education' had a big impact on how I went on to operate in the world around sex. It was 'bad', and I wasn't supposed to be doing it, so it followed that the people who did it were *also* bad. Having a high sex drive, I could risk going to Hell myself, but obviously the girls and women who did it with me were bad.

Even years later, with partners I respected, on some level I would be judging them. And women that actually *enjoyed* sex, I judged even more. Somewhere along the line, I picked up that women weren't supposed to enjoy it.

And with masturbation being a secret, and hence having to be done quickly, it informed my attitude towards sex in adult life. Sex was something that had to be done – a need. Something to *get* from women. There was very little thought of it being a union until much later in life. Sexuality wasn't something I respected. It was something to be used.

. . .

There was a guy called Gabriel at St Mary's youth club. He was a good guitar player and knew plenty of hit songs. I hadn't progressed any further with my guitar playing since we'd left Wolverhampton. In fact, I'd given up. (My brother Pat, meanwhile, had a bass and amp, had learned to play well and was in a local band.) Gabriel was forming a group with his mate John and they had a gig a couple of months' hence at St Mary's youth club. They were both on guitars and vocals, and needed a bassist. I told them I could do it. The truth was, of course, I couldn't play. I could maybe play one very simple and easy riff, that Pat had taught me, but that was it. 'Join the group,' they said.

'OK.'

I'm not sure *what* my thinking was, because I lived in such fantasy, but apart from ignoring the fact that I would find it hard to get out of the house for rehearsals, I was also overlooking the fact that I couldn't play.

I didn't practise, and I didn't turn up for the rehearsals. I think by that time, I was seeing any kind of guitar playing as beyond me.

Incredibly, on the night of the gig, I had the cheek to turn up. There was another guy playing bass. During the interval, the singer came over to me with a rolled-up tie and flicked it at me, saying angrily, 'What happened to you?' I couldn't answer.

At the same youth club, I met another young musician, Richard France. Everybody knew he played guitar. He almost always carried one and would stop and play a tune if anyone asked him. He dressed a lot like the pop stars of the day (long hair, flares, reefer jacket), unlike the rest of the locals who were short-haired and vaguely Moddish.

I got talking to him. He said he was forming a band and was looking for a singer. In a moment of bravado, I volunteered my services.

'Great. Let's go round to my place now,' he said. 'I've got a microphone; we can run through something.'

'Eh, sure,' I said.

We went to his house, where he had a room full of musical equipment. He set up the microphone, plugged it in and started playing 'The House of the Rising Sun' on his electric guitar. I started to sing, and this awful sound came out of the speakers. It was screechy and horrible. I hated it.

I was so embarrassed, I made my excuses and left. It baffled me that I had been a confident singer when I was a young kid in Wolverhampton, but now I didn't seem to be able to make a decent sound at all. Richard wasn't as down on my singing as I was, and encouraged me to continue, but I couldn't.

. . .

The *Batman* series was on TV at the time. All the kids watched it. The theme music went, '*Batman, de-de de-de de-de de-de de-de de-de de-de de-de, Batman!*'

One day in our school lunch hour, Brian O'Houlihan got a couple of our friends to sing the theme tune to me, but changed the words from 'Batman' to 'black man'.

Later, when he was on his own, I asked him, 'Why did you do that?'

He laughed as he said, ''Cos you're a bit darker than the rest of us.'

On another occasion a boy at school, who I would have considered vaguely a friend, certainly not an enemy, was talking to a group of us, saying it was a nice area, but there were too many 'wogs' round here. Then he turned to me and in all seriousness said, 'No offence, Kev.'

That one *really* threw me.

There was no intention of humour. The 'no offence, Kev' was said with concern for my feelings. After being in school with me for nearly two years, this kid's perception of me was that I was black.

It would of course be insulting to be called a 'wog' if you were black, but a downright headfuck to someone who was being told they were Irish and, to my knowledge, not born of any black ancestry. I'd often been taken for anything but Irish, ever since I could remember, but now the curls in my hair seemed to be getting much tighter, almost African. One kid said my hair was like a Brillo pad. Also, my skin seemed to be getting darker in the summers. It was highly confusing. Secretly, I lived in fear of these moments, which happened from time to time – people would make comments about my appearance, which to them were innocent but for me were like daggers.

Sometime later, when my hair was a little longer and getting bushy, an uncle said, 'You want to watch it, Kev, you're going to start looking like a n****r.'

It wasn't a joke. He was trying to give me helpful advice. I began to think I must have some African ancestry way back, or there was something that I wasn't being told.

I decided to ask my mum, 'Am I adopted?'

She said, 'No, of course not,' and told a couple of my siblings to stop teasing me about my big nose.

From around that time, and throughout my mid-teens, I did my best to keep out of the sun. Comments or questions from others about my heritage would be more frequent in the summertime.

Dad would attribute my darkness and my ways to my mum's side of the family, the Brownes/McDonnells. He was forgetting that his younger brother Paddy also had black hair and brown skin. He made it clear that he saw the dark complexion as a negative.

On occasion I tried to use it to my *advantage*. I decided to nick a bike in the school lunch hour and cycle home on it to Harrow. I walked through the back streets of Willesden until I saw one in a front garden of a terraced house. I got on it and started pedalling. Just at that moment, the front door burst open and a couple of athletic black guys, a few years older than me, came bounding out. The bike was old and wasn't fast. Plus, one of them was a hell of a runner, for although I cycled for all I was worth, he caught me. They took me back to the house and brought me inside. After their anger subsided a little, it turned into a strange situation – I wasn't free to go, and they were still vaguely telling me off, but they were also being quite friendly to me and we were all watching the cricket on TV.

In an attempt to gain favour, I told them that I was half-Jamaican and that my mother was born in Kingston (I'd heard my Jamaican friend Fordy talking about it). The guys seemed sceptical, but I was heartened when one of them, asked by the other if he believed me, replied, 'Could be – could be.'

Then the same guy said, 'You want to go back to school, or ya want to watch de cricket?'

It was nice of him to offer but I was worried about not getting back to school or being late. I felt uncomfortable about turning down their hospitality, and it was really hard to say, 'I have to get back to school now.' They said OK, and off I went with my tail between my legs, once again somewhat headfucked that I'd passed for mixed ethnicity.

I was mates with two black kids at the school, the aforementioned Fordy and also a boy called Mason.

Fordy was very funny, in that every morning he would walk to school with *such* a miserable look on his face. The boy hated school. Then at lunchtime, on his way home for his meal, he would be full of energy and happiness. Again, on his way back to school for the afternoon lessons, he would be depressed and dawdling, but after school, that kid would be so happy again! He was a great boy.

Barrington Mason was a big, slightly sulky Jamaican guy. He didn't speak much. He barely even looked up. On his first day at school, the form teacher was making a new register and trying to work out exactly what his name was.

'Is it Barrington Mason, or Mason Barrington?' the teacher enquired in his formal tone.

'Enawan [anyone],' Mason replied, in his deep Caribbean tone.

'No! Which is it, Mason Barrington or Barrington Mason?' said the teacher.

'Enawan' was all Mason would say.

The teacher got annoyed, but Mason didn't change his response. No matter how many times he was asked, he only replied, 'Enawan'. The school never found out which it was.

The three of us would sometimes sit together and talk about our main interests, music and sex. They would also tell me about life in the Caribbean (they had both only recently arrived in London) and the latest Blue Beat and rocksteady records their parents owned.

The teachers, including the head, were openly racist to Fordy and Mason and the other black kids in the school – calling them all kinds of names and making comments about the jungle. We were taught in school that Africans were uncivilised cannibals.

It's hard for young people to understand this now, because times have changed so much, and for the better, but in those days, the mid-sixties – before black people in the UK started to actively en-masse stand up to the racism they were being subjected to, and before they began to proclaim being black and proud, which in the suburbs of London happened in the early 1970s – black and mixed-ethnicity people were seen as absolutely bottom of the pile. I recently spoke to a mixed-ethnicity friend who grew up near me around the same time. He told me that when he was a kid he wished he was white. I can see why.

And I'm ashamed to say that the fact that I was close to Fordy and Mason didn't stop me joining in the disgraceful racism that was so prevalent back then. When the geography teacher showed us a map of Africa, I described Nigeria as 'N*ggereria' to get a laugh out of the class, and to the anger and disappointment of Mason and Fordy. They were good people and didn't deserve that shit. I'm lucky Mason didn't beat me up.

I had been programmed to believe that black people, like the Irish, were of less value than British people. It was pretty much impossible to grow up in London at that time and not be racist.

· · ·

One Sunday morning as I walked home from Mass, I passed a ladies' hairdressers. I decided to go around the back of the building and try to find something to steal. I noticed a tiny window open. Being still small and skinny, I was able to get inside. I climbed in, headfirst, full of excitement. I slid down onto a shampooing sink and lowered myself in. It was quiet and I was scared, but also somehow turned on. In fact, I had an erection. It was a ladies' hairdressers, and that made it exciting. I liked the smell of the place. It said women, glamour, care and soft things. I felt like I was sneaking into a world that was out of bounds.

I couldn't find anything to steal, apart from two shillings (10p – the price of ten fags) but I enjoyed being in the place and I stayed longer than I needed to.

· · ·

Our Lady and St Thomas's Catholic Youth Club was usually a great evening. It was held every Tuesday, though I was only allowed to go once a fortnight. It had a simple format: a small room, low lights, good records and slow dancing. It seemed a lifetime since I was a small boy and getting compliments about being good-looking. But now, girls were liking me.

We would dance and rub against each other. Sometimes I'd dance with several girls in a night. Rhythm seemed to come relatively naturally to me, and in a darkened room I was far more confident.

One night, a non-Catholic girl from the Harrow Estate, Sue, came down with one of her pals. She was 14, the same age as me, but looked 18. I got off with her and we groped each other on the dance floor. As I walked her home down the side of Harrow Hill, we stopped at a park bench. She was wearing a black bra under a white see-through blouse.

She had the most beautiful fully formed tits. We were really connecting sexually and she was happy when I took her breasts out. I pulled up her skirt. She was wearing black knickers over a black suspender belt and stockings. I was massively excited. I pulled down her knickers and touched her cunt. It was lovely, warm and wet. But what turned me on most was the sight of it. It was the first time I'd seen one. I'd previously groped girls by sliding my fingers inside their knickers, but now I was looking at her cunt and lovely pubic hair surrounded by her suspenders and stockings. Wow!

I put in one finger, then two. It felt good and she was enjoying it.

I took out my cock. She didn't mind. I started to get on top of her. I was desperate to fuck her.

'No, no, not on a fucking park bench in the middle of Harrow!' she said.

'Oh, come on. What's the difference between two fingers and my dick?'

'No.'

'OK.'

I couldn't understand her logic. I carried on fingering her and kissing her. I tried again.

'No, come on. We're going.'

She got up, laughing. 'Come on! Let's go.'

'Ah, please.'

'Come on! Bloody cheek!' She laughed.

Sue was a lovely girl. I did call round one time after that, but she wasn't in. She was growing up fast and soon started hanging around with the local greasers (rockers), a good few years older than me.

To my shame, I had the belief that girls who that were open, sexually, were 'slags', especially if they were non-Catholic. I *liked* them – in fact, I fancied some of them like mad – and it didn't stop me going after them but, as far as I was concerned, they weren't nice girls and not to be confused with Irish Catholic girls.

My school life was a mess anyway

I was now up for doing just about *anything*! Boys from posh schools were a particular target for my violence. They were easily identifiable by their brightly coloured school blazers. I would walk up to them in the street, or in a tube station, and punch them straight in the face without even speaking to them.

I regularly broke into the likes of Scout huts and stole the members' subscription money when I was supposed to be at school, or during my lunch break. Scout huts were easy and there would always be a few bob in them. I did one in Queensbury. It was next door to the fire station. Not only did I steal the money, but after I'd finished, I set the hut on fire. I was so excited and laughed all the way home, as I visualised a passer-by seeing the Scout hut on fire and running to a phone box and making the emergency phone call to the fire station.

Passer-by: 'Hello. There's a fire!'

Queensbury Fire Brigade: 'Where?'

Passer-by: 'Next door!'

Queensbury Fire Brigade: 'Next door to what?'

Passer-by: 'Next door to you – the fire station!'

I found the concept hysterical and was disappointed when I walked past the next day to find the hut still standing.

I also carried a knife, and any time I found myself in a tube carriage alone, I would rip as many seats as I could, and smash the light bulbs. When people were sitting near me, I would put the knife under my coat or bag and secretly rip as much of the seat as I could. It was like a drug. Same thing in the cinema. It was of course dark, and easy to rip the seats. I would sit alone in one quiet section of the theatre, rip all the seats around me, including the one I was sitting on, then move to another empty part of the cinema and do the same thing there. On some occasions, I would rip as many as 20. I would set myself targets. The more I ripped, the better I felt.

Small art galleries were a target for theft when I was bunking off school. They were usually staffed by women and their purses would be in the back area. I would walk in, wearing my school uniform, pretend to be studiously interested in the paintings – then when my chance came, I'd steal a purse or whatever I could from the staff area.

I wasn't actually having fun. I was doing all the things Pat and Joe had done a few years earlier in Wolverhampton and much more, but I wasn't enjoying it. I felt lonely and desperate.

None of that excuses my behaviour. I didn't show any care for the victims of my crimes – the women in the art galleries, who would have to do without because I'd stolen their money, for cigarettes or whatever, or the woman who worked at my after-school job, opening her purse to find her ten-shilling note was missing.

I had no regard for the consequences to others. My dad wouldn't buy me a bike, so I stole one, and told my parents I'd made it from old scraps. The truth is, some other kid had to do without his bike because I'd stolen it.

On one occasion when I was bunking off school alone and hanging around in a Piccadilly amusement arcade, an old guy came up to me and said, 'There's a man over the road, he'll give you money. I'll take you over. He'll pay you. Come with me.'

I *knew* what he meant, and had it not been for the fact that I was already late in leaving for home (the end of the school day), I probably would have gone. I found it almost impossible to refuse any kind of attention. Positive or negative.

• • •

On a beautiful sunny September day in 1968, I heard 'Hey Jude' for the first time. I couldn't believe its sheer beauty. How could someone come up with something like that?

I'd just started a new school, St James' in Burnt Oak. The headmaster of Willesden Builders had said in my report there was no point in me going back there. Dad was, of course, furious. I could legally have left school at that point, but Dad wanted me to study further. St James' was Catholic, and I already knew a few of the kids from the Scouts and church in Harrow, but other than that, most of them didn't know me. It was a chance to reinvent myself.

I seemed to be pulling it off OK. No one challenged me for a couple of weeks and I successfully fronted out one potential candidate. Then one Friday afternoon, a playful teasing in the classroom got out of hand. It was with a kid called Caufield. His mate was goading me and encouraging Caufield.

I threatened him. But Caufield didn't back down.

Shit. Now what am I going to do?

It was on: after school. I began to feel scared. Caufield seemed confident! He was positively relishing the prospect of a fight.

Fuck! Maybe he's harder than he looks. I would sometimes labour under the illusion that the hard kids wore cool clothes and the square-looking ones, like Caufield, were weeds. And I often got proved wrong.

Four o'clock came, and the whole school was up for watching the fight. They piled out of the gates and towards Watling Park for the 'bundle'. On the way down I said to one of the hardest kids in the school, nervously, 'Is he a good fighter, mate?'

What I really meant was 'Fuck, I'm terrified. What shall I do?'

The school hard nut shrugged his shoulders as if to say, 'I dunno!' and he turned his back.

All the kids were ecstatic and Caufield was having happy exchanges with them. I didn't feel happy. They all ran towards the park, screaming, shouting, punching the air. Everyone loved a bundle! But before we'd even reached the park, their anticipation got the better of them, and they stopped, forming a big circle on a patch of grass outside a house on the estate. The circle was at least three deep and everyone was baying. Those not at the front were pushing and jostling to get a better view.

Caufield and I were pushed into the circle.

He came at me and thumped me hard in the face.

Fuck! He wasn't afraid to have a go, *and* he could punch.

Next thing we were on the floor, rolling around. Neither of us on top of the other for any length of time. Both punching hard. I couldn't see myself winning this one. Caufield was strong and he had the edge. He was getting on top of me.

Then: relief! An adult grabbed Caufield and pulled him off me. It was the history teacher.

Phew! I secretly thought.

Thank fuck. It was over. But it was arranged that we would reconvene at lunchtime the following Monday in the park, well away from the school this time. *Shit! Still, maybe I can think of something over the weekend.*

There was mud all over the back of my school blazer, which inevitably drew questions at home. Dad said, 'What happened ye?'

'I had a fight.'

'Did ye win?'

'It was a draw.'

'A draw? There's no such thing as a draw. Ye lost, didn't ye?'

'It was a draw! The teacher broke it up!'

'Ye lost, didn't ye? Admit it.'

Then he said something that confused me.

'Well, I'm glad to see you've got a bit of spunk in ye.'

I was confused. I thought my dad's criticism of me was that I had too *much* 'spunk' in me. I'd already been in plenty of trouble. But maybe this comment was about what I suspected was a concern of his, that I was too feminine.

That weekend was horrible. I was so nervous and couldn't stop thinking about Monday lunchtime. I told Pat, and asked if we could maybe find out where Caufield lived and go round and beat him up over the weekend. Pat agreed. I went through the phone book and rang all the Caufields listed but couldn't find him. I was getting more and more tense as the weekend went on.

On the Sunday, Pat's mate Alan came around, who had been at St James' a few years earlier. I told him about it. I was still trying to find out where Caufield lived and was hanging on to the vague hope that we could do something before Monday came. Alan was down on the idea and said bluntly, 'You only get trouble if you deserve it. No one picks on you unless you ask for it.'

As the weekend drew on, I could feel the strength was being sapped out of me. I guess it was the anxiety.

That Sunday night, Pat and I hatched a last-ditch plan. I would wear my hobnail boots (steel toe-capped) so that I could kick him. Also, we looked in Dad's toolbox and I pulled out a coal chisel, a heavy, solid iron implement with a spade-like shape on the end. It was about three inches wide, and usually used with a hammer to split house bricks or the like. The plan was to hit him a hard first blow with the coal chisel and end the fight quickly.

Monday morning came and I felt ill with fear. I wanted to do anything but fight. I wore the hobnail boots and hid the coal chisel in the inside pocket of my blazer. The boots and coal chisel couldn't have been more incongruous with the way I felt.

Lunchtime came and we all went down to the park. Caufield was ready and confident – again making jokes with his pals and taking the whole thing lightly. I was alone and didn't talk to anyone.

They stopped at the playground. I saw one of his friends whispering to him and looking at my boots. I knew the tarmac wouldn't suit my footwear (which were leather-soled with many nail heads, making for very slippery soles and heels), but I couldn't seem to speak up and ask for the fight to be on the grass. In my mind, I had already lost.

I was afraid to do anything. I meekly leaned forward in a pretence at throwing a punch at Caufield and the coal chisel fell out of my pocket and dropped to the ground. It clanged as it hit the tarmac.

I recall the faces of St James' hard boys staring at me like I was the village idiot, and the awful feeling of humiliation.

Caufield laughed. I'd been sliding around in my hobnail boots. I had been trying to make it look like I was putting up a fight. There existed a principle at the school – it didn't matter if you won or lost; you would be respected if you had a go. But I was hopelessly out of my depth. Caufield and the others mocked me and laughed, making jokes to each other right in front of me. Blood rushed to my head. Then I heard the most pathetic words come out of my mouth: 'My brother's hard. He'll fuckin do ya.'

My pretence at being a hard boy was well and truly over.

That afternoon, as I sat sheepishly in my class room, waiting for the lesson to start, a weedy kid who wouldn't normally cheek me walked in and said, 'Hello, Oliver.'

'What? Why are you calling me Oliver?'

''Cos you keep asking for more!'

. . .

Now I've just turned 15 years old, and I'm standing in Elephant and Castle Police Station, begging the police not to tell my mother about the motor scooter that Skippy and I had just stolen.

This is my third arrest and it's looking like it'll be my third appearance in juvenile court. I'd been arrested and charged three months earlier for stealing a moped and prior to that for forging a tube and bus pass.

The thought of the belting I would get from Dad was scary, but the prospect of breaking my mother's heart bothered me much, much more. *Mum would be so upset that she wouldn't want to speak to me. She would be so hurt that she wouldn't be able to take it. This would kill her.*

Skippy and I had taken the day off from St James'. My new school was less organised than Willesden School of Building and didn't send letters home if you missed a day. Now, instead of wandering around Soho on my own, as I had been, I had found a compadre. He was a

Polish boy in my class who had, to us, what was an unpronounceable name, so all the kids called him Skippy.

We happened upon each other one morning as we both walked into Burnt Oak tube station at the same time, instead of going the extra quarter of a mile to school. We had both been bunking off on our own in the West End, unbeknownst to each other. Now we were partners.

On this particular day, we'd got the 140 bus over from Harrow, intending to go to school, but we couldn't quite force ourselves to walk past the tube station to get there. We had a better idea. The West End!

I didn't take these decisions lightly. Not for a minute. I was tortured by them.

Sometimes I'd really *want* to go to school. I would leave our house with every intention of going, and most times I *would*, but sometimes I just couldn't seem to get there. I knew it was dangerous, that there would be hell to pay if my parents found out. But it was so hard to resist, and on at least a dozen occasions during that autumn term in 1968, I succumbed to that feeling: half excitement, half fear.

My school life was a total mess anyway.

Apart from the fighting, I was supposed to have learned a Shakespeare speech off by heart for my English literature class. When I was unable to recite it in front of the class from memory, as each boy was required to do, the bullying, miserable teacher told me to write it out ten times and bring in the results the following day.

I got as far as three copies. My hand was sore from writing. It was about ten o'clock that night. I'd started late.

Bugger this, I thought, and got six sheets of carbon paper. I put them under six sheets of blank paper, and wrote one more. Now I had ten.

The teacher wasn't as stupid as he was mean and spotted it quickly. He seemed to delight in giving me 'the strap' – St James' punishment of choice – a heavy, three-inch-wide leather strap that looked a lot like the kind of thing a barber would sharpen his cut-throat razor on. Although the strap was painful, it didn't bother me as much as the humiliation, and the fact that now I would have to write out the original ten sheets, as well as learn the next bit. As I walked back to my desk after getting the punishment, a kid laughed, seemingly at the intolerable pressure I was being put under. I should have hit him.

The following morning, as I got off the bus in Burnt Oak, I knew I didn't have the pages I was supposed to. It was a depressing thought – more humiliation. As soon as Skippy and I made the decision not to go to school, I felt as light as a feather.

The tube journey to the West End was damned exciting: the Northern Line from Burnt Oak up to Leicester Square, adrenalin now building with the thought of all the possibilities that lay ahead. Change at Leicester Square for the Piccadilly Line, and *there it was*. Piccadilly Circus tube station and the West End of London!

Coming up the stairs and out into the street: the noise, the colours, the people! Man, it was the most exciting place in the world. Freedom! Sex! It was all here.

A record shop would often be first on the agenda. In those days you could go into a listening booth and hear any record you chose.

Breakin' down the walls of heartache, baby,
I'm a carpenter of love and affection.

Then we'd walk around, explore, and take in the atmosphere. Before long, if we had the money, we'd be in a strip club – one or two opened at midday (Skippy, like me, was obsessed with sex). I loved to go down St Anne's Court where the sexy prostitutes would hang out of the windows. I was full of lust and hadn't had full sex at this point. Skippy even knew the names of some of the women.

'That's where Mimi lives,' he said, as he pointed to an upstairs window.

On this particular day, we decided to bunk a train from Victoria to Brighton. In my mind, I felt like a Mod a few years earlier, going down to Brighton. But as we left London, I suddenly remembered the time. Shit! It was 2.45! I would be in real trouble if I wasn't home for five o'clock, 5.30pm at the very latest, and if we were going down to Brighton, there was no way I'd make it back to Harrow in time.

The train had left Victoria 15 minutes earlier. Suddenly it slowed down, almost to a stop. We could see a row of semi-detached suburban houses below the bank on which the train was riding.

'Quick, let's go,' I said.

We opened the door. The train was barely moving now. We jumped out and rolled down the bank.

Neither of us were hurt, and we were exhilarated from the experience. We laughed as we brushed ourselves down. 'But where the fuck are we?' God knows.

'Let's take a walk down that street.'

We saw a motor scooter parked in a front garden. It looked old but OK. Scooters were cool. Mods had ridden them. But we were both only 15 and didn't have licences.

'Are you sure you can ride one?' I asked Skippy.

'Yeah, I've ridden a couple.'

Skippy quietly wheeled it out of the garden and a little way down the street without starting the engine, so as not to alert the owner. About a hundred yards down the road, he said, 'Right, let's go.' He kick-started the bike and the engine roared.

Off we went, excitedly, both in our school uniforms – Skippy riding, with me on the back. Of course, we didn't look like your average motor-scooter riders, but Skippy was confident he could get us back to Harrow. We saw a sign for 'Central London' and followed it.

'Great. With any luck, I'll be home at the normal time.'

I was impressed with Skippy's confidence, determination and scooter-riding prowess.

As we went around the Elephant and Castle roundabout, a police-man on a motorbike rode up alongside us. He stared at us and, after a few seconds, signalled us to pull over. Damn! He slowly got off his Triumph 650 and walked towards us. We dismounted. He was wearing full-length black leather motorcycle boots.

'Is this your scooter?'

'Yeah,' said Skippy.

'Where'd you get it?'

'I bought it.'

'Where from?'

'From a bloke who put an advert in the paper.'

'OK. Which paper?'

'The *Daily Mirror*.'

Shit, Skippy! I thought. *Everyone knows they don't have classified ads in the* Daily Mirror.

'Right,' he said. 'I'm arresting you on suspicion …'

Skippy started to run. I stayed. I was too nervous.

The copper remained with me as he radioed for support. One minute later Skippy was back; he had run straight into another policeman.

We were taken, handcuffed, in the back of a van, to Elephant and Castle Police Station. It was becoming clear that this was serious. They brought us in through the rear entrance. We were very much under arrest.

'Please, officer, don't tell me mum, she's not well. The shock could kill her,' I said.

'What's wrong with her?' he said.

'She's really bad with her nerves and this will be too much for her.'

'What's your name?'

'Keith Radney.' (The phoney name I always gave.)

'Address?'

'316 Imperial Drive, Harrow,' I said. (There *was* no 316 Imperial Drive.)

'Are you on the phone?'

'No.' Another lie.

Maybe there's a way I can get out of here, I thought.

They took us into separate rooms, and we made statements, admitting what we had done. They took our fingerprints. One of the coppers brought me sausage and chips and a mug of tea. I enjoyed the meal. It felt like a comforting reminder of normality.

The one who nicked us said to one of his colleagues, 'Right, Charlie, you'll have to drive over there to get his parents.'

That'll take about two hours. Maybe I can escape somehow? I clung to that hope.

The officer said, 'Come on,' and motioned me through the open door. Then he opened another door, a big heavy one. It was dark in there. I was scared.

'Is that a cell?' I asked. I hadn't been in one before.

'Yeah, get in,' said Charlie, the fat unpleasant one.

'No, it's not, son,' said the nice one who'd nicked us. 'It's just a detention room.'

It was a cell.

And off they went. It was dark and depressing in the cell. There was only a toilet and a hard wooden bed to sit or lie on.

I couldn't see any way of escaping. Maybe I could talk them into letting me go, especially on the grounds that Mum would be too upset if she knew.

Skippy was in the cell opposite me. After about an hour, I realised that I could see him through the tiny window, but it took me about 20 minutes to attract his attention and make him realise that I was trying to communicate with him. I couldn't make him understand. It was purely to relieve the tension, or to give each other hope. He tried to communicate something to me, but I couldn't make out what it was, and after a while, we both gave up.

I thought about the kids in St James' and wished I was with them. They'd just be coming out of school now, without a care in the world. Walking down the Orange Hill Road, laughing, joking, going for a cup of tea and a fag in the caff.

Why the fuck couldn't I just have gone to school? I asked myself. *And soon my mum and dad will know that I've been arrested, again! Fuck!*

Skippy had happily volunteered his dad's work phone number and was out after about two hours. Not long after that, Charlie returned and was furious.

'I've just wasted three fucking hours driving through the traffic, and there's no 316 Imperial fucking Drive in fucking Harrow!'

Charlie's partner, a young bloke, stepped behind me and laced his arms inside my elbows, pulling my arms up as high as he could. Charlie laid into my stomach with his fists.

This time I gave them the correct name and address, but I *still* didn't tell them that we had a phone. I reasoned that it would be at least another hour before Mum and Dad would know – another hour where I'm not in deep shit, as opposed to two minutes with a phone call. I know that logic sounds crazy, but that was how I thought.

Dad got there at about 8pm. He watched as I was charged with taking and driving away.

When we arrived home, the whole family was gathered in the lounge. The curtains were drawn, and there was barely any light in the living room, only a small table lamp. It was like a wake.

Mum was sobbing and inconsolable, stretched out on the armchair, almost lying down, as if ill. In the case of previous beltings, Dad would first ask everyone else to leave the room. Not this time.

Also, usually, Dad would stand with his hands in his pockets, telling me off, then he would slowly take his hands out of his pockets, to reveal a belt already wrapped around his right fist. He would unroll the belt and hit me with it. This time he took off the belt that was holding up his trousers, as I watched.

'Take your trousers down,' he said.

I did. I tried to get myself into the corner of the room, but there wasn't time. I tried to put my arms around my legs to protect them and roll myself into a ball, as the belt came raining down, but then my head was getting it. I was screaming.

On previous occasions, at around this point (a minute or two in), Mum would run in from the kitchen, crying and pleading with him to stop. But not this time. He carried on, as the family watched.

Finally, he stopped, and I went up to bed.

Approved School was looking like my next home. I didn't mind the idea at all. In fact, I welcomed it. I wanted to get out of the house. A couple of mates had gone, and they said it was OK.

. . .

Now it's six days after the Elephant and Castle arrest and I'm about to get nicked *again!*

Skippy and I had both pledged, with genuine solemnity, to our parents and even to each other, that we would go to school and be good, and we meant it. I know *I* did. But we just couldn't seem to carry it through. I would leave home with the intention of going to school. I'd get on the 140 bus and sit next to Skippy, still with every intention of going to St James', but by the time we got to Burnt Oak, school was looking dark, dreary and serious. We looked at each other.

Fuck it!

After bunking into the London Zoo and getting bored with cruelly giving the monkeys lighted fags, which they initially tried to eat, we ended up walking around the outside of Regent's Park, trying car door handles, to see if we could steal anything from the parked vehicles.

We noticed a conservative-looking young man walk past us, and I thought there was something odd about the way he looked at me. But then he disappeared, so we carried on.

It turned out there had been two of them, both plain-clothed. They'd been watching us for about half an hour, as we tried one car door after another. We hadn't even found one that was open. Finally, the two men walked up to us and showed their badges. We couldn't believe it.

After asking us a few questions, one turned to the other and said: 'I'm satisfied.'

That gave me a moment of hope. *Great. He's satisfied with the lie we told him.* We said we were looking at the speedometers to see how fast the cars could go. But what he meant was that he was *satisfied that they had enough information to arrest us.* These were young police officers and feeling very pleased with themselves.

Fucking hell! How could I have done it again? This can't be happening!

They took us to Marylebone Police Station and, after getting statements, they put us in separate cells.

I just couldn't comprehend what my parents would say about this one. I had promised my distraught mum I would go to school.

Shit! Fuck!

All of that said, I found something comforting about being in a police cell as a juvenile. Most of the police officers treated us a bit more gently than they would do older criminals. They gave me the usual mug of tea, and two sausages and chips, which gave me a sense of wellbeing.

Skippy was out in a couple of hours again. Meanwhile, using the silver button on my barathea school blazer as a chisel, I carved 'ROWLAND' in big letters on my cell wall. I'd studied all the other names on the wall. I wondered what they were in for, and if any of them were murderers. I carved my name bigger than all the others.

This isn't real, I thought. *It's just a game. This is some kind of research. Really, I'm talented. I'm not a criminal. One day I'll write a play or something, and all of this will be valuable experience.*

Five hours had passed and still no sign of my dad. The duty sergeant came in and told me that I was going to Stamford House, a boys' home. By law, a youth under 16 couldn't spend the night alone in a police cell. They started to make the arrangements. I was quite excited about it. I wondered what the other kids would be like. I didn't want to go home.

Moments later, the copper opened the cell door to tell me that Dad had arrived. The officer noticed the big carving of ROWLAND on the wall. He got angry, and made like he was going to hit me, but he didn't, I'm pretty sure because Dad was only a couple of rooms away. He *did* tell my dad though.

Dad had Pat with him. We drove home in silence, the three of us in the front cabin of Dad's truck.

I didn't think the atmosphere at home could be any bleaker than it had been the week before, but this time it was even darker. One of my siblings screamed out in tears, 'He's breaking up the whole family!'

I was expecting a serious hiding, like last week – but it didn't come. It was like Dad was in shock, or maybe he had given up. He sent me upstairs.

Just as I reached the top of the stairs, I heard my brother Pat behind me. Before I could look around, Pat was laying into me, pummelling my back and head with both of his fists. I hit him back, but not much.

As I write now, I can't help but be aware that it was Pat who had taught me to steal, and who had enjoyed hearing my stories (some real, some imagined) about who I had beaten up, what I'd stolen, or how I had cheeked teachers, etc.

Everyone was resigned to the fact that I was going away to Approved School.

Of course, I wanted to go. I knew I was doing things that were wrong, and I felt terrible that my mother was so upset – that was the worst thing. But deep down, I must have seen that there was way too much pressure being heaped on me at home, and there always *had* been. I thought I'd be better off somewhere else.

I had wanted to get a lot wilder than I actually was. In truth, I was restraining myself. Two kids at St James' had run away and ended up in Carlisle. *Yes! Fucking great! So exciting.* I was envious of them.

Nothing my dad was saying touched me. All he could do was threaten me with more violence or hit me. I was already getting that. It wasn't going to stop me. And I would have gone even further had it not been for the thought of Mum being so upset. Losing her love was my biggest fear. But I seemed to be in the grip of something more powerful than me. I was on some kind of roll. I didn't actually give a fuck about myself or where I would end up. My life seemed grey and miserable.

· · ·

Now it's two weeks later and I'm standing outside the door of a prostitute in St Anne's Court, wearing my school uniform and hoping desperately for my first full sexual experience.

I had been wanting a prostitute for a while and had made a previous visit with only ten shillings (50p – a quarter of the price) in my pocket.

I pleaded with her. 'Please! I've only got ten shillings. Just let me have *something.*'

'No, son, it's two quid!'

'Oh, but please, please. Let me have something!'

'Son, there's a nice Chinese restaurant across the road. Do yourself a favour and get yourself a nice meal with that ten bob.'

She closed the door.

But now I had the two quid and plenty more. I was taking the day off school and spending the proceeds of a theft of over £30 in cash from a car in North Harrow bowling alley the previous day. It was another of my 'trying to open car-door handle' sessions. This one had proved fruitful.

The next day I walked into school with a wad of notes in my pocket. I invited loads of kids down the Wimpy Bar for lunch, in what was an unconscious attempt to buy friendship.

The day after, I took four or five of the hard nuts up the West End, for strip clubs and prostitutes. It was about midday and the clubs had just opened. We all sat there in the front row, in our school uniforms, watching the strippers.

Later that afternoon, a middle-aged French prostitute first washed her cunt in a bowl and then immediately lay on the small bed, legs apart, with her thighs pulled up to her chest.

'Come on, dahling, put it in,' she said.

It was depressing, and more like a clinical exercise than a sexual encounter. It felt wrong – like I was having sex with someone like my mother.

I tried to kiss her. She turned her head away. 'No, dahling, just fuck.'

I could barely do it. But I did. I went with another prostitute an hour later. This time I couldn't get hard. But the lady was nice and friendly. I gave her the two pounds fee, before we started. As I was leaving, she asked me for a tip for her maid. I refused.

A friend, George, went in with the same woman right after me. When he came out, he said, 'She told me – next time, tell your black friend to bring a tip for my maid.'

I didn't know if he was serious or winding me up.

. . .

Apart from the stress of being around Dad, going to court was actually an exciting day. On the way there, I would wonder what the other boys would be wearing. I quite liked the smell of juvenile courts' waiting areas – a mixture of cigarette smoke and officialdom.

On one occasion, when it was just my mum and me (Dad couldn't get off work), I saw another kid who was for sure the same age as me. He was dressed in a mohair jacket, nice parallel trousers, and he had short hair, but the thing that attracted me most as we all sat in the waiting room, was that he was smoking a fag with his mum and smiling – it didn't seem like the end of the world that he was in court. He looked relaxed as they both smoked, and his mum was clearly OK with his cigarette use. There seemed to be a real intimacy between them.

I got two years' probation for the charges – taking and driving away, and attempted theft. I was disappointed that I wasn't being sent to Approved School. Glowing references from the Scout masters, which I somewhat reluctantly sought, plus our nice house in Kenton, were the clinchers that kept me at home. I remember the copper coming round for a 'social report' (in those days, the police fulfilled that function, not social workers), to look at where and how I was living. As he stood in the hallway, he looked around at the newly decorated space and said to Dad, 'There won't be any problem here, sir.'

Friends of mine who lived in a nearby council estate had been sent away for less.

I had initially liked the notoriety I received in school for going to court but now it was serious: at least one of my friends was being told by his parents to stay away from me. And he was obeying them. I felt estranged from the other kids and from normal everyday things.

I decided to leave school. *I'll have money in my pocket, I'll be a man,* I thought. I was feeling guilty about taking food for free at home, especially since I was making my parents so unhappy.

I started looking for a job in the men's clothing stores on Harrow High Street. I was only vaguely surprised that bringing home the various career leaflets garnered no serious objection from my parents. I think they too realised it was for the best.

PART TWO

All stick, and no carrot

I was 15 years and three months old when I left school in December 1968. I started as a junior salesman at Dunn and Co, selling hats and suits. I liked working among clothes and the staff there treated me well.

On my first day, one of the assistants asked me if I smoked. I said no. (I was acting how I thought they wanted me to be. The truth was I had a daily cigarette habit.)

He said, 'Are you sure? Here, have one if you like.'

I said, 'No, no' (I felt I couldn't backtrack now). Instead of taking the cigarette, I later stole one from his packet! Bizarre behaviour, I know. There were only two cigarettes remaining in the pack when I took one out, meaning it was highly likely that he noticed. The next day I had to go in and say that I smoked 'sometimes'.

. . .

I'm going where the sun keeps shining,
Through the pouring rain,

I'd heard that song from the film *Midnight Cowboy* and loved it. It seemed to say freedom to me.

I saw an advert for a 'Midnight Cowboy' in a cabinet outside a newsagent shortly afterwards. I phoned the number and was asked to go to a house in Kenton. I was greeted by a big black guy, who told me that being a Midnight Cowboy was not just about servicing women. It was about going with men too. He asked to see my cock. I didn't want to take it out, but I did. He touched it and held it, as if he was inspecting it. I got the impression he was enjoying it. I wasn't.

He asked me to phone him if I was up for being a prostitute for men. I didn't phone back.

Despite leaving school and bringing in a wage, my relationship with Dad didn't get any easier – perhaps worse. I was barely given any more freedom. I would go out on a Friday or Saturday night, but I was expected to be in early. He had a stick, which he kept by the front door in the corner of the hall. He would use it on me for coming home late or whatever. When he first produced it, he held it up to me and said: 'This is *your* stick!'

In a perverse way, around this time, I got to almost quite like it when Dad hit me. Not the pain, but the attention. It seemed almost like a game to me. Sometimes, I would push him by staying out late or defying him, until he hit me. On other occasions, I'd be over-compliant with him. I seemed to oscillate between chronic people-pleasing and rebelling against him.

Sometimes Dad would lock the six-foot-high back gate when he was going to bed and I wasn't home by the permitted hour. I would climb over the gate and gain entry through the back door. He then started locking the back door as well.

To get around that, I would climb over the back gate as usual, then throw small stones at our back bedroom window to wake Joe, who would open the window so that I could climb up on top of the outside toilet and into our bedroom, closing the window again. In the morning, Dad would come into our room and, though he didn't say anything, I could tell he was surprised to find me lying in bed.

• • •

A few mates from Harrow and I would often go to the Top Rank, a dance hall in Watford. We arrived late one night, and the bouncers decided they weren't going to let us in. We pleaded with them, but to no avail. They were Irish, and grown men, compared to us 15-year-olds.

To bunk in, we went around the side of the venue and started trying the exits. Suddenly one of the doors sprung open and five or six bouncers burst out, and ferociously beat the shit out of us.

I was *mainly* surprised and aggrieved because there was definitely a perception in our house that Irish people were kinder, warmer, more spiritual. When I got home, I said: 'Dad, a load of bouncers at the Top Rank beat us up, and they were Irish! I thought Irish people were supposed to be good!'

'Huh?!' he said. 'They're the worst of the lot!'

It was confusing.

Dad seemed to have ambivalent feelings towards his Irish roots. He didn't spend a lot of time in pubs like many other Irish men. He didn't go out much, didn't drink a lot, didn't sing much. We didn't normally go home to Ireland each summer like many Irish families. Money being tight was a factor in that, but a big part of him seemed to want to get away from Ireland. Maybe it was the poverty. He was quite conflicted about the whole Irish immigrant thing.

We were never really part of any Irish community. We were always on the outside. That was his choice. Dad's perception of the Irish in England, which became the dominant view in our house, was largely that they were emotional, maudlin, fiery, unambitious, and boozers.

I talked to him about it a few years ago. 'Dad, why were you not keen for us to be part of the Irish community?'

'There was an awful lotta drink in it,' he said.

I couldn't argue with that.

When my sisters Grainne and Sarah were in their late teens, he would sometimes encourage them to date 'refined' (posh) English boys. This they did. But often, after these young specimens of middle-class English youth were brought home, Dad would change his tune and refer to them as 'little pipsqueaks' or the like.

. . .

Now Dad and I are in the hallway. I'm 15 years old. He is telling me off, stick in hand, and getting ready to hit me. Mum is in the kitchen, busy with other things, not really watching, maybe trying to ignore it. As Dad raises his arm to strike me with the stick, I think, *Fuck this! I'm not taking it any more!*

I put my fists up in front of me to let him know that if he hits me, he's going to get at least one back. As quick as a flash, Dad turns to Mum and shouts, 'Look at him! He'd hit his own father!'

Though I was only vaguely conscious of it at the time, it's clear now that he thought it was fine to hit me, but akin to treason for me to hit him back. Also, in that moment, I got confirmation of the vague suspicion that I'd felt occasionally on some deep level, that Dad was competing with me, for Mum.

He would often criticise Mum for defending and spoiling me. But she didn't spoil me. Dad dominated and it was all stick, and no carrot.

It never even occurred to me that maybe Dad was a bit crazy, or that the way he was treating me was wrong. There were no grandparents around, or any neutral adults with a different reality, to check things out with. Dad's narrative was the only one around, and I believed it.

He didn't hit me again after that instance, but the criticism continued. In fact, it intensified.

. . .

My probation officer, Mr Maynard, was a good man. He encouraged me to do the things I *wanted* to do. He was positive and seemed to like me. Later, when I would again get arrested and he would be approached for references, I would feel bad about letting him down.

After about six months of seeing him on a weekly basis, Mr Maynard asked me how things were at home. 'Fine,' I said. It didn't even occur to me to say anything *other* than 'fine'. This was the only experience I had, and if things weren't fine, it would mean it was my fault.

He also asked me, did I masturbate a lot? I *did* masturbate a lot, but felt bad about it, and told him I didn't. He then suggested I 'see someone'. When I asked him what he meant, he said: 'A psychologist.'

'Why?' I said.

'It might be good for you,' he said. 'It might help you. No pressure. It's up to you. Please think about it.'

I told him I would consider it.

I mentioned it at home, at the dinner table one night. No one said anything.

I declined Maynard's offer. Though I wasn't conscious of it at the time, I see now that I was afraid they'd find out that there was something wrong with me, mentally.

A part of me wishes I *had* seen someone now. Maynard was a good man and was trying to help me. I sensed that he could see through the charade. But I was too afraid to open up. Of course, if I had seen someone I might have ended up with Valium addiction, or similar, which wasn't uncommon in those days.

. . .

I saw some lodgings advertised in the *Harrow Observer*. I rang up the landlady and she pretty much agreed on the phone that I could move in. I'd had a bad week with Dad and felt the situation was hopeless.

The catalyst was Dad criticising me for not paying my housekeeping money that week (£3 out of my £6.50 wages). I had just left Dunn and Co and started a new job as an apprentice printer, but I had to work a week in hand, which meant no wages for the first week. It was the only week I hadn't paid housekeeping money since I'd left school. While I was having my dinner at the kitchen table, Dad was standing over me, ranting. I knew there was nothing I could say – I felt bad that I didn't have the money, but also I knew that I hadn't actually done anything wrong. He was accusing me of deliberately trying to hold money back. I wasn't. I told him again: 'I haven't got any money. I won't get last week's money till the end of this week.'

He leaned right into me, putting his face up close to mine, and with a look of pure scorn, said loudly into my face: 'Ya ate last week, didn't ya?'

This was one occasion when I *did* get angry with him. I jumped up and said: 'If I'm going to be *treated* like a lodger, I may as well *be* a bloody lodger. I'm leaving!'

On this occasion, Mum agreed, and took my side, saying angrily: 'I don't blame you!'

Deep down, something told me that I was just in the wrong environment. The people in Dunns had appreciated me and often told me what a good job I was doing and how sad they were when I left, and should I ever want to come back, they would welcome me. I had responded to their encouragement and worked hard for them, as I had with Peter Kent-Baguley, the good teacher at school.

I came home from work a few days later, and told my mother I was leaving that evening. I went upstairs and started packing. I was quite excited. Independence felt good.

Soon afterwards, my dad came home, earlier than usual. Mum had obviously phoned him. They both came upstairs while I was finishing my packing. Mum and Dad now had a completely different attitude. Dad was soft, gentle.

'Don't go, Kevin,' said Mum. 'We don't want you to go, love.'

'Ah, it's for the best, Mum,' I said.

'No. Don't go, love.' Then she said: 'Why don't you move into Pat's room?'

Pat had moved out and gone to teacher-training college in Birmingham. I had been asking for months to sleep in his small, empty box room, at least while he wasn't there, instead of sharing a room with Joe. But Mum and Dad had firmly said, 'No!'

Now, they were *offering* it to me. It seemed like a really big gesture. I was feeling extremely guilty for wanting to leave. Like I was breaking their hearts, particularly Mum's.

It was guilt and fear that made me stay. I couldn't resist the magnitude of Mum's gesture, and Dad was now talking to me in a completely different way, as if I were an adult, and I was afraid of losing what now seemed like a real opening for a much better relationship between us. If I left, I would feel like I'd be rejecting his olive branch. I stayed.

It was a mistake. Wanting to leave home didn't mean that I didn't love my parents. I did love them, but I needed to get out. I just didn't have any emotional intelligence back then. I had no idea that I could still love them but do what was right for me. I couldn't even begin to separate those two things.

I moved my clothes into Pat's room and ended up not leaving home until I was almost 19 and had a geographical reason to do so.

Things didn't improve. In fact, in an argument shortly after, Dad said, 'Have I got to be nice to you, to keep you here?' It was like he regretted his moment of softness with me.

Dad was different around other people. A couple of years prior to this when I was still at school, I had wanted to go to a boxing club. I asked Dad and he said, 'No, go in the front room and do some homework.' I went in the front room and, after a bit of daring from Pat, decided to leave the house, via the front-room window. I went to the boxing club and enjoyed it.

The guy who ran the club gave me a lift home in his truck. He pulled up outside the house and we chatted for a couple of minutes. I could see Dad watching us from the front window. When I got inside, expecting at least a serious telling-off, if not a belting, Dad just said, 'Where did you go?'

I said, 'to the boxing club.' He didn't say anything else. I think it was because another adult, an outsider, was involved. In retrospect, I wish there had been more outsiders involved. It would have been better for me. Dad had way too much control, and as a family, it was stifling and claustrophobic, certainly as far as I was concerned.

I had, by this time, lost trust in my own perception. I made my decisions based on what I thought were other people's values (Dad's, mainly, but also other members of the family, as well as outsiders). If I was asked a question, I would have to think about who was asking it and what answer they would want to hear, or what answer would get me the least stressful outcome. It was confusing. And bloody hard work. I had become an over-thinker – inevitable in those circumstances. Looking back, I see that I felt there was no way out. My situation was internal. I was defective. *That* feeling would increase in intensity in the years that followed.

Rolo of 'Arra

Summer of 1969 was when a load of factors came together – 'Ivy League' clothes going overground, a new generation of 'junior Mods' coming of age, and the explosion of so many great reggae records.

We would meet in Wealdstone Wimpy bar on Saturday nights, hang out there for an hour or so, and then off to wherever the dance was that night.

From the moment we arrived in London, I had longingly looked at the local Mods, with their coiffured haircuts, doing their fantastic Mod walks, or riding their scooters – you didn't have to wear helmets in those days and no self-respecting Mod would. They sat incredibly upright on those Italian machines.

But now I recognised that 1969 was *our* time, just like the Mods a few years earlier, and the Teds before them. We had our own look and our own music – reggae.

There was no name for the look at that point, but 'Peanuts' was the description we'd sometimes give ourselves. Skinhead was a joke term. You would good-naturedly say 'Oi, skinhead!' to a friend who had just returned from the barbers having had their hair cropped almost bald, GI or astronaut-style (particularly popular in the summer of '69, with the moon landing). Not all of us had that haircut at the time, but many did. Skinhead wasn't the name of a youth cult until the media labelled it later.

I was conscious that one or two of the 'Harrow' were ex-St James' and knew some of my previous cowardice. But I was part of it. Sometimes one or two of the harder boys would consult me about style or dancing, both of which seemed to come naturally to me.

We were 'the Harrow' ('Arra) and it was great. Dressed beautifully in long white raincoats, over perhaps a cardigan with a striped or check

Career Club (or similar) shirt, Sta Prest or pleated trousers, white or sky-blue socks, and beautiful highly shined black or oxblood Royal's cordovan, wingtip brogues or plain caps (shoes).

Wingtips were cumbersome, yet beautiful. When I first saw a pair in the Squire shop in 1968, I was shocked that they were so big and awkward-looking, but I soon also recognised that they were beautiful. Like a great song or a work of art, they haunted me. I'd think about them at night as I lay in bed, trying to sleep. I found the statement of wearing shoes like this, against the background of 'swinging sixties London', incredibly radical, to the extent that it made me howl with laughter at how subversive it was, even though I had no idea what that word meant. I knew intuitively that this was an amazing statement.

Before it hit the media, only the cool kids would understand it. Everyone else would think you were square. These massive, cumbersome shoes were the antithesis of what was supposed to be fashionable in late 1960s London. Up to that point, cool had meant dainty, even slightly effeminate. Not now! We dressed like middle-aged Americans, astronauts or soldiers.

The whole look would be finished off with an immaculate, razor-cut college-boy or cropped haircut. There were no unwanted creases in the trousers or shirts. The fact that the look was so 'conservative' meant that the mainstream didn't even notice it. But we noticed each other and that was what counted.

Everyone was 16 – or 15 at the very youngest. But 16 was *the* age.

It's hard to understand now, but things were very different in those days. Now, 16 sounds incredibly young, but it wasn't then. You would already have been working for a year, and would have a disposable income; 18- and 19-year-olds were considered past it. They would generally have stopped going out dancing and would instead go to pubs and stand around and chat. By 21, 22, 23, you were expected to have settled down. That was the societal pressure at the time, and I felt it. Ridiculously, if a woman was 27 and not married, she would be considered 'on the shelf'.

With regard to what the media called skinheads and suedeheads, there has been a lot of misinformation over the years, mostly written or spoken by people who weren't there – too young, or not in London.

Yes, there were all sorts of later permutations that happened outside the capital, and some of them were interesting, but if you are into how and where things start – and I am – it was very much a London thing. And if you were 10, 11 or 12 years old in 1969, you didn't experience it. It was a youth cult. 'Youth' (not child) being the operative word.

There was a walk – or rather, an attitude, a way of being that was around in London at that time. It's difficult to describe, but it involved walking in an exaggerated way, leaning slightly forward from the hips, and swinging your arms back and forth (but diagonally in front of you and behind you too, as you moved). It was a statement, that I've only ever really seen in London.

This thing was all over the capital, but still underground. You couldn't read about it in magazines and you didn't hear reggae on the radio. The names of the clothes shops and records were passed on by word of mouth only.

Five or six of us boys would dance in a line, pretty much exclusively to reggae. I picked up the dancing quite easily. If a girl was interested, she would dance nearby. That would be a sign to move towards her when a slow or slowish record came on, and do a close, sexy dance, groin to groin, with both of us alternating putting one thigh in between the other's legs – it was a dance we had learned from the Jamaicans.

The first media article appeared in the *Daily Mirror* on August bank holiday Monday, 1969. The feature was titled 'This Is a Skinhead'; there was no photograph, only a cartoon of a boy wearing a white T-shirt, braces, jeans and boots. There then followed a glut of articles.

Though a big part of me was initially pleased about the media recognition, it was disappointing that only one aspect of the style was portrayed and presented. That was actually just one facet that came 'in' for a few weeks in the summer of '69.

The bonehead thuggery that was being reported in the media had nothing to do with the look itself. Yes, like with any group of young working-class people, if circumstance demanded, or if invited, there could be a fight. But it wasn't about violence. That was just the sensationalist media.

It was a very sophisticated way of dressing. 'Fashion' was in the West End – tasteless orange or purple shirts with silly, shaped collars, horrible hipster trousers with nasty three-inch belts. The kind of thing the dancers on *Top of the Pops* would wear at that time – naff in the extreme. The cool look was in the suburbs.

Ultimately, it was killed off by the distorted media coverage. One of the papers came up with the word 'suedehead' and touted that as the next fashion development. A bunch of 11-, 12-, maybe 13-year-olds, as well as some un-hip older youths, picked up on that, and started describing themselves as such. Then, a cash-in writer, who had previously produced a similar book on skinheads, put out a book called *Suedehead*, and a myth was born. To this day, you will hear people talking about suedeheads as if it existed as some kind of style cult. No one who was anyone called themselves a suedehead at the time.

What actually happened, was in the late summer of '69, as a reaction to all the sensationalist media coverage, the coolest kids immediately started growing their hair long. To the extent that by summer 1970, their hair was almost shoulder-length, though they were still wearing Ivy League clothes. Next, they would undo the collar buttons on their button-down shirts. Then they started wearing the likes of penny round-collared shirts, but still with straight trousers. By the start of 1971, they were wearing flat-fronted A-line wide trousers and roll-neck sweaters, until in '72 the look was completed with chunky Toppers shoes, and feather-cut hair. It had completely changed. What some people call 'suedehead' was nothing more than a transition period.

The saddest thing for me was that as a result of the media sensationalism, the Ivy League thing, which was just progressing into something *really* interesting, was killed off.

The proper Ivy League thing was about loose-shouldered jackets, with raised edging and straight patch pockets with flaps. Jacket vents would be four inches and off-centre, worn with a nice loose pleated shirt (sewn-in pleats were for the high street), and a pair of flat-fronted, slim-cut trousers with a one-inch leather belt, topped off with loafers or brogues. But the haircut that was about to come into fashion was the thing that was really radical. It was one thing to have your hair cut short all over, but this new and barely seen development meant leaving it a fair bit longer on the top, with the side parted neatly, and tapered to nothing at the back and sides. It was nothing more than an Ivy League 'short back and sides' and was totally outrageous! Only the most discerning eye would get it. Mainstreamers, including most teenagers, would have taken one glance and written it off as completely square. It was so brave for the time. I was really excited about it. But it was not to be.

Dexys later did that whole look on the *Don't Stand Me Down* album and its surrounds. It looked particularly good on Billy Adams, Dexys' guitarist, as this photo shows.

. . .

Now I'm 16 years old and standing outside Harrow Wimpy Bar with a few other boys. Smelly pus is coming out of my ears, and I'm very embarrassed about it.

For the last few weeks, both of my ears had been leaking pus. It was literally falling onto my shoulders, and it had an unpleasant smell. After a few weeks, I went to the Ear Nose and Throat Hospital in King's Cross. The specialist treated me for external otitis and told me it was caused by stress.

An older face, about 19, that I didn't know very well – Bob Magill – joined the gathering. He was stylish, and dressed similar to us – sheepskin coat, short hair and a trilby. He was a *real* hard man, and in a different league to the rest of the 'young Harrow'.

I was having one of those days when I was hoping no one would notice me, and the dripping ears didn't help.

'Wassup wi' yer ear?' Bob Magill said, noticing me tending to it.

Ah fuck, I thought.

'Ah, nothing much,' I said. 'I got this external otitis thing.'

He looked at me intently for about 30 seconds, as if he was studying me. I was sure he could see into me and wouldn't approve of what he saw. Finally, he spoke.

'You got nerve aggro, int'ya?'

My natural instinct was to deny it.

'Nah, I ain't. Nah. I'm all right,' I said.

'Yeah, you 'ave.'

'Nah. I ain't. I'm all right.'

Then he surprised me by saying, '*I* used to have nerve aggro. It's bettah now though.'

Later, I realised he was trying to be kind. But it was too late.

I didn't see Bob again until about a few weeks later. I was sitting in the ABC cinema alone, having just bunked in, and was starting to rip seats. Bizarrely, the cinema had employed Bob as a bouncer, to stop people getting in without paying. He came over and told me I had to leave. A few weeks later, one of the Harrow boys, Les, said to me, 'Bob

Magill told me to tell you, he was sorry he 'ad to kick you out a' the ABC. He had no choice. The managers were watchin'.'

I was really touched and amazed he even knew who I was. Twenty-odd years later, I read in a newspaper that Bob had been shot dead in a gang killing.

. . .

Booze was a release for me. It freed me of many of my inhibitions and gave me confidence, and it would get me singing. I would walk home from the pub alone through the quiet suburban streets, singing at the top of my voice. 'River Deep – Mountain High' was a favourite.

I had some good nights out on the booze, especially with the 'Arra. By now, we had progressed to meeting in a pub, usually the Red Lion in Harrow Weald. We'd have a few drinks before heading off to wherever it was happening that night. In those days, most landlords didn't check whether we were underage.

Though I've always been ambivalent about the anticipation and inevitable anticlimax of Christmas and New Year, at 16 and out with my mates, it was great fun.

New Year's Eve was a strange one. As soon as the clock turned midnight, all these little hard nuts would walk up to people they would previously have hit without a second thought, now shaking their hands, and with a great big smile on their faces, say, 'Pur' it there, mate. 'Appy new year!'

I thought that was hilarious. And I still find it hard to understand how people can get so excited about something that is only a day in the year.

Of course, the 'Arra boys' goodwill had a very limited timespan. The following day, it would be back to business as usual.

When some people think of Harrow, they think of Harrow on the Hill – the area where the public school is. But Harrow and Harrow on the Hill were very different. Harrow was rough, in those days certainly. I think the London suburbs were at least as violent as the inner-city areas. It was hard to walk down the street in those days, if your face wasn't recognised, without somebody challenging you. 'Who you screwing [looking at]?'

Some of the 'Arra didn't like to travel out of the area, as it could easily mean a fight. It wasn't that they were scared of fighting. Far from it. But they took fighting very seriously and didn't like losing. Hence they would sometimes be reluctant to travel unless there were enough of us to take on other crews. I came to find this frustrating. I didn't want to sit in a pub all night. I wanted to meet girls.

About twenty years ago, I was at the funeral of a lovely, true Harrow legend and absolute gentleman, Pete Brown. Another ex-Harrow boy, whom I hadn't seen for 30 years, was also there and said, 'Do you remember me, Rolo – Melvin Bracewell?' I clearly remembered the name, but couldn't match his face to it until later. 'You fucking should do,' he said, good-naturally. 'I got you out of enough scrapes!'

He was right. If we went to another area, it was very important to not stand out too much, or it would often mean a fight. Being 'too flash' was a serious accusation. I was naïve in that it wouldn't even occur to me to rein myself in. I would dance and go for girls without proper consideration of my surroundings and the dangers. Some of the more sensitive local guys would quite often take offence and confront me. I would mouth off, and people like Melvin would jump in.

But my affair with the Harrow pretty much ended one night when I clashed with one of the main leaders, who I will call Aden O'Boyle, who was from one of the hardest and biggest families in the area.

Trips to the likes of the Top Rank in Watford were becoming less frequent. For a few weeks now, we'd almost completely stopped travelling out of Harrow, and sometimes we would just stay in the public bar of the Royal Oak in Wealdstone.

I was getting bored and had been voicing my displeasure about it, saying openly that I wanted to get out of Wealdstone and meet some girls. Quite a few others agreed with me. I don't think Aden was pleased about it. He was concerned there might not be enough of us if we needed to fight, given that a few weeks earlier a load of us had been jumped by the Watford and had come off worse.

On this night, at my instigation, we decided to go to the Rank. The ill will among our gang, which never seemed to be too far away, would often fall on someone, and on this occasion it was my turn.

Aden had got it into his head that I was being disloyal in some way by expressing my desire to get out of Harrow for the evening. He was making snide remarks, as were one or two of his close confidants. I got the strong feeling I might get attacked. I tried to speak to him about it. I said, 'Look, Aden. We're mates. We fight alongside each other.'

He was choked up and said, 'I feel like fuckin' cryin'.'

But he continued drinking heavily at the bar and brooding, and before long he was openly scowling and I could see him confiding to one or two others and looking in my direction. It was remarkably similar to that scene in *Goodfellas*, where Jimmy Conway is getting more and more broody at Mo' and you can feel the sense of macabre in the air. It was clear I was going to get it.

I made out I was going to the toilet and slipped out of the Rank quietly. I just managed to catch the penultimate train back to Harrow; Aden and the crew always caught the last train.

On arrival at Harrow and Wealdstone station, I bumped into a girl who I knew had been up for me for some time. I took her around the back of some shops opposite the station and we had sex. Fifteen minutes into which, we could hear O'Boyle and his mates coming out of the station and shouting, 'Rolo, you fuckin' cunt. Where are ya?' It was an eerie and dark moment, and I knew that my time as Rolo of 'Arra was over.

Trying a few different jobs

I got a job selling menswear in C&A in Oxford Street.

The lady who interviewed me seemed very positive and had a good vibe about her. She told me the company philosophy was about providing good-quality, stylish clothes at affordable prices, so that everybody would have the opportunity of dressing well, regardless of budget. I loved that idea! She said it was a Dutch firm, but very international, and that they had a progressive approach towards staff and that there were good prospects for those prepared to work hard. It sounded great.

But my experience in the store was very different. On my first day, the menswear department supervisor, Mr George, gave me a booklet describing what was expected from me as a C&A employee. Being serious about the position, I asked him if I could take the booklet home to study it. He said, 'No,' in what I took to be an authoritative, yet petty tone.

'Staff rules state that these booklets must remain here.'

I decided he was a berk and within a short space of time, I realised that this company was anything but what it said it was.

For the summer sale, instead of reducing their current stock, as many retail outlets do, they brought in the cheapest, nastiest-looking casual jackets I'd ever seen, specifically for the sale. These 'windcheaters' were badly made Terylene and absolute rubbish. It was obvious this firm was just interested in making money, and not the philosophy that the personnel lady had sold me.

I complained to my immediate supervisor, Mr Hale. 'I thought C&A was about selling good-quality clothes at prices affordable to everybody. Why are we selling this crap?'

'The company is just making some money in the sale,' he said.

I didn't like it. During a moment when the other assistants were busy, I took one of the rubbishy, off-white jackets into the changing room, took out my black pen and wrote the word CRAP right across the back of it, in big letters. Then I put it back on the hanger, at the front of the rail so the writing was clearly visible to any customers.

About an hour later, Mr Hale was standing with my main boss, Mr George. They were holding the jacket I'd defaced and looking at me. It was obvious I was the culprit.

I began to hate the company and started to look for ways to amuse myself.

C&A brought a German guy over from Hamburg to work in the menswear department. They often brought trainee executives onto the shop floor, to give them some store experience before they went on their management path. This fellow was decent and about 27 years old. He had only a basic grasp of the English language. On his first day he came over to introduce himself to me in his strong German accent. Looking at the C&A name badge on my jacket lapel, he said, 'Hello, Mr Rowland, my name is Gerhard Lange.'

'Hello, Gerhard,' I said.

Seeing the letter 'K' before 'Rowland' on my badge, he said, 'What does this "K" mean?'

'What does it mean?' I said. 'It doesn't mean anything, it's my initial for my first name.' I was playing for time and sensing an opportunity for fun.

'Yes, but what is the first name?'

'Ah, you're asking, what is my first name?'

'Yes!' he replied, earnestly.

'Kunt,' I said.

'Kunt?' He'd never heard the word – he'd only been in the country five days.

'Yes. Kunt Rowland is my name,' I said.

'Very good. I am pleased to meet you, Kunt.'

'Nice to meet you too, Gerhard.'

We were both working on the trousers section and he was senior to me. Sometimes he would shout instructions across the busy store, 'Kunt! Please come and help me with these trousers!'

Or if he was feeling impatient with me, he would say, 'Come on, Kunt, hurry up!'

Old men and women would look up, startled and unable to believe what they were hearing.

. . .

There was a mainstream fashion look at the time that I absolutely hated. It was basically a very short, petite leather jacket and tight-bummed, black flares, often worn with a dark polo neck and a longish, blow-dried haircut. It was usually finished off with nasty slip-on, square-toed, patent-leather or snakeskin Chelsea-style boots.

It was very much a West End thing and wasn't tolerated in the suburbs. C&A did a very average, 49-shilling Terylene-mix, black flared trouser that appealed to these mainstream types. They were selling by the shedload. I grew tired of filling the coffers of C&A, this so-called progressive, caring company, who seemed only interested in selling the same uninspired, boring clothes to unstylish people.

'Do you have black flares, please?' a customer asked me one afternoon. I had been asked that question for the zillionth time that day.

In order to ease my boredom, I said, 'No, we haven't. They went out of fashion at 10.45 this morning, so we took them all downstairs and burned them.'

The guy's jaw dropped. 'What?' he said.

'We don't do them any more, mate. They're out of fashion. Didn't you hear it on the news?'

He stared at me in shock.

'No, I'm only joking, mate, they're over there.'

That night, I told Pat about the conversation. He thought it was hilarious.

Another source of annoyance was the stupid tier system in the canteen. The maintenance/manual workers would sit at one end of the dining hall, with the shop-floor sales assistants (us) nearby. The store management would sit in the middle, and the managing director and his guests for that day at the top of the hall. They would be served by a waitress. The rest of us would queue up at the self-service counter.

'Why is there an order of seniority in the seating arrangements?' I asked Mr Hale.

'There isn't an order of seniority,' he said. 'It's just the way we choose to do things.'

'Well, I'm going to choose to eat my lunch up there,' I said.

'What do you want to do that for?' he said.

After collecting my lunch from the self-service counter, I walked up to the top management section and ate my food there.

There happened to be no managing director in that day. After I'd finished eating, I joined my coworkers for a cup of tea. Mr Hale said, 'Are you satisfied now?' There was no answer to that. These guys didn't like to rock the boat.

Before I left C&A, I met a lovely girl named Jean. She was doing temporary work during her sixth-form college holidays. We fell in love and dated for over a year.

Many a tear has to fall, but it's all in the game.

• • •

Next I got a job in the accounts department of a company manufacturing dental equipment in Harrow.

I was comforted to find out that the boss of the accounts department, a middle-aged guy called Wilf, was from Stourbridge, close to Wolverhampton, and had an accent very similar to that of the broadest Wulfrunians. Unfortunately, I think he developed a crush on me. He was very pleasant to me when I first started there. Then he seemed to get stressed out. There was no way I was ever going to make an accounts clerk (again, I was just doing what I thought I *should* do) and perhaps my ineptitude caused him grief. But there seemed to be more to it than that.

He touched my cock one day when he was showing me how to do an equation. As he did, he said, 'Sorry,' as if it were a mistake. But it couldn't have been. I was seated as he stood over me, and his hand had to drop about 12 inches from the adding machine to my groin. I liked Wilf as a person, but not in that way, and the situation made me feel awkward. I just pretended it wasn't happening.

After a couple of months, I said to Wilf's assistant, 'Wilf seems very unhappy and impatient. Is he always like this?'

He replied, 'Only lately. Pretty much since you've been here, really.'

I deduced that he meant Wilf was infatuated by me. His gayness wasn't spoken about, but I sensed the others knew. Of course, the other guy could have meant that Wilf was stressed because I was a useless accounts clerk! In any event, I left the company.

I tended to get a lot of attention from gay men – touched up on the tube train twice, accosted in the cinema, and followed all around Selfridges one time by a big 40-year-old German-looking guy. I would deal with it by trying to get away from them. Of course, I didn't tell anyone at home. I felt that I would be blamed for looking too effeminate.

. . .

After trying a few different jobs, and watching Pat, Sarah and now Grainne getting educated, and with that being the number-one priority in our house, I concluded that Dad must be right about *everything*, and I'd better try and get some education.

Dad and I went to see the principal at Hatch End Sixth-Form College. I cringed as Dad asked him if I could be in a boys-only class to avoid the distraction of girls. All the classes were of course mixed. I'd already attended an all-boys school (Willesden) and not done well there. As it was mid-September, the term had already started, and the full-time places had all gone. It was decided I should go on two separate day-release courses totalling two days per week and take O levels that way. I would do other jobs on the remaining three days, for instance work for Dad on the building site, or work evenings in the local cinema.

I felt far more stupid than Pat, Sarah and Grainne. I even felt different to my classmates, who were all on day-release from proper jobs – they were just doing a single day at college each week. I wasn't the same as them. I was revising at home a lot during the other three days of the week, while they were doing their jobs.

It's so obvious to me now that I was completely on the wrong track, and just trying to be like my sisters and brother Pat (all of whom would become school teachers). I had no interest in furthering my education. My whole reason for being there was based on me thinking, *I'm wrong*.

What I should have done was a hairdressing apprenticeship or something like that – something that I was actually interested in. But I was completely out of touch with myself.

I ended up doing that day-release college thing for two years and finally got two O levels in English and sociology. For me, that was a big deal.

. . .

With Mum, I don't know if it was because I'd caused so much trouble for her, or she just thought I was OK and didn't need attention, but she seemed distant a lot of that time. She had recently started work part-time at the local hospital as an auxiliary nurse. It was the first job she'd had since before having kids. She may also have been menopausal at this time.

I'd sometimes have a desire to put an arm around her to hug her, but when I did, she'd always turn her shoulder and pull away. I wondered if I'd broken her heart. I thought of the Irish song, 'The Wild Colonial Boy'.

There was a wild colonial boy, Jack Duggan was his name.
He was born and bred in Ireland in a place called Castlemaine.
He was his father's only son, his mother's pride and joy
And dearly did his parents love the wild colonial boy.

I liked the idea of the song, but I felt so far away from the idea of parents loving their son that I didn't believe it was possible. Not in my case.

I lived for weekends. I would just about have enough money to go out once a week.

Early one Saturday evening, Dad and I had an argument about something or other. I told Dad I was leaving home and walked out of the house. It was a cold winter's night and I didn't have anywhere to go, nor any money. I hadn't thought it through.

I phoned a mate and asked if I could stay at his parents' place that night. I could tell from his tone that he wasn't up for the idea. In any event, I didn't have anywhere to stay and very little money. I went to the local pub and had a drink. Now leaving home didn't seem such a good idea. I phoned home. Mum answered. 'Can I come home?'

'Yes,' Mum said.

I walked in about 20 minutes later.

I wanted to talk to my dad about what had happened to try and work something out. I suggested we talk. He made it clear he was busy watching television and didn't want to discuss anything.

My sister Grainne told me later that Dad had briefed them all: 'When Kevin comes in, don't say anything. Act like nothing's happened. Don't talk about it.'

And that has been my family's attitude to any difficulties or issues I've tried to raise subsequently.

I really wish that I'd had some dignity in those days and left home and even roughed it, or did whatever I needed to get out and stay out. I was tortured, between how I felt and what I was being told to do. But how I felt was not the strongest voice.

· · ·

One of my part-time jobs during this period was at the local hospital, as a porter. One of my first duties was to take someone who had just died down to the morgue. I'd never seen or touched a dead body before. It was a woman, and she was already wrapped in a white sheet. The senior porter told me to take the legs, while he took the head. That body haunted me, I had nightmares for some time afterwards.

One day, I was walking through the hospital grounds and got chatting to an older porter. He was about 50 years old, Irish, easy-going and friendly. For some reason, I opened up to him and told him how the episode of taking the body down was troubling me. He said, 'Sure, it's not the dead people that'll hurt ya, son. It's the live ones!' He was of course right.

Somehow we also got talking about Irishness and I told him that although both my parents were Irish, I didn't look Irish, because I was so dark. He also had dark hair and skin, but not as dark as mine.

There were a couple of female kitchen orderlies who happened to be passing.

'Ladies, excuse me,' he said.

'Yes,' the old Cockney ladies replied.

'What nationality do I look?'

'Ooh, Spanish, I'd say.'

'Well, I'm Irish!' he told them. 'This Irish fella here [pointing at me] doesn't think he looks like a Paddy.'

'Ooh, well, they're more like the Italians, aren't they?' she said.

It was a chink of light.

· · ·

I hated my hair at this point. The short-haired 'skinhead' look had suited me perfectly, but the smart dressers were now growing their hair. I had been aware that long hair was coming 'in' before most. I started to grow mine, but it got frizzier and frizzier. I tried everything, from my mother's hairdryer to putting giant rollers in, but nothing worked. Volume was the issue. I felt very self-conscious about it. In a moment of weakness, I had my hair cut short again. Almost as soon as it had been cut, I regretted it. I found it torturous to have to walk around Harrow with short hair, when long hair was fast becoming the cool thing. That might not sound like a big deal to many, but to me – 'Mary Quant', as one of the Harrow hard nuts had christened me – it was hell.

I started to grow it, and finally figured a way to sort out the frizz. One Saturday I walked into a hairdressers in Wembley and asked if my hair could be straightened. The Greek barber said, 'Hmmmm, once a week with a hairdryer should be enough.'

I was sceptical but allowed him to try. He washed it, trimmed it then blow-dried it – a relatively new technique at the time, of tightly gripping and stretching each section of hair in a Denman brush, while simultaneously drying it with hot air. By the time he had finished, it looked great: no curls, no frizz, no volume, just flat, shiny, healthy-looking longish hair! Wow! A miracle.

I had a new confidence those first few days, then it started to get a bit curly. I went back to him every Saturday from then on. It made me feel like a different person. And I started to do better with girls.

My new longish hair (a kind of feather cut) worked well with my clothes – big wide A-line trousers that were flat-fronted and bellowing out into a wide flare. Jumpers would be small tight crew necks, over penny round-collar shirts. All from Take 6 (a high-fashion shop) or the like, and usually stolen – a friend and I had developed some effective techniques.

Shoes were at first zip-up boots with heels, then chunky round-toed Toppers shoes that were a mixture of suede and leather and had thick crepe soles. I wore a herringbone, heavy trench-style, big-collared and belted flared overcoat that came way down below my knees. It was a great look. The rules of what was now stylistically acceptable had been completely turned on their head.

Mum and Dad in the mid-1960s.

Me at one year old.

Age six on the left
and age eight on the right.

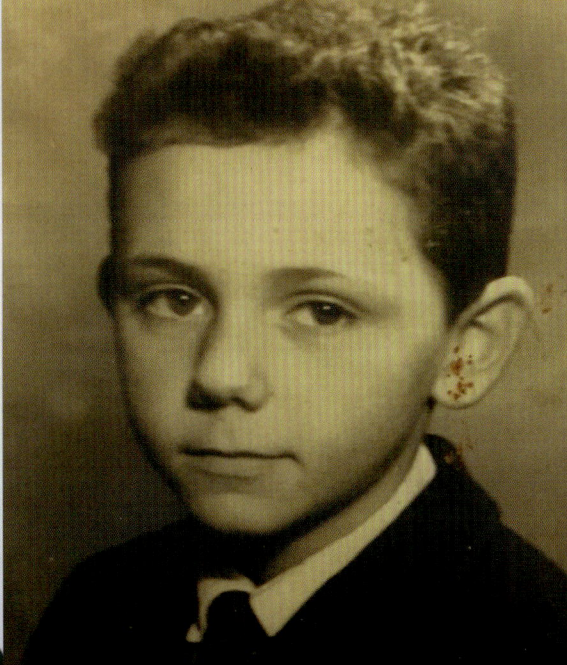

With friend Kevin Fagan in a
Harrow photobooth in 1969.

1970, 16 years old,
Oxford Street.

Pat's band, New Blood. Left to right: Pat, Trevor, myself.

October 1976.
Getting ready to form a band.

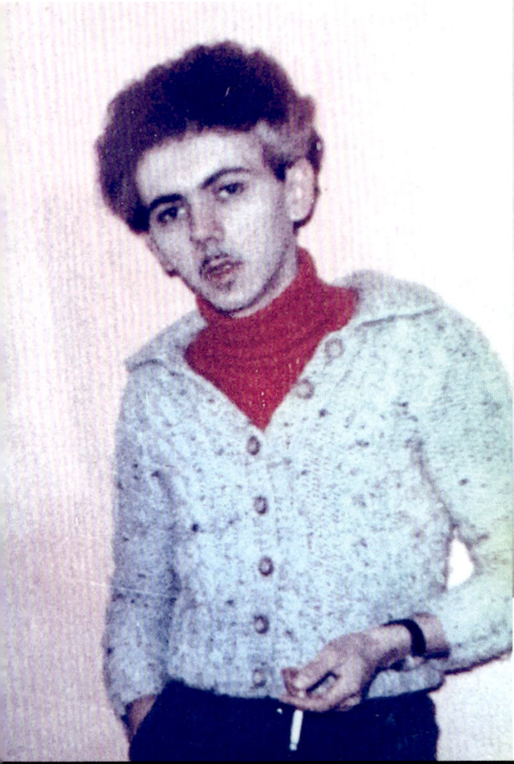

Killjoys gig, 1977

Sadly, the only photo we have before we changed our look. Our style still wasn't fully developed here, but it was getting there.

Late 1979 – Two Tone Tour.

New Street, Birmingham, December 1979.

First *Top of the Pops* appearance, January 1980.

July 1980

Kevin Archer and myself.

1981

The Projected Passion Revue.

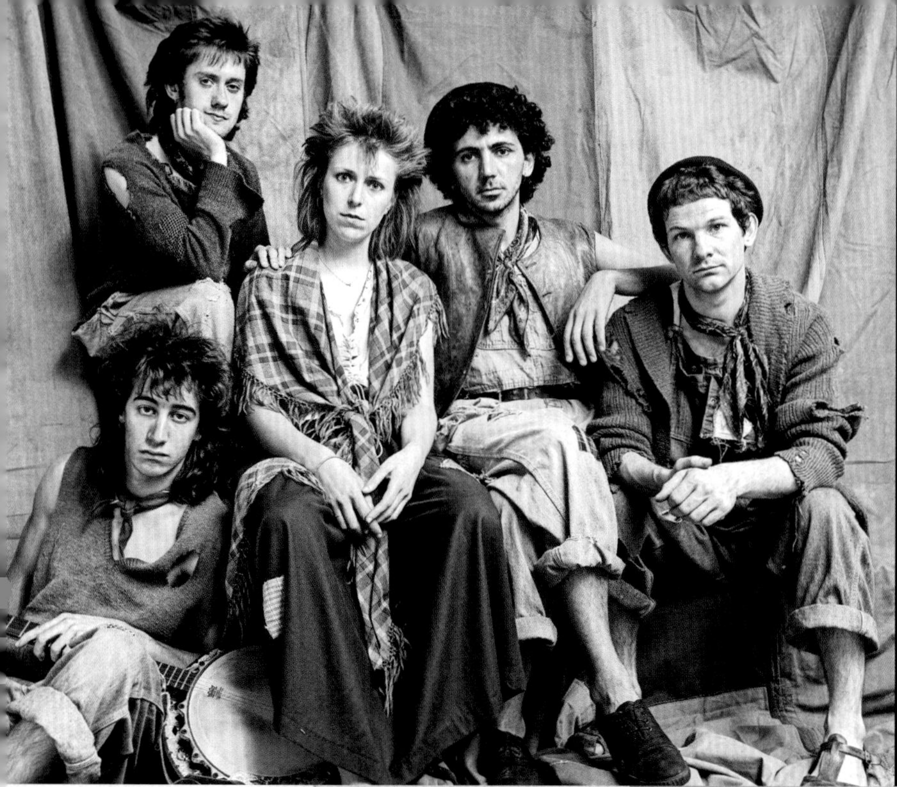

Summer 1982

November 1982

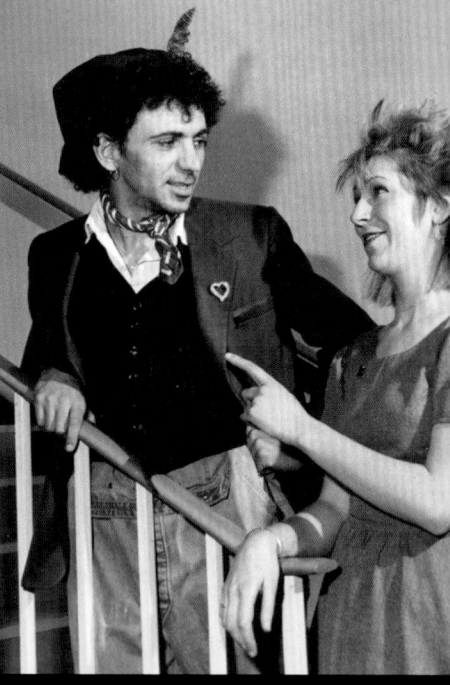

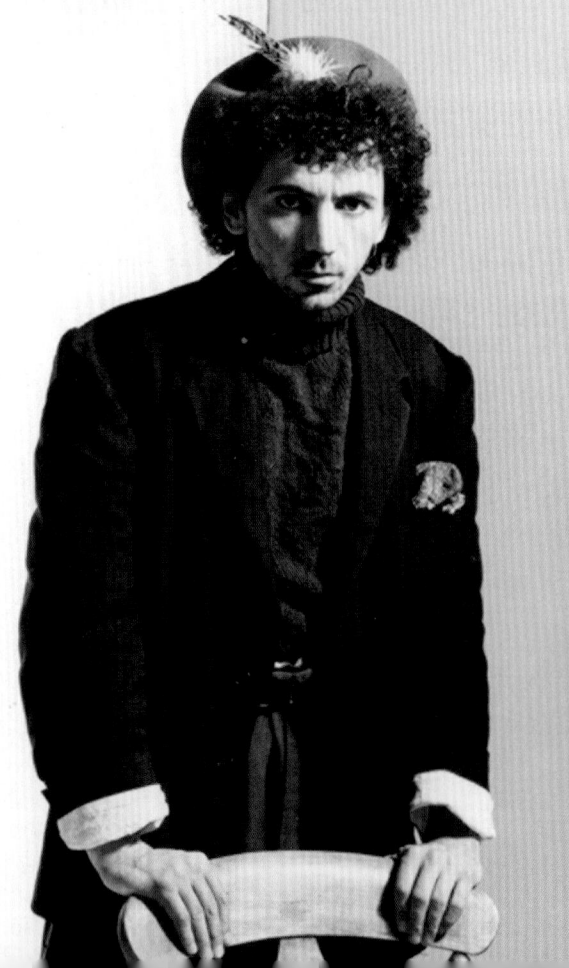

May 1983

'Virginia Plain'

Butlin's Holiday Camp in Clacton, Essex, sounded like paradise, and I was delighted when, in the summer of 1972, I was accepted as a kitchen porter.

Freedom! The summer! Girls! I was 18, and couldn't wait!

'All the Young Dudes' would be magically drifting out of a staff chalet as I took my morning walk to the café where I worked, feeling exhilarated after having had a few drinks and sex the night before. It was easy to meet girls there – many of them were more interested in the staff than their fellow holidaymakers.

My work wasn't demanding. I wasn't assigned to the main canteen kitchen, where they worked tirelessly. Instead, I was a kitchen porter at a café on the site called Holiday Fayre, a place where campers could buy small meals and snacks.

After about ten days of washing-up, I asked the pleasant, northern supervisor if I could have a turn pushing the trolley through the café, picking up the cups and plates. She agreed, and *that* was even more of a cushy number and a great way to meet girls.

Fashion-wise, the summer of '72 was a strange time. Things kind of merged, briefly. Suburban boys and girls, who definitely weren't hippies, were wearing necklaces called love beads (tighter on the neck than the hippy version). Cheesecloth shirts also featured, with big A-line trousers or wide jeans – previously these clothes would have been the exclusive domain of the 'hairies'. I enjoyed that look, even though I tended to wear a more coiffured version.

I met a guy called Billy McKnight at Butlin's. He was a Scouser. He too was dark of hair and skin but had Scottish blood. We hit it off immediately.

That summer, I found freedom, peace, and even a sense of belonging. People seemed to like me. Girls did. And Billy and I really connected.

Both Billy and his mate, Pete, wore hippy-style clothes (loon pants, flared-sleeve T-shirts), but were very different from any hippy-looking guys I'd met in London.

They were clearly working class, for a start (all the hippies I'd seen in Harrow or the rest of London were all pretty much middle class). Bill and Pete took drugs, but they didn't do it in a hippyish way. When they smoked a joint, it was as if it was a normal cigarette. It was no big deal. These days that's normal, but it was very unusual at the time. The posh hippies around Harrow at that time would make it into a big ceremony – only taking one pull on it, then gently passing it round as if it were made of precious stone. Bill and Pete didn't call each other 'man', or employ any of the other hippy traits. They were down-to-earth. I liked them a lot.

Also, I had a fascination with Scousers. I loved the accent. It was clearly quite close to an Irish dialect – loads of words were similar. They would refer to their dads as 'me owl' fella' and say 'yous' for the plural of you, just like the Irish. And of course, the Beatles had come from Liverpool! It seemed like a magical place.

. . .

On Thursdays, I would always watch *Top of the Pops*. There were no televisions in any of the chalets, but there was a communal TV lounge for campers and staff. One particular Thursday, the first ten minutes or so of the programme was OK – but nothing special. All the hippy Butlin's employees were nodding their heads as Hawkwind's 'Silver Machine' came out of the TV. I wasn't up for it: my brother Pat had told me it was just slowed-down rock'n'roll. Besides which, the sight of the 'progressive music' fans swinging their hair at the back of the room in appreciation rather than enjoying it was enough to put me off.

Suddenly, an intro to a song I'd heard once on the radio. It was catchy and unique. 'Virginia Plain'. And then I saw them: Bryan Ferry in his leopardskin jacket, hair greased back, almost Sha Na Na-style (a retro fifties band of the time), but futuristic. Andy Mackay with his space-age quiff. The whole thing sounded and looked great, as if it was from another planet, but at the same time somehow familiar. The band were older-looking than most other groups, and that set them apart, in a good way. They had weight, experience. They were clearly good musicians, but so fucking stylish. And they were fully formed – all bases covered.

David Bowie was the big thing of that summer, according to the music press. And Bowie was a great artist. But when I heard 'Star Man', his big hit of that time, I didn't think it was anything special. Undoubtedly a pretty good song, but not amazing, and not a step forward sonically or musically. It had a very traditional structure and arrangement. Even the vocal style was evocative of the Beatles. A while later, I got into Bowie, first through *Hunky Dory*, then *Young Americans* – and retrospectively discovered *Ziggy Stardust*. But Roxy Music were doing something else entirely.

I knew intuitively that this wasn't just music; it was art. It had more dimensions than normal music. I've tried to explain the subtleties of Roxy and the genius of Bryan Ferry to many, but it's often futile. Some people just can't see it. There was real soul and yearning in the music, yet it was avant-garde, stylish and out there, which took nothing away from its integrity. It was incredible.

That was a great summer for music. Billy and Pete introduced me to Bob Dylan. Although I'd quite liked a couple of his sixties hit singles, I had never listened to any of his albums. I kind of felt that was the domain of students or whatever. But now I was getting an education into his genius by these two Dylan fanatics.

With your silhouette, when the sunlight dims
Into your eyes, where the moonlight swims

Butlin's was my first time away from home and it was an amazing experience. It opened me up and gave me confidence. But soon the summer was coming to an end, and there was melancholia in the air. 'You Wear It Well' by Rod Stewart was on the radio and summed it up perfectly:

I'm gonna write about the birthday gown that I bought in town
When you sat down and cried on the stairs.

Billy and I wanted the adventure to continue. Some Butlin's staff were talking about going to Spain, but that sounded like a big deal – we didn't know how to get passports or anything. We'd heard about an all-year-round skiing resort in the north of Scotland called Aviemore. We thumbed our way up there, taking two days, and arrived in the middle of a cold night. Finding a car that wasn't locked, we got in and had a few hours' sleep. We woke the next morning, freezing and practically broke.

We applied for jobs and were given employment and live-in accommodation as kitchen porters in the big Post House Hotel.

Although it was a culture shock for us (all the other staff were Scottish and from places like Glasgow and Dundee), we were quite happy there, until one night, after about a month, we drunkenly wandered into a party that was for the hotel management only.

A particularly snooty high-level company trainee approached us and belligerently announced that we must leave at once. I drunkenly told him that this was a clear case of class distinction and that I would do no such thing! He became more and more insistent that we leave and, in my perception, more and more irritating.

I thumped him. The police were called and soon I was being held from behind by one of the officers, while the management trainee told me that I was sacked with immediate effect.

I would be allowed to spend the rest of the night in my room but I would have to be off the premises first thing the next morning. A policeman escorted me to my room and repeated the hotel manager's instruction. I agreed, and he left.

Bill and I decided we'd thumb down to Brighton the next day, where we'd been told there was an all-year-round Butlin's Hotel.

Just then, we heard the sound of a few of the Glasgow boys having a small get-together in the next bedroom. We joined them. It soon became obvious that as well as drinking and smoking joints, they were about to drop LSD. Bill said to me, 'Have you ever tripped, Kev?'

'Sure,' I lied.

Soon we were all tripping.

We were listening to a small transistor radio. Peter Skellern's 'You're a Lady' had just been released. It was the first time I'd heard it. The lyrics sounded bizarre.

You're a lady, I'm a man.
You're supposed to understand

It seemed as if he was massively overstating the obvious. I felt like laughing out loud at how ridiculous the statement was.

Everything went strange. I was sitting on a single bed with three hard Glasgow boys. Billy was on the floor. There was a Dundee boy sitting in the only chair in the small room. I went into myself. I was wondering what these Glasgow boys were thinking about and if any of them would pick on me. I thought they might start criticising my effeminate clothes. But when one of them started being friendly to me, it seemed that he was needlessly over-justifying himself. Why was he doing that?

We all decided to go to a club on the complex where we'd often been before. Billy and I were straggling a few yards behind the others. As we approached, a manic-looking local guy, about 30 years old, appeared from nowhere. He grabbed me tightly by the hand, stared intently into my eyes and started talking to me.

'I saw you last night, kicking that guy!'

His voice seemed strange – exaggerated, spooky! I was alarmed.

I'd had another fight the previous evening. I had been trying to pull a posh girl in the club. She was maybe a couple of years older than me and I offered to buy her a drink. She ordered a brandy and Babycham (a very expensive drink at the time, especially in this club, and a lot for someone on kitchen-porter wages). As soon as she had custody of the drink, she made it clear she was leaving my company. I was annoyed.

I had a pint of beer in my hand. I raised it above her head, and slowly poured it over her hair. The beer dripped down onto her shoulders. She was drenched. It was a mean thing to do. A guy who was standing close to her raised his arm as if to do something. As quick as a flash, one of the Glasgow boys, who had been sitting at the bar watching the proceedings, grabbed his arm tightly and gave him a look that said, 'Proceed and you're dead!' The guy retreated, as the girl ran to the toilets to try and sort herself out.

Paddy, the Glasgow boy, grabbed my arm and, with the warmest smile, said in his broad patter, 'Well done, pal! That was real Glasgee! Ye boys are all right! Ah wasnae' sure about ye, at first, but now I know you're all right. Put it there, Kevin!' as he shook my hand again.

That was how we bonded with the Glasgow boys. They had been decidedly frosty to us before that.

That same night, as we left the club about an hour later, I was physically challenged by a guy who was either in the brandy-and-Babycham girl's company or wanted to be. He wasn't hard and I finished the fight quickly.

But now, tonight, I was tripping for the first time in my life, and *this* guy, whoever he was, was going on and on about it. Billy looked on from nearby. The guy was speaking very intensely, looking close into my eyes. *Shit! Is he going to hit me? I'm in no position to fight. I'm too spaced out from the trip. Was it him I hit last night?* I wondered.

No, it couldn't be. The other guy was a posh Englishman. This was a local working-class bloke.

He looked a little insane. He spoke for what seemed about ten minutes – telling me how very wrong I was for fighting. I started to feel deeply guilty and sorrowful, almost tearful. I desperately wanted to get away from him but he seemed to not want to let me go, and had a tight grip on my lapel.

Is he going to nut me, I wondered. *I'd better ask him.*

'Was it you I was fighting with last night, mate?'

'No,' he said, very slowly and eerily. 'But it *couldae* been! Do ya understand? It *couldae* been me, rye [right]!'

'OK, mate. I'm sorry. I was wrong for fighting.' I felt genuinely full of remorse. The feeling was so intense that it frightened me. I was afraid that it would swallow me up and consume me. I was seeing myself as bad, evil.

Finally, he left. 'Billy, what the fucking hell's up with him? He was weird,' I said.

'I think that was the trip, Kev,' Billy said.

'How d'ya mean?'

'It's making everything seem more insane and not real.'

Billy was a seasoned tripper.

And if *that* was a strange experience, the end of my first LSD excursion was odder still. A few days previously, we'd befriended a local girl, Mary. She was a nice girl, and about our age. She would come and hang out in one of our rooms, or those of the Glasgow boys. She loved music and always carried her portable cassette player. On the night before the acid trip, she offered to leave it with me overnight so that I could have music to listen to. I was happy about that. I had nothing else to listen to music on and portable cassette players were a big deal at the time.

After the acid trip, Billy and I returned to my room to find the cassette player had gone. Someone had taken it. We didn't know who: the locks were poor and it was common knowledge that any bedroom key would fit most of the others.

It was now morning, and we were trying to get an hour or so's sleep before packing our stuff and getting off the complex. Then Mary turned up. I told her the cassette player had gone and said I was sorry. I also mentioned that we were leaving. She didn't seem overly distressed about the cassette player, and certainly appeared to accept the situation. We talked for a little while and said our goodbyes.

Billy and I tried to sleep. We both got into the only bed in my room, a single. It felt a little surreal. We couldn't sleep. The acid was still active. Just as we were about to get up and start packing, there was a knock on the door. It was the police, demanding to be let in.

Fuck! Now we're in trouble.

We had broken into a hotel in the village, a week earlier. We had walked down there in the dead of night, suitcases in hand, forced a window open and got into the hotel bar. It was a chalet, and independent of the main hotel. We had leisurely poured ourselves a pint and, in between drinking beer, loaded our suitcases with bottles of spirits, cans of beer and cigars, and stashed them in my room.

Should I throw the booze out of the window?

No. We were on the ground floor and there was gravel outside. The copper would be certain to open the window. There was no hiding place, so I let him in.

It was the same local village bobby who had escorted me out of the party the night before. I felt acutely embarrassed that Billy and I were both in our underpants and that he might suspect we were having sex (we weren't, of course, but we had obviously both been in the only single bed). He had come to investigate the disappearance of the cassette player.

Mary stood sheepishly outside the door. We had no idea where the cassette player was and told the policeman. He insisted on looking around. He of course found the booze, then went to Billy's room where he found more. He radioed for help and we were arrested and driven to the local police station. Our fingerprints were taken and we were interviewed separately.

We each had the presence of mind to give the same story, that we had bought the booze off a guy and we were so well tuned into each other that we both gave the same description – that freaky guy who had grabbed me and lectured me outside the club the night before.

Billy was taken off in a cop car to try to find the 'vendor' while I was interviewed by a detective who had been brought down from Inverness, the closest city. The young duty constable also sat in on the interview. Of course, the whole situation was particularly surreal given that I was still on the acid trip – until you've slept, you're still tripping. The young constable was in fact a nice fellow. They were both quizzing me and I was doing my best to lie convincingly.

And after one of my more pathetic lies, the young constable turned his face away in embarrassment as he stifled tears and said, 'If you're going to pursue a life of crime, Kevin, you're going to have to become a better liar than that!'

He said it in a way that communicated total compassion to me. Of course, I don't know how much of my perception was down to the trip and how much was genuine. Either way, I was moved. That deep, sad remorse again. But still I stuck to my story.

They put me back in the holding cell. A short while later the detective from Inverness unlocked my door and brought me back into the interview room to give me 'the results of some tests', as he put it.

'I don't know about the other fella yet,' he said. 'But you were definitely there.'

'What?' I said.

'We can tell.'

'How?'

'We've done some tests. You left some fibres behind.'

'How do you mean?' I said.

'Your clothes. You left tiny particles at the hotel.'

It's obvious to me now that although such detection techniques were probably available at the time, they certainly wouldn't have been widely used for the solving of the theft of a few bottles of booze from a hotel in Aviemore. But, at the time, I believed him.

'OK, I *was* there,' I said. 'But I did it on my own.'

I felt such relief! I liked these policemen, especially the young constable. They were a cut above those I had experienced in London. And I felt glad to be admitting it to them.

I was halfway through making my statement, when Billy, returning from his search, walked into the main room escorted by his accompanying policeman. I called over to him.

'It's all right, Bill. I've admitted it. That I did it, alone. I've told 'em. It was just me.'

'What? Fuckin' hell!' he said. He looked so disappointed.

'No, it was me, Bill. On my own. I've told them.'

'Ohhh, fuckin hell!' he said again.

I was confused. Admitting I was solely responsible had seemed like the right thing to do. It hurt me to see Billy so disappointed. For reasons I still don't understand, Bill admitted he was involved too.

We were charged, taken to Inverness Police Station, and put in separate basement cells. It was now Friday afternoon, and as there was no court over the weekend, we would have to wait till the Monday to be dealt with. Each morning they gave us a cheese sandwich and a steel mug of tea for breakfast. Lunch was the same. In the evening, it would be a luncheon meat sandwich and another mug of tea. Again the coppers were generally pleasant and, initially at least, I felt a sense of peace being in that cell.

It was a very old police station, built at least a hundred years earlier. I wondered about its history and who had been in there. I thought about all the murderers who might have been incarcerated there. Soon I was depressed. I could hear the sound of happy children playing outside – having fun, being free. *What's the matter with me? I've been nicked again!*

It looked like I was going down this time. This was going to be my sixth court appearance. Surely, I wouldn't be able to escape it again.

The duty sergeant gave me the previous day's newspaper. It was the *Scotsman*. I'd never seen it before, but over those three days I read every word several times. There was a cartoon called 'Oor Wullie'. It was funny, sweet and innocent. A million miles from how I felt – soiled, dirty.

Each visit from the copper was relief from the boredom, it usually meant food or some news. Finally, on Monday morning, we were taken to the Sheriff's Court. We of course pleaded guilty, and though the prosecutor was gunning for us, the sheriff was a decent man. I was contrite and spoke to him from my heart.

'If I'm allowed out of here, sir, I'll go back to London and apply for a job at the Ford Motor Company in Dagenham.' (That was my genuine intention: I'd seen an advert for workers in the *Mirror* newspaper. There was an attractive illustration of a man looking happy and wearing a nice bib and brace overall.) Billy said something similar.

The sheriff said, 'Rowland, as you are the older boy [I was eight months older than Billy and 19 by now], you should have known better.'

'Yes, sir,' I said, fearing the worst.

Then miraculously, he said, 'I'm fining you £15 and I suggest you go back home to London. Immediately.'

'I will! And thank you, sir.'

The prosecutor wasn't happy: 'But in view of the seriousness of the crime, sir!'

'Well,' said the sheriff. 'These boys are young, and a long way from home, and I think the best thing for them is to return to their families. William, you too should go home. I'm fining you £10.'

We couldn't believe it! Suddenly we felt as light as feathers. We were free to go! I for one was not expecting it, and I truly appreciated the kind way we had been treated.

Though I hadn't in the past been enthusiastic about paying my fines, I resolved to pay *this* one. These people had shown us kindness and dignity.

We *ran* through Inverness town centre, even though we had our suitcases with us, feeling ten feet tall and floating on air. We happened upon the duty sergeant from Inverness Police Station, the one who had brought us our sandwiches and tea. He was directing traffic in the middle of the town. We rushed over to him excitedly.

'Hello. We've just been released. We're going home!' we said happily.

He greeted us with a big smile. 'Ah, that's great, boys. Look after yourselves now, lads, and keep out of trouble.'

'We will, sir. All the best.'

Our faith in human nature had been restored.

'You lads shouldn't be here'

Billy and I decided we'd each thumb our way home. But as we got further from Inverness, I knew deep down that I wouldn't be able to settle at home. We decided we would keep going and head down to Brighton together.

By this time, we had very little money left, but Billy had a mate, Tommy, who was already living in Brighton. We would be able to stay there. The only problem was, Billy couldn't remember Tommy's address.

'It'll come back to me, Kev. Don't worry,' he kept saying. But it never did.

It was a cold October night when we arrived in windy Brighton. We hid our suitcases behind a high wall in an old churchyard and wandered off into the night. Brighton looked exciting. The plan was to try and pull a couple of girls that we could spend the night with. We hit a couple of pubs but weren't successful.

Soon it was 11 o'clock and we were freezing. We walked around, trying to find somewhere to sleep. We came across a block of council flats, and after walking up a flight of stairs, we lay down on the floor and went to sleep. Early the next morning, we woke to the sound of milk bottles rattling – the milkman was doing his morning delivery. He stepped over us, and we went back to sleep. Half an hour later, the police arrived and escorted us out. The milkman must have phoned them.

Into the town we went, retrieved our suitcases, and then into the local department store toilets for a good wash and change of clothes. I pretty much stripped off to wash in the lovely hot water. It felt good to be clean.

First stop, Butlin's Hotel. Surely we could get jobs there.

We spent almost all of our remaining money on bus fares out to the big old hotel on the outskirts of town, and asked to see someone from the personnel office. A posh young woman came and spoke to us and told us there were no vacancies.

Shit!

'Are you sure? Nothing? We worked at Butlin's in Clacton!'

'No. I'm sorry. There's nothing.'

Damn. What are we gonna do now? We had no money and nowhere to stay.

Coming from Liverpool where there was high unemployment, Billy knew how to work the benefits system. He took me over to the dole office, we signed on, then went to the Social Security, and at Bill's suggestion told them that we had nowhere to stay.

After some discussion between themselves, the staff gave us a docket each and told us to go to a 'reception centre'. It was a hell of a walk, right up the steep hill of Elm Grove, made worse by the weight of my big suitcase. I had brought a lot of stuff – Billy had much less.

As we wearily trudged up the hill, we argued about who was going to carry my case. I wanted Billy to take turns with it. He was reluctant. 'They're *your* clothes!'

'Yeah, but you're quite happy to wear them.' I had a lot of clothes and sometimes lent some to Bill. We were tired and hungry and the situation was getting to us.

We arrived at the reception centre to find a load of tramps queuing up outside. They were dressed in very worn-out, dark, dirty 1950s overcoats with scruffy trousers and hair. This was a government-run 'doss house'.

'Fuck this, Bill,' I said. 'Come on, let's get out of here. We're not going in there.'

'We haven't got anywhere to kip, Kev, and we're broke,' Bill said.

'But that's a fucking doss house!'

'Let's just have a look at it,' Bill said.

'Oh, fuckin' hell, all right.'

We went to the door. A manager looked us up and down. 'What are you two doing here? You're too young to be in a place like this. You shouldn't be here. Surely you can find somewhere else to sleep!' he said. I suppose we stood out a mile from the mostly old and dirty-looking tramps.

'You lads shouldn't be here,' he said again.

'Yeah, you're exactly fuckin' right, mate,' I said. 'C'mon, Bill. Let's go.' I started to walk out.

'All right, all right!' the man said. 'Come on. Give us your dockets! You can stay here.'

'I don't *wanna* be here, mate,' I said.

'Right! In ya go.'

The room was dark, and was made up of several units of eight bunk beds, four on each row. We were assigned a bed each, then we followed the other guys into the communal bath. It was compulsory. We didn't mind. It was a great big tub, like rugby players use after a game. We dried off with stiff white government towels and were given a big bowl of soup and a doorstep-sized slice of bread. There were about 40 other men there.

As we sat on top of our bunk beds, the men chatted about everything under the sun. Initially they didn't speak to us. We didn't mind; we were happy to listen. Mostly they talked about where they'd been, how many miles they'd walked that day, how to get the most out of the system – giros, etc. They also shared their considerable experience on which were the best doss houses. Occasionally, the conversation would turn to how 'old so-and-so' was doing, or that 'old Mickey' had died, or had anyone seen so-and-so? General stories of the road, and I was fascinated.

I grasped quickly that some were alcoholics, but by no means all. The rules at the reception centre were that you were allowed to stay for three nights only. Then you had to move on. You weren't allowed to return until a further four nights had elapsed. There was no admission after 5.30pm, and anyone who'd had a drink was not allowed in. Some of the alcoholic men were simply on a dry spell, others were recuperating from a binge.

As the night wore on, a few of them started talking to us. One of them, a friendly old Geordie, was quite taken with my new, fancy, double-bladed razor. He asked to borrow it. He was absolutely delighted when I said yes. It was no big deal to me.

One Londoner did a bit more than talk. His bunk was on the same upper level as mine and he was facing me. We were all by now chatting away happily. He was telling me where he'd been; I recall him saying that he'd come direct from a similar establishment in Peckham Rye, which all the other men seemed to be familiar with. After about ten minutes, I realised he was playing with himself as he looked at me. I turned and told Bill, who was in the bunk next to me.

'Yeah, I know. I saw 'im,' Bill said. We ignored the fellow and continued talking with the others.

There was an old Irish guy there, who was clearly a drinker, but was in between binges. He was bald with a pointed face and piercing bright eyes. He was charming and had a poetic vibe about him. He held the attention of the whole room with his stories.

It was clear that he was a committed 'gentleman of the road', as they called each other, and that he and many others had no desire to have a home. He loved the open air and being free. The way he talked about it made it sound romantic and exciting.

Some years later, I was to learn that he and a few other mostly Irish men were the last of a dying breed known as 'long-distance men'. They would walk from town to town, often work on a building site for a few weeks, then go on the booze. They would then walk to another town or city and do it all again. I also later learned that the establishment we were in was commonly referred to by the gentlemen of the road as a 'spike', and that there were many others dotted around the country. There is mention of a spike and the long-distance-man lifestyle in the Irish song, 'McAlpine's Fusiliers'.

But there were *some* men who wanted to get 'back on their feet', as they called it – to get back into society, find a flat and a job. Some of them had simply fallen through the net and were neither alcoholics nor suffering from mental illness. One middle-aged guy had been thrown out of his home by his wife, and because the house was in her name, he didn't have anywhere to go. He couldn't get a job without an address, and he couldn't get a place to live because he didn't have a job. This man was serious about getting on his feet, and every morning he would carefully polish his shoes (with the brushes and polish provided by the centre) and try to make himself look as presentable as he could as he went out into the world, trying to get back into the society he had fallen out of.

. . .

After a morning bowl of porridge, another doorstep slice of bread and butter and a mug of tea, we were all sent out.

Bill and I stood outside and watched to see what the other men did. One or two of them were 'not quite the full shilling', as my mum used to say – not seriously mentally ill or anything, just a little wacky, perhaps.

Two friends in particular interested me – a couple of Irish guys, about 40 years old, one of whom was a 'Dub' (Dubliner). He had the gift of the gab, and was streetwise and charming. As he left us that morning, he joked, 'I don't know what today will bring, but I hope it will be food, and I don't mean fucking apples!'

We all laughed. It was right at the end of the apple season.

His pal was from a rural part of Ireland and didn't seem to be able to quite cope with life. He stuck very close to the Dub and hung on his every word, often repeating what the Dub had just said, to emphasise the point. Or, with a serious look on his face, he'd chime in with 'That's right!' after the Dub's every sentence.

I was touched by their relationship. As I watched them saunter down the hill towards Brighton centre, the collars of their long, dark overcoats turned up, they reminded me of the relationship between the two friends in Steinbeck's *Of Mice and Men*.

. . .

As we entered the reception centre for our third night there, the manager pulled us into his office and said, 'Right, you boys are staying at the YMCA from tomorrow. Take these accommodation dockets and go there in the morning.'

We had no idea what the YMCA would be like. We asked some of the other men, who were now our friends. They didn't know much about it either. One said, 'You might be in cubicles, or you might be in dormitories. I don't know.'

Billy whispered to me, half-jokingly, 'It's probably all right, 'cos these fuckers don't know anything about it!'

I sat on my bed and started chatting to the old Geordie guy who I'd lent my razor to. I was excited about going to the YMCA and a new start. I told him the good news. He was pleased for us.

I said to him, 'This is the last time I'm ever gonna stay in one of these places.'

'I said that 20 years ago, son,' he said.

That shook me.

By the end our third night stay there, I'd had an education into a part of society I hadn't seen before. I'd learned about 'the gentlemen of the road'.

· · ·

The YMCA was full of people who were around our age. Billy and I shared a room and we were given three meals each a day. It was a whole lot better than the reception centre. Sometimes we'd run into the gents of the road in town, usually on the dog-end trail or in the dole office. We'd stop and chat.

Soon after, we found ourselves kitchen and table-waiting jobs in a couple of hotels and settled into the YMCA.

One night, there was a few of us lying around in one of the resident's rooms, smoking dope. We were talking about where we were from, and I was telling the others how I had left home. This London guy who was about 17 and had been in children's homes most of his life, suddenly said, 'You mean you didn't have to leave home and you still did?'

'Yeah.'

'Your mum will be worried sick about you,' he said, with a look of concern on his face.

'It's not like that,' I mumbled, and then trailed off.

He looked sad. He was a good kid. He said, 'Sorry.'

I said, 'No, it's OK, mate.'

. . .

Billy and I kept our hotel jobs for a few weeks and had some mad times.

One night we met some people and went back to their flat to smoke dope. Most of them stayed awake through the night, but I dropped off to sleep at one point. I awoke to the sound of laughing. They told me that I had been talking in my sleep, but not in English. They said it sounded like some foreign language. One of the girls was laughing and asking me where I was from.

I believed that I was different to all of them. In my mind, this episode confirmed to me that I had relaxed too much in front of people. I had let my guard down and been found out. I'd need to be more careful in future.

A few days later, we did a tab of acid, and though I enjoyed some of it, my overall feeling was that I was losing my grip on reality. I felt as if I was going crazy. Looking back now, I'd say it was just fear and insecurity. I was heavily conflicted about the life I was living. Mum and Dad had sent me a letter telling me that I was a drifter and was throwing my life away. It seems incredible now, that a 19-year-old be judged in that way, simply for not having a clear plan for his life. That said, my mum had a brother who left home young, and ended up being a gentleman of the road for most of his life.

But it felt like a battle. I was very afraid of what would become of me. I decided to go home. As I told my boss I was leaving (I'd started work as a waiter in a small hotel, run by a lovely Greek man), he said, 'Are you sure? I can give you a room here.' It was a lovely offer. Plus, as he spoke, one of the waitresses was smiling strongly at me. And to top it all, the sun was shining! It was a beautiful Brighton morning. As I write this now, I see that maybe the universe, or whatever you want to call it, was saying, 'Stay!' But I had zero awareness of anything like that. I listened to the fear that was exaggerated by my previous night's LSD trip. The real truth is, we were just a couple of young guys being wild and doing silly things, but at the time, it seemed like a matter of life or death.

A favourite means of mind alteration

I got a job in King's Cross, selling office supplies on the phone. It was winter, it was dark, and I missed Billy. London seemed flat and dull after our adventures. I found myself putting on a Scouse accent and pretending I was from Liverpool to new people I met.

I contacted a few old mates, and on Saturday nights we would often go to a club called the Californian in Dunstable, Bedfordshire, which was a good place to meet girls. The fact that we were from London meant we had it over the local boys. Old friends like Don from my youth-club days had now started tripping too. One week it would be acid, the next it might be Mandrax or speed. Sometimes my brother Joe would come out with us.

One night, we picked up some acid on the way to Dunstable, dropped it, and drove up the M1 from Harrow to the 'Cally'. I hadn't even thought of the implications of tripping in front of Joe. I just imagined we would all go to this club together and have a great time. I hadn't thought it through.

But we *didn't* have a great time. This was very strong acid! When we got to Dunstable, those of us who were tripping could barely get out of the car. When we did, I took one look at the bouncer and was convinced he was going to seriously harm us. The paranoia was totally overpowering. We went back and sat in the car. After a few minutes, we got out again. But now the car park tarmac was rising up to meet us, like squashy foam. I couldn't walk.

I started to feel very conscious of my brother Joe. He wasn't tripping, but he was with four guys who *were*. I began to realise how seriously I had misjudged this situation. *What was I doing to Joe?*

He had been quiet all night, then he spoke, 'Why are we feeling like this?'

He said it good-naturedly, jovially. I think Joe was having what I now know to be a contact high. He was, to some extent, feeling the effects of the trip himself, simply from being with us.

My heart went out to the man. I had envisaged us all being inside the club, and us not feeling noticeably different to Joe. But we were. We couldn't even leave the car. And I hadn't even thought to tell my brother Joe we were on acid.

By not telling him, I felt I was treating him like he didn't exist. That is so easy to do with Joe, because he doesn't expect anything from anyone. But the man deserves so much more.

I couldn't stop thinking about how thoughtless I'd been to Joe. There was now no possibility of any enjoyment that night. It all seemed very dark. I started to think about how shit and meaningless all our lives were. Then I had a clear thought.

'Listen,' I said. 'What do we do? We work all fuckin' week, then we come here on a Saturday night and get pissed or off our nuts. Then we go home, work all week again, and then come here again on Saturday night, get pissed or whatever, pull some girls if we're lucky, then we do exactly the *same*, the *following* week. And week after week, that's all we fuckin' do. What's the point? It's shit, isn't it? It's fuckin' shit!'

'Yeah!' everyone agreed. 'It's shit.'

'Right!' I said. 'Why don't we take this fuckin' car and drive it down the motorway the wrong way, and that'll be *it*. No more. End the fuckin' thing.'

There was silence … for about 30 seconds. Then:

'What? Don't be such a cunt!' one of the boys said angrily.

'What?!' I said.

'Listen to what you're saying. You're fuckin' nuts, ya cunt!'

I felt even more guilty now, for having suggested such a stupid thing. We all sat there in silence for a few more minutes. Then the same boy said, 'Come on, let's all go home.'

We all knew it was a good idea. Don drove us back to London.

When Joe and I walked in, Mum had just come in from her usual

Saturday-night drink with Dad and their friends. She was in the kitchen making sandwiches and preparing drinks. She looked up.

'Hello. You two are in early,' she said brightly. She was always cheery after a couple of glasses of wine. 'Is something wrong?' she continued. 'You're home *very* early.' It was only about midnight and we would usually come in at two or three in the morning.

I couldn't look at her. I put my head down. 'No,' I said. 'I'm OK.'

She came up close to me. She had emerald-green earrings on and they were flashing like green Belisha beacons.

'Are you sure there's nothing wrong, love?' she said, trying to make eye contact. I couldn't look at her.

'Yeah, yeah, I'm all right.'

'We've got some people in the front room. They're over from America. Come in and meet them.'

I really didn't want to do that.

'No, I'm OK. I'm a bit tired.'

'Just come in and say a quick hello,' Mum said.

'OK,' I said, and went in with Joe and got out as fast as I could. Joe stayed with them.

I went to bed but couldn't sleep. I could only lie there thinking about unpleasant things, in particular some cow gut I'd seen in Crossmolina when I was three or four years old. Me and some of the other little kids had stood and stared at it. Now I remembered it in great detail. It looked disgusting, but I couldn't get it out of my mind.

• • •

I got a job as a sales rep for Pantene, a hairdressing product manufacturer. They were still a small company in the UK at that point, and I was enthused by the quality of their goods. Plus, they gave me a brand-new car – a Renault 4. I had passed my driving test a year previously, courtesy of four attempts and, in the final analysis, a few Valium.

The job required me to drive round to hairdressing salons in London and the south of England and sell them Pantene products. I loved it.

It was the early summer of 1973. About a month after I'd started the job, one Saturday night, I went out with Don and a couple of girls on a blind date.

That night, as well as booze, we were on Librium. I can't remember how many pills I took, or how much I drank, but I know that at 3am I was kicked out of the girl's flat in Colindale by her mother for repeatedly getting too frisky.

I commenced the drive home, but it would be a couple of hours before I got there.

I came to at five in the morning, sitting in my now smashed-up new car, on a flowerbed literally *on* a roundabout in Queensbury, just outside Harrow. I managed to get the car off the roundabout and drove it home.

Because of the Librium, I slept solidly. Mum and Dad were at Mass when I woke up at midday on the Sunday.

I felt awful, of course, and drove the car round to Don's to see if anything could be done with it. He was good with cars, but it was too far gone. The panels were all crushed and mangled down one side. It would need a lot of professional work.

Mum and Dad were understandably angry. That Sunday evening, as I was sitting alone at the dinner table, about to start eating, Dad was positioned on one side of me, Mum on the other. They were both shouting at me at the same time.

I felt a build-up of internal pressure. I was feeling bad enough about what I'd done. They didn't need to tell me what an idiot I'd been. I knew.

I couldn't handle the incessant ranting in each ear. I snapped in anger, turned my dinner plate over, spilling the food onto the table-cloth, and got up from the table and walked upstairs.

There had been lots of arguments and bickering with Dad over the last few months anyway. There and then, I decided to pack in my job and go to Liverpool. Maybe Billy and I would go to Butlin's again. I started putting my clothes into my suitcase. Mum and Dad followed me up to the bedroom and carried on going on at me, asking me what I was doing, but I wasn't listening.

'I'm going!' I said.

'Where are ya goin?'

I didn't answer.

Joe handed me some money. 'Here y'are, Kev. Take this.'

It was so kind of him. I could tell he was sad to see me go.

'Ah, so you're going off tramping again for the summer!' Dad said.

I walked out, got into the car and drove off.

First stop was Greenford, to give the car back to Pantene's area manager. I was relieved to find he wasn't in. I wrote a note explaining that I'd crashed the car and that I was leaving the company. I put the note and the car keys through his letterbox, and left the car outside his house. I walked back to Greenford High Street, suitcase in hand, and got a 140 bus to somewhere near the M1 motorway, where I started thumbing. It was by now about 9pm on a sunny Sunday evening.

I'm going where the sun keeps shinin', through the pouring rain.

A couple of lorries gave me lifts through the night and I arrived in Liverpool at 6am the next morning, and saw the city wake from its slumber. I could smell the summer optimism and excitement. Liverpool is a magical city at the best of times, and on that summer morning, it looked beautiful.

I'd just had my monthly pay, so there was money in the bank. It was too early to go to Bill's house and his mum didn't have a phone, so I put my suitcase in the left luggage at Lime Street station. I killed time having breakfast in a caff, had my hair cut at the Adelphi Hotel, and even gave blood at the transfusion centre, until finally, at about 10am, I got a bus out to Bill's house in Garston. His mum brought me in and explained that Billy had just moved into a flat, a few miles away in Lark Lane.

I made my way over and found him. He was sharing a place with another guy, Jimmy. It was great to see Billy again. I soon discovered that he had a good life there – a decent job in a bakery, on night shifts, and a nice little flat. Bill was earning good money, and didn't want to give it up to go to Butlin's.

'Why don't ya stay here and get a job at the bakery?' he said.

I stayed with Billy and Jimmy for a few nights then got a bedsit across the street and embarked on a series of short-lived careers – sweeping the floor in Billy's bakery: one month; delivering soft drinks in a truck: one week; selling cars: two months.

I'd phoned Mum and Dad a couple of days after I'd arrived to let them know I was safe. They weren't happy. I also phoned the boss of Pantene. He wanted me to come down south to finalise everything. I wouldn't. He sent me an accident report sheet and I filled it in, badly and carelessly. I wanted to ignore the past, which was irresponsible. All of that said, I really did feel as though I'd escaped.

Over the next few weeks, we generally had a good time. Liverpool was great in the summer, especially around the mostly bohemian Lark Lane. If any drug-taking was happening, it was usually around there. Nothing was too serious. We worked, we drank, we took drugs and we went after girls.

Phensedyl was a favourite means of mind alteration. It was a cough medicine that could be bought over the counter from chemists. It tasted disgusting, but we would drink the full bottle in one hit, and then quickly slug a glass of lemonade to be rid of the bitter taste. The medicine made us very drowsy, in a pleasant way. I remember having a long and detailed conversation with someone I thought was sitting next to me, before realising there was no one there.

On one particular night, we decided to trip.

Billy and I, along with his mate Jimmy (whom I hardly knew), planned the operation meticulously. Each of us was to drop the tab at exactly 11.30pm, in different locations. Billy was to bunk off his night shift early, as he usually did. Jimmy would stay back at the flat, and I would be in the pub with my coworkers after finishing my late stint at the car showroom. All of us would arrive back at the flat by midnight, just as we would be about to come up on the trip.

It was a good plan. But it didn't work.

I took my pill and arrived at the flat at midnight. Jimmy and I were coming up on our acid, but there was no sign of Billy. Maybe he'd been held up, but he would surely be here soon, I thought.

Billy didn't show, and I ended up tripping, on very strong acid, in a small bedsit, with a guy I barely knew.

I got so freaked out that I felt I was losing my sanity and would never regain it. Jimmy wasn't helping matters. He seemed to be trying to psych me out. We played records, Jimi Hendrix's *Axis Bold as Love*, and Pink Floyd's *Dark Side of the Moon*. But Jimmy seemed to be laughing at me. I was convinced he resented me, for being flash – I wore brighter clothes than he and Billy and flashiness was a criticism that had often been levelled at me, down the years.

We listened to music for two or three hours. Jimmy kept saying, in a very low and what sounded to me like a sinister voice, 'Let's go outside to the park, Kevin. I think it will be better if we go outside.'

He appeared beyond sinister – evil. I was very scared of him. I didn't want to go. I was convinced he was going to harm me. Maybe even kill me. It was 3am.

'Let's go to the park, Kevin – it'll be better if we go to the park. Come on, Kevin,' he kept repeating in the most horrible voice. He seemed like the devil.

'No. It's all right. I'll stay here,' I said.

I thought he could see inside me. That he had found me out. That I was weak. All my defences were down. The charade was over.

'Come on, Kevin. Let's go outside. It'll be better.'

'OK. OK, let's go, just for a few minutes. But I don't want to go to the park.'

The streets were deserted, bleak and eerie, and it seemed there was menace in the air. We walked along the side of Sefton Park. Although Jimmy tried his best to coax me, there was no way was I going in. There was a lake there and I felt a very dark danger was waiting for me. I was terrified of him and desperately trying not to show it. After what I judged to be a respectful amount of time, I insisted we go back.

I went into the bathroom and looked in the mirror. I looked awful, hideous.

The pretence was finished. Jimmy and everyone would be able to see the real me. They would see who I really was: a phoney, weak. Jimmy would undoubtedly tell Billy and I'd be a laughing stock. I'd been found out!

As I sat in that small room with Jimmy, one thought went round and round in my head. *Pat. He is my only hope now. I'm lost. I've got to find Pat.*

I made it through the night. Dawn was breaking, but the intensity of my feelings remained. The fact that it was light meant that I could pretend to Jimmy that my trip was over, that I was coming down. I wasn't. I was still tripping heavily, but I could now justifiably go back to my bedsit.

'I think I'll go back to my own place now and try and sleep.'

Once I got back to my own bedsit, I looked in the mirror again.

Oh no! I was a horror. My hair had gone curly again, and it looked really short. I looked awful, completely different! The others hadn't seen me with curly hair before.

They think my hair is long! I've got to fix it quick. I've got to try and make myself look better!

I got my curling tongs out and plugged them in. Before I had a chance to straighten my hair, Jimmy knocked on my door, asking for a cigarette. There was no time to hide the tongs. (Jimmy and Billy didn't know I used curling tongs to straighten my hair. They would surely think curling tongs were poofy.)

Jimmy came in, sat down and we talked for a minute. He looked at the tongs.

'What's that?' he said, looking aghast.

Oh no. He's seen them. 'It's a hair thing,' I mumbled. 'I just wanted to see if it was working. I'll unplug it.'

'A hair thing! What do you mean? It looks mad. What is it?'

'Oh, it's just this thing that I had in my bag. I wanted to test it to see if it's working,' I mumbled. 'I'll put it away.' I tried to distract him by talking about something else.

At that moment, Billy stormed in, breathless. He had been running. 'Lads! I'm so sorry! The fucking area manager turned up and we all had to work the whole night!'

'Did you take your trip, Bill?' I asked.

'No – I knew by 11 that there was no chance of getting off and I had no way of getting in touch with you. I couldn't get away to make a call. I'm exhausted. I'm going to bed. Sorry again.'

'That's all right, Bill.'

I didn't have money on me. But I still had some of my wages from Pantene in the bank. Money always made me feel better.

It was 9.30am. I told Jimmy I was going down the road to the bank. I wanted to get away from him, but I was afraid to *not* invite him. It was like he was my master now. There was surely an unspoken understanding that he was far superior to me.

'If you come down the bank with me, I'll buy you a cup of tea in the caff afterwards,' I said.

I often visited that caff. The old ladies made good strong tea. Maybe that would help. We went to the bank, and Jimmy sat in the corner giggling manically as the banker phoned my branch to check if it was OK to cash my cheque. I was sure Jimmy was laughing at me.

As we sat opposite each other in the café, I was internally cringing – trying to avoid eye contact, terrified that he was looking right into my soul. I wanted to disappear. He seemed to be constantly on the edge of bursting into hysterical laughter, at me. The problem was, I didn't have any doubt that he was 100 per cent right for doing so. I was a farce.

After the tea, we went back to my bedsit. I wanted rid of him. Again, after what I judged to be a respectable amount of time, I faked a yawn and said I was tired.

I was torn, because on the one hand I wanted Jimmy to go back to his flat, but on the other, I was anxious about Jimmy and Billy being alone together and what they would say about me. Jimmy would surely tell Bill that I was weak, a phoney. But I had to get away from Jimmy. I yawned again. Jimmy left.

I tried to sleep that morning, but I couldn't. I kept thinking about Jimmy and Billy having that conversation. They were now together, in their flat. They would surely be talking about me.

That evening, when I had a few moments alone with Bill, I nervously mumbled something along the lines of, 'Jimmy was a bit weird with me last night, Bill. I was a bit freaked out.' (A massive understatement.) I was hoping I'd got my side in first with Bill, though I thought it very unlikely. I didn't want to tell Billy the truth, and let him know that Jimmy had found out about me. What I wanted to learn from Bill was what Jimmy had said to him, and maybe try and get Billy on my side a bit.

'Was he?' Bill said.

'He was trying to get me to go outside to the park, but he seemed to be talking in a weird voice, I think he was trying to freak me out, Bill.'

'He coulda been, Kev. He probably would enjoy that,' Bill said.

I was pleased he was taking my side. I didn't tell Billy that really I felt the whole thing was my fault, because I was a phoney.

We later found out that this acid was from a small batch that was three times stronger than usual.

That was my last LSD excursion, other than years later, in the eighties, when I thought I was taking an ecstasy tablet, and it turned out to be a trip. The same thing happened – intense paranoia and fear.

I don't think I was ever the same after those trips.

I was in turmoil

I got a job in a men's boutique, as they called them in the early seventies. It felt good to be around nice clothes. The shop stocked good-quality styles of the day – not the absolute height of fashion, but decent. There were a lot of personalities to deal with. Not least mocking Scousers, wondering what a 'Cockney' was doing moving to a very economically depressed Liverpool in 1973.

Not long after arriving in Liverpool, I met Sophia. She was a good-looking, open-minded, positive girl and we hit it off immediately. She moved into my little bedsit, and while I was at work, she would cook food for when I came back for lunch or at the end of the day.

The Peters and Lee song 'Welcome Home' was in the charts at the time.

Welcome home, welcome.
Come on in and close the door.

We fell out as the summer drew to a close, and then, a few weeks later, got back together. I was unsure whether it was the right thing to do. We seemed to have run our course, but to be truthful, I was lonely.

By then I had moved to another bedsit, at the end of her street. She would visit me, and I would spend many evenings and nights at her parents' house.

Staying with Sophia's parents was weird for me. We would sleep together in her bed and her *dad* would bring us a cup of tea in bed in the morning! I never got used to that. My parents and I had never even spoken about sex. It simply didn't exist.

And now Sophia was pregnant. She had been on the pill but had forgotten to take it. I was shocked. I didn't know what to do. I suggested an abortion. She was open to the idea, but it never seemed to materialise. Sophia and her mum started talking about her having the baby.

'OK,' I said. 'I'll do the right thing.' Which in those days, was to get married.

Sophia's mum started planning the wedding. She said it would be a small affair, and that two of my family could come.

Sophia had previously talked about how a baby of ours would be lovely and dark (she was dark too) and I would agree, not for one minute thinking it would happen.

Coincidentally, at this time I was summoned back to London to be a witness for a car accident I'd seen while working in King's Cross. I stayed at home in Harrow for a few days. Everything was still on with Sophia, but I didn't phone her while I was back home.

I started to have second thoughts about getting married and recalled previously hearing Dad saying that when a young unmarried girl got pregnant it wasn't always best for the couple to get married, as it could ruin three lives. His point of view surprised me at the time. But in any event, I had started to think differently. I was 20; Sophia was 19.

After a few days, I said to Sophia, 'Please, babe, have an abortion. I'm not ready for a child now. Maybe if we're still together, we could think about it again at some time in the future.' I was trying to pull out all the stops.

God, and my daughter, please forgive me for wanting to have my child aborted. I didn't think of it in terms of a human life. At this time, I saw children as nothing but a nuisance. The idea that having a child could be something enriching was an alien concept to me.

Sophia agreed to end the pregnancy and said she and her mum would look into it. Apparently, though, there was a problem with the waiting list. Then her mum told me that, although Sophia was still planning to have the abortion, they had also booked a bed at the hospital to have the baby, just in case.

After a while, it became clear that Sophia was going to have the baby.

Over the next couple of months I went backward and forward, telling Sophia I was going to stay with her and look after her and the baby, then changing my mind and backing off. Each time I pledged to commit, I meant it.

I was in turmoil. It was obviously even worse for Sophia. We argued like crazy – blazing, screaming, crying rows, sometimes in the street.

Finally, I backed off and stayed backed off when she was five months pregnant.

I decided to move to Birmingham.

Pat and I had fallen out over the way I'd left home, but now we'd made up again by letter, and in April 1974 I left Liverpool and went to live with him in Smethwick, west of Birmingham, where he had just qualified as a teacher.

The idea of staying in touch with Sophia and the child, while not being in a relationship with her, was never discussed. It wasn't even remotely an option. Life, then, wasn't like it is now, where a young father might visit his child on the weekend. The choices from Sophia's family were black or white – stay and marry our daughter or get out of the picture completely. I chose to be out.

Over the following years, I expected a visit from the Child Support Agency (or their equivalent at that time). All credit to Sophia and her family – that visit never came. Of course, if I had been responsible, I would have saved and sent money. But I didn't. I spent whatever I had.

Two years later, when my daughter would have been two, I called round at about 9.30 one night, accompanied by a friend, Tommy, whom I'd met through Billy, asking to see the baby. It was rude and selfish of me to just turn up without giving notice. Sophia came to the door and said the baby wasn't there. Understandably, she wasn't friendly.

I had told most of my siblings about Sophia and the baby, but not my mum and dad. Telling my parents that I had got a girl pregnant was unthinkable. Completely out of the question.

But 13 years later, in 1988 at the age of 33, during a particularly scary and turbulent Atlantic flight where I feared for my life, I decided that I should tell my parents that they had a 13-year-old granddaughter whom I had never seen. I realised in that moment that if anything were to happen to me, my parents might never know. I guess the fact that I had, by then, somewhat made my way in the world helped me find courage for the conversation.

I went up to their home in Coventry (they had moved back to the Midlands). It was about 11 o'clock at night. I'd planned to tell them earlier, but I just couldn't seem to do it. Now it was almost bedtime.

I said, 'I've got something to tell you.'

'What?' they both said.

'Would ya sit down and have a drink?'

They had a brandy each.

'Well, what is it?' Dad said.

They looked a bit concerned.

'OK. Do you remember when I was in Liverpool?'

'Yes.'

'Well, I went out with a girl called Sophia.'

'I remember,' Mum said.

'Well, it's hard to tell you this, but … we had sex.'

'Yes,' Mum said.

'And she got pregnant. And she *had* the baby. It's a girl.'

'Where is she now?' Mum said.

'In Scotland. Billy tracked her down for me.'

'Are you sure she's yours?' was the first thing Dad said (I smile now at the thought of typical Dad scepticism).

'Yes, I'm sure. Billy has seen her and told me there is no mistaking her.'

Then Mum surprised me. 'This kind of thing has been going on since time began, love,' she said, with great understanding and warmth. I was shocked and relieved. We'd never talked like this before.

Dad was understanding, too. Then he slowed right down, looked worried and, in a way that was uncharacteristic for him, said, 'The only thing is – is she all right, like? Because she's no different to them kids around the corner!' Pat and his family were living nearby.

'To the best of my knowledge, she is, Dad. I'm told that Sophia married a decent guy.'

I explained to them that in 1982 when Dexys did well and I started to earn some money, I phoned Billy and asked him if he could track Sophia down. This he did. Billy learned that when my daughter was four years old, Sophia took up with a good man. They stayed together and married.

I also explained that after Billy had found the address in Scotland, I wrote to Sophia and offered money to help with whatever was needed for my daughter. She would have been eight at that time. Sophia and her husband wrote back saying they didn't want help, that my name wasn't on the birth certificate, and should I contact them again, they would engage a solicitor.

· · ·

Meanwhile, Birmingham was very, very different to Liverpool, and I found it hard to settle. I was thinking of moving on, maybe back to London. But events of the next few months would conspire to keep me there.

PART THREE

Infidelity and trust

My brother Pat had formed a three-piece social-club band who played at weekends, called New Blood, after an album he liked by Blood, Sweat and Tears. I enjoyed going to see them and was proud of Pat, standing there, playing his bass and singing:

Moon river, wider than a mile
I'm crossing you in style someday

I had pretty much given up on the idea that I would ever get on a stage and be a musician. I was very conscious of the fact that I hadn't been able to adequately master an instrument. I felt stupid for that, and I was more than aware that time was slipping away for me, and it probably wouldn't happen now.

I could play maybe four simple open chords (C, F, G and A minor), but I couldn't play barre chords. And anything that went further up the neck was a mystery to me. Concentration, as always, was the problem.

. . .

Now it's my 21st birthday party, at my parents' place in Harrow. Saturday, 17 August 1974.

Twenty-first parties had traditionally been quite a big thing in our house. Pat's, Joe's and Sarah's had all been biggish affairs with extended family of all ages, as well as friends, in attendance.

Mine was shaping up to be the same, although because of the strained relationship between me and Dad I felt unworthy of having a party, what with Dad having to buy all the booze etc. From our interactions leading up to it, I sensed that he wasn't very happy about it either.

Pat and I had come down from Birmingham. Our relationship was a little strained at that point. Nothing serious, but we had started to bicker.

I took my girlfriend Jackie to the party. I'd started seeing her a few weeks before I left Liverpool. She'd moved to London about the same time that I'd moved to Brum, and we had met up whenever I was in London.

At that point, we hadn't had full sex, but were very close to it. Jackie was a virgin. I remember being surprised when she told me she hadn't had sex but had taken drugs. Most other girls I'd met had lost their virginity before taking drugs.

My teenage sweetheart Jean, for whom some years later I would write 'Reminisce Pt.2', was also at the party. She was the girl I'd met when we both worked at C&A, five years earlier. We had dated for a year. I loved her, but eventually felt hemmed in and began to resent the fact that I was in love. I felt too young at 17 to be committed to one girl.

'I'll Be There' by the Jackson 5 was in the charts at the time Jean and I were breaking up.

You and I must make a pact, we must bring salvation back,
Where there is love, I'll be there.

I dismissed the song as corny and over-sentimental, because I knew deep down that it was pure and true and beautifully expressed the fact that love is the most powerful and important thing in the world. I knew I'd had love in the palm of my hand and was walking away from it. I also didn't want to let that song in because I knew that if I did, I would cry and cry, and by that time, I believed that I shouldn't cry.

Jean hadn't wanted our relationship to end and made that clear over the next 12 months or so. I was torn but my long-term plan was to sow some wild oats and then return to Jean.

The sowing took longer than anticipated and, after a year, I still wasn't ready for commitment. Jean had started to move on, but I was still arrogantly confident that I could get her back. We would run into each other occasionally in clubs or bars in London.

However, it became clear just before my 21st party that Jean was now over me. In fact, she was engaged to be married and would be coming to the party with her fiancé.

I liked seeing my new girlfriend Jackie, and certainly fancied her. But at the party, I was torn, and darting between Jackie and Jean, whose fiancé seemed to be allowing her some space. It was a balancing act for me. I wanted to spend time with Jackie, but I knew it would be my last chance to have any time with my teenage love, Jean, before she married.

I neglected Jackie. I was freaked out about Jean moving on. I was preoccupied with getting her on her own and asking her if she was sure about getting married.

Jackie and I had been on a few dates, and I felt it was sealed between us. She was in the front room chatting to my granny and great-aunt. Occasionally, I would sit down with her to see how she was doing. Everything seemed to be OK.

I went and talked to Jean for a while. She was polite and friendly, but she wasn't taking me too seriously – quite correctly, of course. She had allowed me plenty of time, but now she was committing to somebody else.

I walked into the back room and saw Pat and Jackie slow-dancing in a clinch, hips grinding together.

I wasn't crazy about the idea, but I wasn't unduly concerned. People *did* that. It was common to dance with someone else's girl, and grinding hips was the dance of the day. I'd taught it to Pat a couple of months earlier.

But, I *did* feel embarrassed and unsure what to do. I left the room and tried to put it out of my mind. I came back a few minutes later. They weren't there. I said to no one in particular, 'Where's Pat and Jackie?'

My uncle said, jovially, 'Ooh, they've gone outside together.' He seemed to be enjoying the drama. His laughter hurt.

I went out to the back garden and looked for them. I couldn't see them. I tried the garage – not there either. I looked in the shed, outside the house. No sign of them.

I went back inside and waited. Finally, I went upstairs but they weren't there either. I hung around on the landing for a while and chatted to other people, pretending nothing was wrong, but I was totally preoccupied.

I went back downstairs. Now, they were both sitting in the back room, but at opposite ends of it. They weren't making any eye contact with each other. It was so obvious.

I didn't know what to do. I walked out of the room, then came back in. I started dancing with Jackie, I don't know why. I suppose it was an attempt to regain some ground. Then I asked Jackie to accompany *me* outside. She agreed. I really don't know why I did that! I started kissing her, passionately. Wondering what Pat had done with her. I wanted to see what she'd let me do.

A couple of hours later, upstairs, Pat and I argued about something completely unrelated, and I hit him. He didn't hit me back.

The next morning was very uncomfortable. Jackie had stayed overnight, and we all went to the local pub. We were standing in a horseshoe shape at the bar. Jackie was initially standing next to me, and closest to the bar. My female cousin was standing on the other side of me, unaware of the dynamic and constantly asking me questions. I wanted to talk to Jackie, but I didn't want to be rude to my cousin. And I didn't know if I *should* speak to Jackie. I didn't know if I was supposed to be angry at her, or what?

Pat was on the opposite side of the horseshoe. I was feeling stressed about the whole thing. I stretched my left arm to lean up against the bar, in front of Jackie, almost barring her. Suddenly, she ducked under my outstretched arm and went across to the other side of the horseshoe, to stand next to Pat. It seemed to be happening again!

After the pub, I dropped Jackie off at the train station in Harrow. There was a 20-minute wait for her train. I waited with her. It didn't even occur to me to ask her what had happened last night, any more than it did to ask the same thing of Pat. I just couldn't.

Just before she got on the train, I mumbled something sarcastic, like, 'Pat would probably like to see you.'

She didn't say anything.

The next day, I went back to Birmingham with Pat as if nothing had happened. I was still living in his house. I talked with him a little about being sad about Jean getting married, though I see now that I was avoiding facing what was really going on. What really, deeply bothered me was the Pat and Jackie thing. But on the surface, I probably wasn't even conscious of it – so accomplished was I at lying to myself.

And so began a debilitating lifelong obsession with infidelity and trust. From that night of my 21st party onwards, my confidence with women was gone – as in, completely gone. Any swagger from then on was pure make-believe.

I loved Pat and I still found myself longing for his encouragement and approval, as I always had, but deep down, a part of me also really despised him. I was in so much turmoil. I went inside my head and stayed there.

I had no concept of how to deal with pain, or even *acknowledge* it. So instead I tortured myself about how weak I was and, as well as resenting Pat, I became intimidated and jealous of him.

I went all out to pursue Jackie. It's hard to say this, as I don't want to hurt anyone, but although Jackie was and is a great girl, and I really fancied her, a large part of it, initially at least, was about me trying to prove I was good enough for her. I didn't speak about the situation with Jackie, nor anybody else. I just pretended that it hadn't happened.

Jackie moved to Birmingham and we were together for the next three and a half years, off and on, with almost as much time off as on. During the off times, we both saw other people.

As I've said, I didn't deal with my feelings. What I did do, was become a controlling nightmare to Jackie.

Not too long after the 21st thing, I started to instigate conversations about marriage with Jackie. I guess, again, a large part of it was about wanting to 'win' her. The truth is, I wasn't capable of real love. It's not that I didn't care for Jackie – I did – but I was in no state to have a relationship with anyone at that time, though obviously I didn't know that.

· · ·

In November of that year, out of the blue, Pat said to me, 'If you can learn the guitar on all of the songs in New Blood's set in six months, you can join the band.' Steve Skidmore, the guitar player, had just given six months' notice to leave.

It seemed like an incredible opportunity – I could be in a band, on a stage! My dream! I didn't even think about the ramifications or my *real* feelings towards Pat. I had blanked them out to such an extent that I wasn't even conscious of them. I jumped at the chance. I already felt that I should have made a start in music by that time.

Of course, the dignified thing for me to do would have been to step away from Pat's band, and trust that I would find another way into music. But I didn't have the kind of integrity required to make those sorts of decisions.

We would rehearse around Pat's house on Saturday mornings. On one occasion when Pat popped round to our place and suggested to Jackie that she should come to the rehearsals and cook us lunch, I said, 'No, I will be too nervous in front of Jackie.' But the truth is, I wanted to keep those two apart. I'm not saying there was anything going on, other than my paranoia.

· · ·

Playing the guitar in Pat's band was my chance be on a fucking stage! I *had* to do this. I *had* to make it work. But it wasn't going to be easy.

I started learning the songs. I would get the chords from Pat or from a music sheet, and I would work them out from the diagram in my chord book. My fingers hurt and they wouldn't seem to stretch far enough.

Pat said, 'Take it easy. If you just do half an hour's practice every night, you'll be good enough.'

It was good advice. I managed to find the focus, concentration and discipline that I had always lacked. The fact that it was something I was really interested in, and that I could see the goal, made a big difference.

I'd work on a song for 30 minutes, then come back to it the following night. If it started to get too much, I'd move to another song. It was working! I was certainly not going to be a great guitar player at the end of the six months, but I would be adequate – just about good enough to get on a stage.

Steve Skidmore and Pat's encouragement helped a lot, and I got some guitar lessons from a really good local player and friend, John Mark-Lew.

During the rehearsals, we also started to introduce a few new songs. In one of them, a Beatles song – 'And I Love Her' – I suggested dropping the main instruments out of the middle eight and bringing them back in on the last bar. Pat loved the idea and told me that as a result he had said to Mum, 'Kev has more talent in his little finger than the rest of the family put together.'

. . .

In my day job , I was working as a rep selling mats. After a while, I was transferred to the Nottingham branch of the company, which meant I was required to spend four nights a week in that city. I worried about what Jackie might do while I was away. At weekends, when I was home, I would edgily try to find out details.

I was insecure and angry about the men Jackie worked with. If she mentioned them, I'd slag them off, even though I hadn't met them.

One of my married colleagues at work was shagging somebody else's wife and was bragging about it in the office. He said, smugly, 'If a dog doesn't get his meat at home, he looks for it somewhere else!'

I wanted to fucking kill him. I took situations like that very personally. Similarly, I hated watching films where women were unfaithful. It seemed to confirm my world view that you couldn't trust anyone. Everyone was deceitful. Everyone was shit. And worse than that, I'm the kind of guy that people do that to: a loser.

There are two kinds of people in this world, I thought: those who do the hurting and those who get hurt, and if other people know that I'm one of those who *get* hurt, they will hurt me, badly. My life will be unbearable. The more I thought about it, the more uptight I became.

. . .

We continued our New Blood rehearsals over the next few months. This was late 1974, early '75. If Pat called over to our place when Jackie was there, I was rigid with fear and couldn't be myself. Afterwards my mind would go into overdrive.

From then on, if I was with a girlfriend in a social situation with another man, I would be paranoid that she liked him more, especially if it was Pat. I would feel exposed and defective, and my mind would be doing her thinking for her, imagining at what point she would realise I was a phoney and start to get interested in whoever we were with. That has continued.

I tried everything I could to manipulate situations so that I would look strong – trying to make sure that nobody more confident, more charming or better-looking, or who would humiliate me in front of her, would be in our company. But of course that was impossible. I would try to *deceive* a woman into thinking I was a whole, well-rounded man. Keeping that act up was a strain.

I was determined not to get hurt again, but it seemed to keep happening. People say you attract what you fear, and it's true. Shortly after joining Pat's band, and during an off period with Jackie, I brought a date along to a gig. She got drunk, and while we were putting the gear away at the end of the night, she made a play for Pat. I couldn't believe it, but I just concluded that I was simply the kind of person people did things like that to.

On another night, a friend of Alan, our drummer, came along to a gig. He and Jackie were talking a lot while Pat, Al and I played the set. I was in torment as I watched from the stage – they seemed to be getting on well. Jackie was due to come to our gig the following night, and doubtless had mentioned it to this guy. The next night, I insisted Jackie didn't come. Shortly after we started our set, Alan's friend arrived. Seeing that Jackie wasn't there, he left soon afterwards. I took that as all the confirmation I needed.

I started to wake up earlier and earlier in the morning. Unable to get back to sleep, I couldn't stop myself thinking and worrying intensely. I would be all wound up before I'd even got out of bed.

I wanted to be part of a scene

I did my first gig with Pat's band in the summer of 1975. I was as nervous as hell. This was my first time on a stage as a performer.

I had been planning it for months. It was a working men's club in Nuneaton. We turned up at the venue to find the stand-in drummer, Tony, blind drunk. Not just blind drunk, but falling-over drunk. He could barely speak.

Pat was alarmed, and I was too, initially. But pretty soon, I realised it was a blessing – it took the pressure off *me*. We did the gig with Tony tapping along occasionally as best as he could, given the fact that he was almost falling off his drum stool. The audience focused on him – they were laughing and could see that he was 'fluthered' (as my mum would call it). All the talk that night was of how our drummer was blind drunk, not about the incompetent guitarist.

Great! I'd got my first gig out of the way!

On those first few nights, I knew my playing was stiff, but I loved the fact that I was in a group. I lived for it. I thought about little else all week.

I was single-minded and intense about my performances. And after maybe three months, I started to move around a little bit onstage, especially after seeing a friend in Liverpool (Steve Torch) performing in a band that was playing in a similar circuit to New Blood – that is, social clubs at weekends. Steve moved all over the stage, like a true showman. The fact that *he did*, gave me confidence to move around myself. I'd always believed that how performers look is really important, and now that I was less rigid with fear, I could put it into action.

We all – Pat, the drummer (first Alan then Trevor) and I – wore white suits: I already had one that I'd been wearing socially.

At my suggestion, Pat and I would start the intro to the first song of the night ('Hello, Mary Lou') with our backs to the audience. Then just before it was time for Pat to sing the opening line, we would turn and face them. Little things like that helped take the focus off my very basic guitar work.

I started thinking about singing and selected an old Cole Porter song, 'True Love', and another standard, 'Try to Remember'. I ran them by Pat, who was happy that they would fit in well.

I made my onstage singing debut at a working men's club in Tamworth. The song and my vocal had sounded pretty good in rehearsal, but it was fucking awful on the stage – screechy and unmusical, just as it had when I'd auditioned for Richard France's group at 14 years old in Harrow. That put me off singing for a few months. I returned to doing the occasional backing vocal behind Pat.

. . .

Roger Chapman was, and is, such a great performer. I'd just heard the last Family single before they broke up, 'Sweet Desiree'. And I only decided to go and see him live at Barbarella's on a whim.

He walked out onstage looking more as if he was going into a street fight. It was the first time I'd seen anyone with an attitude like that on a stage.

Most musicians at that time were middle class, gentle and academic. Here was a performer with the mannerisms and spirit of the hardest kids I'd seen in London and it was spilling out into his every move.

As soon as he walked onstage, the atmosphere in the club changed, from a hippyish, laid-back, slightly studenty vibe, to intense uncertainty and excitement. We were watching a *real* star.

He was wearing Levi's 501s with small turn-ups (unheard of for musicians at that time), Dr. Martens boots, and a check shirt. He also had short hair – again, almost unheard of for musicians. His singing was something else:

And my friend the sun, he looks well on the run
He's there in the distance, if you care to see.

The way he sang it could only have come from someone with Roger's experience and pain.

If there was any justice, Roger Chapman would be a massive star. He is, of course, highly respected by music lovers, but in my view, he should be one of the most popular singers in the world. He is certainly one of the greatest.

. . .

My younger sister, Grainne, had moved up to Birmingham to go to the Catholic teacher-training college that Pat and Sarah had both attended. She was to stay in a room in the house that Dad had bought a few years earlier and that Pat was now renting out to students.

At the time Dad bought the house, I was 16. He said he was going to give us all a small percentage of it. As he talked, he warned us that we must stay united and work as a team. He said that no one of us should go against the others and try to take out their financial share of the house.

Sarah said, 'I wouldn't, Dad.'

Pat said, 'I wouldn't either, Dad.'

'Nor would I, Dad,' I said.

'You'd be exactly the one to do it!' he said loudly. 'You'd say you wanted to get your money out! There'd be something you *must* have the money for.'

Now, it's a few years later, Grainne is moving into that house. Mum and Dad brought her up in the car one Saturday and, as I lived only a few miles away, I popped over to say hello.

Looking back, I think the reason I worked so hard at keeping in touch with my parents, despite all the signs that I didn't fit, was because I was still trying to prove to them (especially Dad) that I was all right. It was futile.

Mum, Dad, Grainne and I were sitting in her room, drinking tea. I found myself arguing with Dad about some small thing or other. The conversation became heated, and it turned into a stand-off. He had said something like, 'If you don't like it, then what are you doing here?' I walked out in anger.

I stood outside the house for a few minutes. Then I sheepishly walked back in and sat on the bed.

I cringe now at the fact that I had zero self-worth or dignity. Deep down, I must have felt that something awful would happen to me if I wasn't close to my family. The truth is, being in that dynamic was killing me.

. . .

I carried on practising my singing and doing the occasional backing vocal in Pat's band. We did a country song together called 'Parade of Broken Hearts'. Pat sang the harmony on the choruses, and our voices blended well.

Take everything, you won't be back.
Poor broken hearts, come on, let's hit the road.

Gradually, my confidence grew and I again attempted to sing something on my own. This time it was the Kris Kristofferson song, 'Me and Bobby McGee'. It went better. It wasn't amazing singing, but it was passable. I delivered it with a Bryan Ferry lilt.

Soon after, I wrote a song myself, called 'Girly'. A simple thing, nothing special. Pat let me put it in the set. I appreciated that because this was a working men's club band. The audience hadn't come to hear original songs; they wanted to hear songs they were familiar with.

One night, as we packed away our gear after a gig at Castle Vale Working Men's Club, Pat and the club entertainment secretary (who was a bit drunk) were standing on the empty stage, working out some dates for future gigs. The entertainment secretary said, 'And if you can't mek' any o' these dates, gimme plenty of notice. Everyone gets sick once in a whoile.' Then he pointed at me and, in a serious tone, said, '*He* looks like he's gonna fuckin' die tomorra.'

Do I look that bad? What's the matter with me? I thought.

After the bloke had gone, I said to Pat, 'He's a cunt,' or something similar.

Pat said strongly, 'Look, that bloke has just given you £150!'

He was referring to the future booking's money, but I wasn't talking about that. I guess I was hurt that he pointed out I looked so bad. I was very thin and pale, presumably due to the worry and stress. I just pretended to agree with Pat, that it didn't matter. But it was confusing and unpleasant and more proof that there was something wrong with me. *I'm not even as healthy as other people*, I thought.

On another night, when my family were up from Harrow, we were sitting in my Uncle Jimmy's pub, near the centre of Birmingham. There were some plain-clothes policemen drinking in the corner. It was always easy to tell plain-clothes police in those days – their clothes would be just that, very plain. Dad said to me, 'You could be a copper.'

'No, I don't think I could.'

Dad pointed out one of the policemen, who was in his forties and of thin build. 'You never know. Look at that fella over there. *He* doesn't look that strong.' The guy he was pointing at looked pale.

Dad was telling me this as if he was doing me some kind of favour. I accepted that I was less healthy than the rest of my family. I wondered if wanking was the reason. From the age of about 15, it bothered me a lot, but I wasn't able to stop or moderate the habit. I would try to abstain and would sometimes manage three or four days before I would again give into the temptation, sometimes feeling self-loathing as I was actually wanking.

• • •

I started to feel resentful towards the working class. I had never felt like this before. If anything, I'd revered and even romanticised them, and was very class-conscious. Now I was viewing many of the working-class people I met as slovenly, hopeless – without grace, intelligence or style.

At a gig that Pat and I did in Winson Green I looked around the room and didn't like what I saw. Blues (Birmingham City) and Villa fans, arguing about their football teams.

They looked old-fashioned. Their lives looked dull and grimy, and yet they were making a big deal about Villa or Blues. Their whole identity was tied up in Blues or fucking Villa! *Are you stupid?!* I thought. *Who gives a fuck? What have Blues and Villa ever done for you?*

Obviously, I saw Wolves and Albion fans in the same way, and in fact all football fans. It seemed to me that the players were being paid a lot of money, while many of the fans had abandoned their own lives to support the footballers' excessive lifestyles.

I realise now, of course, that this was a very jaundiced view. I guess I was generally full of anger at this point and would find myself getting in fights, often in clubs, usually over women.

· · ·

Wearing 1940s and 50s clothes and haircuts in the mid-70s was different. Nearly every young man was still wearing the feather-cut, baggy flares and tank-top look that was initially exciting in 1971, '72, but was now nothing but depressing, as far as I was concerned.

Bryan Ferry was a massive inspiration. He wore a white tuxedo in early 1974. It was pure genius and way ahead of its time. Of course, he had the best clothes designer, in Antony Price, but Ferry understood the looks and wore them incredibly well.

I would get clothes made, or pick up dead stock from old men's shops or from charity shops. Wearing an American GI outfit, or a forties suit, with a short-back-and-sides haircut to a normal club in late 1975 and early 1976 was a culture clash. Girls would often think I was an off-duty soldier. In a perverse way, I quite liked that.

I was going to normal funk clubs, and occasionally seeing another guy or girl with similar ideas. But very few of them would be as passionate or take it as seriously as I did. Sometimes I'd see a girl in a forties dress and think, *Oh, she's a kindred spirit.* After some Dutch courage, I'd attempt to talk to her, but I found that most people were just wearing these clothes as fun. It wasn't serious, like it was with me.

I wanted to be part of a scene, like I imagined Ferry was. But there didn't really seem to be anyone in Birmingham who felt the same way about clothes that I did. Then I found the Romulus – a club on the Hagley Road, where in the downstairs room, on Saturday nights, a small dressing-up crowd would gather.

It was really good to see like-minded people. The girls were wearing forties or fifties outfits and would have their hair dressed up. The boys would usually be Ferrys or Bowies circa *David Live* (Martin Degville, later of *Sigue Sigue Sputnik*, was one), and there were a few James Deans.

Suits would be forties or fifties style, worn with quiffs or wedges, which would often be blond on the top, and coloured purple all around the graduation at the sides and back.

The DJ would play Roxy and Bowie at the peak of the evening, and forties swing. I had been getting bored of going out and dancing to soul music; it seemed to be getting lighter, less tough, as it moved nearer to disco, and didn't have the same impact for me as the likes of the Fatback Band or War, from 1973 and '74.

I felt good at the Romulus and would look forward to it all week. Saturdays would be great. I'd do a gig with Pat's band and then quickly pack away my gear and head to the club.

Typically of me, I didn't really get talking to anyone there. I was too insecure and self-conscious. Instead, I focused my energy on trying to convince Pat and other guys I knew, like Trevor (who played drums with us and was later briefly in Dexys), that this was a great and valid scene and that they should come along and start dressing this way. They weren't very interested.

Around the same time, I got into hairdressing by way of a six-month government training course. It seemed almost too easy to be true – a crash course and, at the end of it, I would be a qualified barber.

As the interview ended, they told me I'd been accepted onto the course. I walked out of there feeling as light as a feather. It was good to get away from the sales stuff that I'd been doing. It wasn't me. When people refused me a sale, I took it personally. Hairdressing felt natural.

I was moving forward. First, performing in a band, and now this.

That said, the course was quite basic. The likes of Vidal Sassoon had revolutionised hairdressing in the sixties and early seventies, and the techniques I was being taught, though good, were pre-revolution. It was essentially a barbering course, and although the standard was high, we weren't shown any contemporary cutting skills or women's styles. At the end of my six months' training, I was sent upstairs to the job placement office, not feeling very hopeful.

When they asked me where I would like to work, I said, 'Brown's, in an ideal world [the coolest and best hairdresser's in Birmingham], but there's no way they'd take me on!'

To my amazement, the job placement girl phoned Brown's and immediately got me an interview with the owner.

It was on one of my shining days. I felt and looked good in my lovely navy peg-leg trousers, a red Hawaiian shirt, light brown pointed shoes and James Dean haircut.

Paul Burton, the owner, interviewed me, and appeared to like me (I even liked myself on that day). He asked me to return the following week to do a trial haircut. As I was leaving, he said, 'I'm gonna give you a job anyway. I like your personality. I just want to see what level you're at.'

When I returned to do my trial haircut, I wasn't having a shining day, at all. I was awkward and nervous. He seemed to pick up on it and became impatient with me.

The haircut didn't go well. I would have usually done better. I sensed that he was now regretting the fact that he'd offered me a post the week before. Nevertheless, he started me.

I was to spend my days watching the top stylist, Heather, for my first month, and also, under close supervision, cut models' hair in the evenings. I knew I was lucky – the juniors, who were only a few years younger than me, had to shampoo hair and sweep the floor all day, then they would be taught how to blow-dry, and then and only then would they start doing cuts in the evenings. I was basically given a good hairdressing course, on full pay!

I studied and worked hard. I loved it and, because I was so passionate, I was a quick learner. Even after being there all day and doing supervised cuts in the evenings, I'd sometimes do friends' hair after that. I was living and breathing it.

Soon I was cutting hair in the shop for paying clients and, within a few months, I had built up a client base – mainly women, but some men too. I was given a station on the upper tier of the shop, right in the front window.

Wedges and fireflies (similar to the wedge, but shorter), and short layered cuts were the styles of the day. For slightly older women, I liked bobs – they were great to cut, requiring a lot of precision. The hair had to be cut in the finest of layers, to avoid *any* graduation. It was all about the back of the hair, and sometimes a woman would have her head down for at least an hour while the cleanest of lines was implemented. I never saw a woman complain. It was a serious haircut.

I loved the sensuality and trust of cutting women's hair. It felt intimate. It helped me socially, too. As soon as a woman knew you were a hairdresser, you would usually have her full attention.

Despite my full stylist status, and the fact that I was getting busier, my wages at Brown's were still only £25 a week, the pay I had started on. I began to think I should be getting more.

I asked Paul, the owner, for a rise of a fiver a week. He explained to me that as he'd only recently trained me on almost a full wage while I was bringing in zero revenue, I was only now doing haircuts to the weekly value of £125, £130 a week. Therefore, he wasn't actually making any money on me yet.

His explanation made total sense, and I felt bad that I had asked for the rise. 'I totally understand what you are saying and I'm withdrawing my request,' I said. 'Sorry, I shouldn't have asked.'

But now he was insistent that I *should* have the rise. There ensued almost an argument, each of us insisting the other was right.

'No, I'm not taking it. You're right. It's too early.'

But he wouldn't take no for an answer, and I left work that day thinking, *What a great guy.*

. . .

The genius of Van Morrison properly came into my consciousness during that boiling-hot summer of 1976. Prior to that, I had viewed him as another West Coast singer-songwriter type, and not my cup of tea.

Then I heard *Astral Weeks*.

I actually heard the whole album three times in one evening. During one of my long break-ups with Jackie, I was in a wine bar in Birmingham with Rose, my new girlfriend. The woman running the place was clearly very into the album and played it three times in succession. On the first listening, it sounded a little bizarre and tuneless – I was convinced he was making the songs up as he was going along. They didn't seem to have any form. But on the second time, something stirred in me. By the third hearing, I knew I was listening to something incredible.

Down the Cypress Avenue
With the childlike visions creeping into view

This, and one or two of his other great works, like *It's Too Late to Stop Now*, changed my understanding of what music could be.

I'd never heard music that went this deep or made so much sense of the way I felt. I related to the pain being expressed. I didn't know it could *be* expressed with such beauty. That was a revelation, and this was great art.

Van's music was deadly serious, and that was exactly how I felt. Ever since I could remember, people had always been telling me to cheer up. But this music, for the first time, validated the way I felt, and much more. I couldn't understand why anyone would not see this as the best thing they'd ever heard. For example, 'Caravan' on *It's Too Late to Stop Now*:

Switch on your electric light,
Then we can get down to what is really wrong.

Those lyrics didn't even make a whole lot of sense to me, but it didn't matter, because on a much deeper level I totally understood it, in a way that I can't even explain.

Mama (as the band 'doodled' beautifully in the background)

Over there? ...

It's turned on already

and then ...

Turn it up!

BANG! The most amazing soul-style (actually, not far off cabaret) brass riff storms in, played with such conviction and meaning that it transcends all styles. Pure soul, with a depth I hadn't known existed.

. . .

That summer, I felt more fulfilled than I had ever been. I was doing good haircuts at Brown's, dressing nicely, going to the Romulus, and playing guitar in New Blood at weekends. Plus, all that heat and light from the summer was lifting me.

As I walked through Birmingham city centre on my way to work one day, I saw a poster of Enrico Cadillac Jnr, the main singer of a band called Deaf School. The first album cover photo echoed the film *From Here to Eternity*, but in 1976 it said *so* much more. Their look was perfectly retro yet contemporary. They were playing in Birmingham soon and I couldn't wait to see them live.

The show started with moody lighting and fifties-style smoky saxophone jazz music. We could see the silhouettes of two men standing at the front of the stage, Enrico and Eric Shark. They lit cigarettes and talked inaudibly to each other over the music. The fact that we couldn't hear what they were saying didn't matter. We understood.

Then the lights went up, and the rest of the band roared in. Wow. One minute it was rock'n'roll, the next it was 1930s-style English crooning, then we were in a 40s musical, then a bit of Elvis, then there was a Marlene Dietrich vibe from Bette Bright, the female lead singer. The sound was cutting edge and contemporary yet retro. They had used the past to make something completely new and relevant.

They pretty much acted out the songs and there was always something to watch. In fact, you didn't know where to look – there were things going on all over the stage. But my eyes were mainly drawn to the charismatic Enrico and Bette. It seemed they'd taken the Roxy Music thing, developed it and moved it on.

Each member had their own image. There was a Ferry-influenced cabaret showman (Enrico). There was a spiv (Eric Shark). A chanteuse (Bette). A vicar (the Reverend Max Ripple). A Mr Average. An early 60s-styled guitar player (Cliff Hanger). Everybody was committed to their role and all of them could really play, confident and strong. I *knew* this was the future. I was totally inspired and immediately started thinking about forming my own serious band along the same lines.

'Don't try and make it as a musician, man. You'll break your heart trying,' Pat said to me.

But what did I have to lose? Absolutely nothing!

I advertised in the local paper and, after a few weeks, I had something like a line-up. We called it Lucy and the Lovers. It was a reasonably good, art-rock thing, but by the time we were ready to do our first gig, in early 1977, punk was taking off in Birmingham.

Obviously, we identified with the punk thing: it was originally fashion-orientated, and the clothes we were wearing were very similar. A lot of the Ferrys and Bowies from the Romulus had gone over to punk.

All of a sudden, as if overnight, loads of kids who hadn't come to punk from the style end of things were now into it. A few months previously they had liked Black Sabbath or Led Zeppelin. I felt like outing them!

Punk was going overground fast, and pulling people in from all directions, which was incredibly exciting, but from the perspective of Lucy and the Lovers, it wasn't great – punks were making up the largest part of our audience, and only wanted punk music.

· · ·

Early that summer, 1977, my brother Pat suffered an aneurism (brain haemorrhage) and had to have a metal clip inserted in his head. He had the operation a few days before Lucy and the Lovers were due to do our first gig. When I went to visit him in hospital, the first question he asked was, 'How did the gig go?'

It hadn't gone well. The punks thought we were pretentious and some of them heckled us. There was almost a fight, but I didn't tell Pat *that*.

'Yeah, it went good, man,' I said.

Pat recovered. Lucy and the Lovers didn't.

We had started off as an interesting idea, with two girl singers (one of whom was Jackie) dressed in sexy clothes. We had a saxophone player. I wore make-up, a thin pencil moustache, greased-back hair and a 1950s rubber raincoat, and would perform one or two of the songs seated. We owed more to Roxy and Deaf School than punk. And although there was a certain amount of aggression in our sound, mainly coming from my lyrics, the music itself had much more variety in it than punk. We had brave ideas for songs: there were timing changes and there was drama in the music. But Lucy and the Lovers, in that form, wasn't acceptable to the punk audience and, to cut a long story short, we compromised.

We ditched our slower songs and wrote faster ones, and when the sax player left, we didn't replace him. When one of the girl singers left, we didn't replace her either, and eventually I also decided Jackie was surplus to requirements. In short, we dropped everything that made us different. Now we were a guitar, bass and drums band, just like all the others. We changed our name to the Killjoys, in the hope that we would get recognition from the punk audiences. Punk had such momentum that any band who said they were punks could do gigs and get in the music papers. But our change of direction was, of course, a mistake.

An average punk band

Leaving Brown's was hard. Paul Burton clearly believed in me and was about to send me on a Vidal Sassoon training course that I was really excited about. He told me he was grooming me for better things. But although I really wanted to do the Sassoon course, I knew I couldn't let him fork out for it and then leave, so I told him that I was going to do music full-time and departed.

I don't know if I *really* thought that something could happen with the Killjoys, but I guess I saw it as some kind of adventure. Plus, the new fad for Farrah Fawcett-Majors haircuts in Birmingham was doing my head in. It was so mainstream and dull, and I was getting tired of women coming in and asking for the same style.

It felt refreshing to throw off the suburban shackles and not have a job or a regular wage, and instead sign on the dole. In those days, unlike now, you could just about survive on unemployment benefit.

My dad wasn't happy about the new career choice. He was convinced I was a loafer, and advised me that my bandmates, who he hadn't really met, would rob everything they could off me.

'They'll get everything they can off ya!' he said.

Dad, Mum, Joe and Grainne had actually witnessed Lucy and the Lovers' first gig at Barbarella's. They happened to be in Birmingham staying with Grainne that weekend. I was surprised to see them at the gig. Dad told me afterwards that he had his fingers in his ears during the set.

Through the Killjoys, I met John Tully and Dave Cork. John, as well as being a local concert promoter, booked the bands at Barbarella's. Dave Cork knew the Clash. He had promoted them and was friends with Bernard Rhodes, the Clash's manager. John Tully and Dave Cork were like gods to me, and they managed the Killjoys for a short while.

· · ·

In that summer of 1977, my Aunty Beatrice (my mum's younger sister) died. I went to the funeral in Wolverhampton. There I met for only the second time my mum's 70-year-old aunty, Margaret Wilkinson (McDonnell).

At this point, I had blue hair and had been getting stick about it from Mum and Dad, as well as strange looks from some other relatives. Blue hair in Wolverhampton in 1977 was very unusual.

Mum's Aunty Margaret came over to me and in her slow Irish drawl said, 'Hello, Kevin. Nice to see you. What are you doing with yourself these days?'

I thought, *Oh, fucking hell. Here we go. More criticism. I'd better answer carefully.*

I mumbled, 'Well, not that much, I'm doing this and that, and I'm sort of in a band.'

'Oh, in a band? What kind of music do you play?' she said, enthusiastically.

Not knowing what to say, I said, 'Well, it's sort of rock'n'roll.'

'Oh, is it? I love rock'n'roll!' she said with an encouraging smile. 'That sounds great, Kevin!'

I was shocked. I couldn't believe it. *Who was this woman?*

I went up to my mum, pointed at my Great-Aunty Margaret McDonnell, and said, only half-jokingly, 'Mum, are you sure Aunty Margaret is related to us? She's been encouraging me to do music!'

Mum just laughed.

The McDonnells, Mum's side of the family, were considered 'Townies' in Crossmolina. Granny McDonnell, who was actually Mum's great-aunt, had a pub in nearby Ballina. It wasn't a massive pub, but in those days, having a pub was a big deal. The McDonnells were into the arts and renowned as good singers. One of my mother's uncles, Pat, wrote poetry, and back in the days when many of the town's people were illiterate, would compose letters for those who couldn't write.

He was dark of complexion, with black hair. I've been told by older relatives that I'm like him. Paddy McDonnell was a heavy drinker and died young from TB, which was by no means uncommon in those days.

Margaret had ten children, and encouraged all of them to do music or drama.

. . .

I was, by this time, pretty much unemployable. I had tried a part-time job – delivering parcels in my dilapidated old minivan – but I just couldn't seem to do it. I always seemed to get lost or break down.

Deep down I knew that I just couldn't work. I was out of that groove and to say I hated doing menial jobs was an understatement. I couldn't seem to handle it, mentally. I tried to help my mate Steve Millward (who was living in my house at the time) with some building stuff: I couldn't even do a day. I said to him, 'I'm going home. Sorry, mate.'

I was also unable to manage my money. I couldn't seem to make whatever I had last. I would go around to Pat's place in the mornings (he was recovering from his brain aneurism) and his wife Margaret would cook us bacon and eggs. I felt uncomfortable about taking their food. It was more than good of them. They didn't have much more money than I did.

I carried on with the punk band. Nothing much was progressing, but we did gigs and hoped for success and even tried to develop into something a bit more original – we wrote a couple of ballads and I started to dress up a little in jodhpurs and frilly shirts. But everything seemed to be a struggle.

. . .

That same year, I met Kevin Archer. He was in a local punk band, the Negatives, that Pat was looking to manage. Kevin was five years younger than me, and I found him to be very pure and genuine. He reminded me of an authenticity I'd almost forgotten about. I was happy when he joined the Killjoys.

That Christmas, 1977, a programme on punk was shown on TV. I was at my parents' place in Harrow. There was only one TV in the house and, perhaps naïvely, I was wanting to let the family see what I was a part of (not that my band was featured in the show, of course). After some persuasion on my part, pretty much the whole family sat around and watched it.

There were one or two emerging punk bands featured. Towards the end, Dad pointed to the up-and-coming band on the screen, and said, 'How long have they been goin'?'

'About nine months,' I said.

'And how long have yer group been goin'?'

'A year and a bit,' I replied.

There was a pause. And then: 'Well, if they've been going for nine months and they are already doing better than *yer* group ...'

I could see where he was going with the calculation.

That old familiar feeling – an intense frustration, embarrassment and debilitating inability to articulate a response – washed over me. It was of course my own fault. I was looking for some kind of approval and recognition.

Dad seemed to always want to bring me back down to reality – his reality. Or to teach me some kind of lesson – but not with tenderness, always bluntly or brutally. I would later express it in 'All in All (This One Last Wild Waltz)', even though, at the time of writing, I had no idea what it was about:

> *All in all, I'd say things have turned out good*
> *You still don't smile at me, but then I never thought you would*
> *You don't waste time on praise, do you, sir?*
> *But you should be proud to be sure.*

· · ·

Early one morning, I lay in bed, thinking. I'd been awake for hours, anxiously turning things over and over, as I often did. I suddenly had a strong thought.

Fuck it, if I can just get on to Top of the Pops, *then everyone can fuck off! I'll have something no one else I know has. Nobody will be able to put me down if I can achieve that!*

But the harder the Killjoys tried and the more compromises we made, the further success seemed to get from us. We were an average punk band, and we were seen as such. And once you've played your hand and declared yourself as one thing, it's very difficult to get people to view you as anything different.

I started to fantasise about forming another group.

It dawned on me that people would want to dance again. I started to think about a soul band – only in very general terms, but I knew it would have a brass section and that we would dress well, not scruffy.

One day, when Kevin Archer was round at my place, I played him a song that I'd recently written. It was called 'Tell Me When My Light Turns Green'. It hadn't even occurred to me to play it to the rest of the Killjoys; I knew it wouldn't be right for them. But Kevin and I were kindred spirits.

When I'd finished the song, I put my acoustic guitar down and Kevin said, 'That's soul, that is!'

I burst out laughing. It was a laugh of recognition. 'Really? Do you think so?'

'Definitely. That's soul.' He looked very serious. 'Why are you laughing?' he said.

'Well, I'm really glad to hear you say that.'

'Why?'

'Well, because I can see a time when the Killjoys won't be together and, ultimately, this is what I'd like to do. Soul, but in a contemporary and unique way.'

Then I started to feel guilty. Shit! Kevin had only recently abandoned his electrician apprenticeship to join a *punk* band, and now the lead singer was telling him that the band probably wouldn't last.

Bizarrely, my idea at that time was to get as far as we could with the Killjoys – hopefully a record deal – and then to split up and go our separate ways. I would form *this* band, and the others could do whatever *they* wanted – we were clearly going in different directions. I made no secret of that plan to the other members of the Killjoys. We hadn't been getting on, and it was obvious that we wouldn't be able to stay together much longer.

Then two things happened.

Firstly, I came home very late one night from a recording session in Cambridge, organised by John Tully and Dave Cork. The original plan had been to stay overnight and I had phoned Jackie and told her. However, when we'd finished the session, someone said, 'Fuck it. Shall we just drive back to Birmingham?' We all agreed it was a good idea.

I didn't think to phone Jackie to tell her. It had been a long day and I was concerned that I hadn't sung well – nerves had got the better of me, and that was playing on my mind.

The band dropped me off in the van. I opened the front door and threw my bag down, leaving the hall light on. I walked into the room where Jackie and I lived. I didn't switch the light on immediately. I didn't want to wake her. Suddenly, I noticed that there were two figures in our single bed. My first thought was that she had a female friend over. It wasn't unusual. I walked nearer to see who it was. The two were motionless as I got close to the bed.

Then, horror! I realised it was a man in bed with her.

I can still remember the way my heart thumped with fear.

I don't recall exactly what I said, but it was something like, 'What the fucking hell's going on here?'

Jackie said to the guy, in the most matter-of-fact way, 'Get up.'

He got up and started putting his clothes on. The way he was doing it was so casual. That annoyed me. Who the fuck did he think he was? And what sort of cunt did he think I was, that he could come into my home, fuck my girlfriend in my bed, and then not even have the decency to hurry as he put his clothes on, or show any kind of embarrassment? The bloke was totally relaxed. That incensed me.

I whacked him in the face, hard. He tried to fight back – I could see he was a guy who could handle himself – but I was so angry, and the anger made me powerful. He didn't have a chance.

I shouted at my girlfriend in rage, 'You fuck off out as well!'

As she got out of the bed, I noticed she was wearing a new pair of sexy knickers with drawstrings on the side. I'd never seen them before. She sat on the bed and casually said to him, 'Wait for me outside.'

What! How fucking dare you, I thought.

It was like I meant nothing – she was talking to him like I wasn't there! There was no explanation, no 'sorry', just the two of them acting like I didn't count.

'You wait nowhere, cunt!' I said, as I thumped him again on the jaw. He was still putting his trousers on and nearly went over.

'All right!' he protested.

I threw him out of the front door. He didn't wait outside; I made sure of it.

I screamed at her, 'You get out, you fucking cow!'

She was still acting casually and not even looking at me. I pushed her out of the front door. Then I grabbed her clothes from the wardrobe and threw them into the dirt in the garden. I trampled on them, so they would get as muddy as possible. She picked them up and scampered away, carrying a few of her dresses under her arm.

She had been so friendly on the phone a few hours earlier, saying, 'Don't worry if you can't get home, love.'

I went back inside. It was late. I couldn't sleep in those sheets. What really hurt was the fact it had been in *our* bed, the single bed we shared every night. I slept on the chair.

. . .

The next day, I played 'Alison' by Elvis Costello over and over again. It seemed to fit my mood.

Oh it's so funny to be seeing you after so long, girl.
And with the way you look I understand that you were not impressed.
But I heard you let that little friend of mine
Take off your party dress.
I'm not gonna to get too sentimental

Like those other sticky valentines,
'Cause I don't know if you are loving somebody.
I only know it isn't mine.
Alison, I know this world is killing you.
Oh, Alison, my aim is true.

Things had got stale between me and Jackie, for sure. We were more like brother and sister than lovers, but there had been absolutely zero indication from her that we were anything like at *this* stage.

I'd written a song while I was with her, one of the first songs I ever wrote. The chorus went:

I asked for help from above
God sent me your lasting love,
Oh, but I took without giving
And now I'm sorry I'm living.

And that was true. I'd taken without giving. I had virtually no concern or consideration for Jackie. The band was my life. It was all about what I wanted. Getting with Jackie and moving her in with me was mostly to prove that I *could*.

I'd also chased other women. When she was away, I'd tried in vain to get another woman back to my place, and I've no doubt that had I been successful, I would have taken her into our bed. But, despite my wrongdoings, this still really hurt.

My brother-in-law Phil had recently given me some gym weights. Over the next few weeks, I started working out on them, obsessively. *I'm going to be strong. I'm going to build myself up.* I started cooking healthy dinners and taking vitamin pills.

Then, a few weeks later, I bumped into Jackie on the bus. I found her very sexy again – way more than I had in a long, long time. I didn't *want* to, but I did.

. . .

Then, a couple of weeks later, the Killjoys were to do an important gig at the Nashville in London. Howard Thompson, an A&R man at Island Records, was coming. It was late morning on the day of the gig and Kevin Archer was on his way to my place. We would pick up the van from the usual hire company, meet the other three in Birmingham, then drive down to London. I phoned the drummer, Bob, to arrange the pick-up. He said bluntly: 'We aren't coming.'

'What?' I said.

'We're not coming!'

'What? Why not?!'

'We're leaving the band!'

'What?'

'We're leaving the band.'

'Why? Who?'

'We're just leaving. The three of us.'

Wow! The Killjoys' guitarist, bass player and drummer were all leaving, there and then.

Telling me at the last minute felt as if it had been designed for maximum impact. They seemed resentful.

I started panicking. Almost immediately, I thought about forming a new Killjoys. I phoned the music papers, telling them I had already formed a new version. I even made up names of the new 'personnel'.

I was in a state. I'd lost my girlfriend and my band in the space of a month.

Then, a few days later, a thought dawned on me. Hang on, the Killjoys weren't going anywhere. I wasn't happy. It was all stress and hard work, with very little reward. We hadn't got on. And we never *would* get on. And we were probably never going to get very far.

A strong sense of relief came over me. I felt lighter and freer than I had in a long time. Then I realised, *These people have done me a favour!*

The Killjoys had become such a burden. I don't doubt that much of that was my doing. But now I was free.

Us against the world

It was June 1978 and my burden had gone. I was ready to form *the* group. The one I had been dreaming about.

I had tried compromising. I had tried to accommodate people with completely different musical tastes. Now I was going to do it my way. I'd learned a lot in the Killjoys – mainly, how *not* to do it.

But before *anything*, I knew I desperately needed to take a break. I was wiped out from my Killjoys obsession and the Jackie episode. I needed a few weeks for myself, to recharge. Plus, I was broke and in debt. I'd put all my eggs in the Killjoys' basket. I hadn't taken care of my household bills and instead used the money for the band's business. I was living on dreams … but not any more.

I got a job in a local women's hairdresser's, where I rediscovered my love for cutting hair and beauty. I started going to jumble sales, buying beautiful old forties and fifties suits and shirts. I remember getting a great old man's white linen bowling suit – as in bowls that are played on a green. It was beautifully made and cost only a few pence. I dyed it blue. I was enjoying dressing up again.

I started going to discos, not punk clubs. Punk was now grubby, dull. I blow-dried my hair again, which was not welcomed in punk circles.

Wearing beautiful fifties suits, I would go out on a Saturday night, and do my utmost to pull girls, which I did with some success.

Being back in hairdressing made me feel good and reconnected me with the things that I'd completely lost touch with. I was feeling invigorated, fresh, clean and glamorous again. I was still raw after the Jackie thing, but after a couple of months of just cutting hair, enjoying the summer and chasing women, I was ready.

I asked Kevin Archer to help me assemble the band. He wasn't sure. He was planning to form his own electronic group, but he said he would help me get started in the interim. I knew I couldn't do it on my own. My secret hope was that Kevin would find himself more and more involved in our band and would forget about his electronic thing, which was what happened.

I had the idea to look back to sixties soul for musical inspiration, then to do something different with it, hopefully in the way that Roxy Music's first album had taken fifties rock'n'roll as a springboard into something new.

It's hard to understand now, but soul music was *not* hip in 1978. The likes of the *NME* were not talking about it. Soul music was considered old hat. Therefore, it had the potential to be radical.

I *had* a vision, and I was going to see it through. Punk had been great, especially at its peak in '77, but now it felt like the time for different emotions.

Kevin Archer and I started the search for musicians with an advert in the *Birmingham Evening Mail*, describing ourselves as a 'new wave / soul band.' We advertised for pretty much the whole group: a brass section, organist, drummer, bass.

Pete Saunders on organ and a sax player named Carl were the first in, followed by Pete Williams on bass (he was a mate and ex-band member of Kevin's) and then Geoff Blythe (who I christened JB) on tenor sax, and a drummer called John Jay.

The brass section proved a bit more tricky. We didn't know any brass players, so one day we stood outside a city council rehearsal hall and watched through the windows as the Birmingham Youth Jazz Orchestra went through their paces.

'Right, when they come out, you grab that dark-haired one, and I'll grab the blond bloke. Tell them we've got management and a record deal.'

It was a bit like a press gang, and it yielded Steve Spooner, who played alto sax.

We couldn't find a trombone and trumpet player, so we put an advert in the *Melody Maker*. Big Jim Paterson saw it, and travelled down from Portsoy, north of Aberdeen, overnight. We immediately loved him, and him us. He went back to Scotland and returned a few days later with the rest of his belongings. Geoff Kent on trumpet from Leicester saw the same advert, joined up and shared a bedsit in Birmingham with Jim.

The whole band had been told at their auditions that they would need to pack in their jobs and sign on the dole, as we would be rehearsing all day, at least five days a week. Anyone who had reservations about that clearly wasn't right for us.

'You would spend 40 hours a week doing something you hate,' we reasoned. 'Why wouldn't you want to spend the same amount doing something you love?'

Most musicians don't have original ideas, in terms of the direction a band might take, but that doesn't stop them telling you what they think is their own vision – except it's usually based on how some other currently successful band are operating.

We *had* a vision, it was original and we knew it.

We were lucky that, in those days, the benefits office didn't get you in to justify your efforts to find a job, like they do now. As long as you signed on every fortnight, they pretty much left you alone. We saw the dole as our student grant.

In terms of clothes, I knew instinctively that, like me, other people would now want to dress up again. I was already seeing signs of it in Birmingham and London. The people who had been rocking wedge haircuts and forties and fifties clothes before punk in 1975 and '76 were wearing wedges again and retro-inspired clothes.

We went to the Birmingham College of Fashion and met the best young progressive designers, especially one called Vicky (sadly, I can't recall her surname). Usually, we'd have rough ideas of what we wanted, and Vicky would contribute and inspire us.

I let my imagination fly. We had asymmetric haircuts, and wore colourful, flamboyant clothes that would a couple of years later come to be identified with the fashion movement, New Romantic. But in 1978, when we started, this was radical and fantastic. No other band was dressing like this.

In the above picture, you can see that the clothes Kevin Archer (front middle)
Geoff Blythe (bottom right) and myself (second from right at the back) were
wearing would be later known as New Romantic.

Those in the group who had little idea about clothes were advised
on what to wear or, more often, *given* clothes to wear, though it had to
be something they could relate to and enjoy. They were always part of
the decision-making process. I cut everybody's hair. Again, the individual's hairstyle would be a collaboration.

We used the Deaf School idea of everyone having their own
look. We had a scientist, two mods (we eventually settled on one), and
a 1930s all-American boy. Kevin Archer, Geoff Blythe, myself, and later
others, all dressed futuristically.

It was now clear that my whole life had been leading to this. A bold
statement, I know. But that's how I felt. My passion for music, plus my
love of clothes, interesting hairstyles, and my skill for making them a
reality, all seemed to combine perfectly. The whole vision gave me a
new confidence. That confidence surprised even me, and made others
around me believe in the vision too.

We started daily rehearsals in the garage of Pat's house, where
he lived with his wife and young baby, Jack. One day we downed

instruments and had a meeting to choose a name. Everybody was invited to propose suggestions. I had 'Midnight Runners', but couldn't think of a good word to precede it. I asked if anyone could think of one that might work. No one could.

Keyboard player Pete Saunders suggested the name Winslow Boy, after a book he had read. He shared the outline of it and most of us liked it. Winslow Boy was voted in as the band name.

It irked me. While I didn't doubt it was a good book, I felt that, as a name, it was too middle class.

After a few days, I raised the subject again.

'Look, I think the name Midnight Runners suits us better, if we can just think of the right word to put in front of it.' No one seemed to object to re-opening the discussion, so we started coming up with suggestions, but nothing sounded great.

Then Geoff Blythe said, 'Mandy's Midnight Runners?'

I think he meant the female name, Mandy. But I took it to be the slang name for Mandrax, a drowsiness-inducing drug that I had enjoyed in the early seventies.

We can't have a downer-sounding name, I thought. It needed to be an upper, and immediately I thought of Dexys, short for Dexedrine, a powerful amphetamine tablet. I announced the idea and everyone agreed to it.

We lasted a couple of months in the garage, until the neighbours made too many complaints. Then we broke into old disused warehouses in the centre of Birmingham and used them as rehearsal rooms. We would put on our own locks, stolen from the local department store, and claim 'squatters' rights'.

We would usually last a few weeks in each place. It wasn't unusual for the landlords to call the police, who would of course always take the landlord's side. We would attempt to baffle them with our 'knowledge' of squatters' rights. I'd heard a few slogans while in Liverpool but actually knew very little. We acted confidently, though, and would sometimes manage to confuse the police enough to get ourselves a few extra days' rehearsal before being moved on. When asked for our addresses, we told the police we were of NFA – no fixed abode.

On one occasion, we found a nice, old-looking commercial building, just across the road from Barbarella's nightclub. There was no sign of life inside, so we chose it as our next rehearsal space. No sooner had we got in, than we realised that it was in fact an operational furniture storage warehouse. While we were pondering what to do, the police arrived and started trying to get in. We had bolted the door from the inside. They started talking to us on a megaphone.

'This is the police. Come out. You are under arrest. You have broken and entered into a private property. You must come out immediately!'

Even if we'd managed to convince them about our squatters' rights, they would surely nick us for something or other. We decided to sit it out.

The police were now shouting through the letter box.

'No. We live here, we're claiming squatters' rights,' we said.

Police dogs were barking outside. The building backed onto a piece of wasteland and there was a drop of about 30 feet from the level we were on to the ground.

A different police voice shouted into the megaphone: 'We're sending the dogs round the back.'

Jimmy Paterson started laughing manically and shouted back: 'They must be incredible dogs if they can jump 30 feet!'

We all laughed uproariously. I don't know why, but I wasn't really afraid.

We were buzzing. It felt like we were in a siege, and it was fucking exciting! We were taking the police on! I'd tried to take them on in the past and had always lost. But I was alone then. Now, with this crew, we were afraid of nothing.

Eventually the police got bored and left.

Though we didn't realise it at the time, all of this stuff was bonding us together. There was a great feeling of abandon in the group. We had nothing to lose. It was us against the world.

Soundwise, we accidentally stumbled across something unique when Geoff Kent (who was a very good trumpet player) left us. We first thought about replacing him, and even got as far as trying a few trumpeters out, but after a while we realised that, without the trumpet, we had a completely individual brass sound. The combination of tenor and alto sax with a trombone gave it a tougher, rougher and bolder sound, which was exactly right for how we felt.

We worked hard during the day, honing the songs. It was a meritocracy. Everyone was encouraged to write. Those who spent their spare time writing and crafting songs naturally became the band's songwriters, mainly Kevin Archer and myself. Geoff Blythe or occasionally Jim arranged the brass, but the songwriters pretty much always presented the main brass melodies.

When we weren't rehearsing or writing, we'd sit in caffs and discuss what we were going to wear, or how we could hunt down some unusual garment. Everything was done on a shoestring.

The whole thing was a mission. We believed it was going to happen for us. We were unique – we had a great look and sound. We weren't what was going on in 1978, and we didn't want to be. We were the future.

These early days of Dexys were in some ways the best. When we did our first gig, in Wolverhampton, the audience mocked us, but we didn't care at all. In fact, we barely even noticed. We had asked a pub manager if we could play for free one Saturday afternoon. We played to a load of football fans. They were clearly bemused by our wild clothes, radical haircuts and horn-driven sound. Some reacted aggressively. But we weren't seeking their approval. I saw it all as just practice. By playing live in front of them, we had got just a little more used to being in front of an audience and resolved a few technical issues. Job done! Thank you very much!

And we had adventures. We worked hard but had good times too. For some of us, me included, the band was also our social lives. In fact, it was our *lives*!

Bunking the trains was a laugh, and it opened up avenues that would have otherwise been completely out of bounds.

A friend, Keith Millward, had put us in touch with a man named Alper, a promoter from France who said he wanted us to do a gig just outside Paris. He gave us a date and told us he would come over to England to pick us up and take us back to Paris. I only took it half seriously – people often said things and didn't come through. I went to bed the night before, thinking he probably wouldn't show up.

At nine o'clock the next morning, I was awakened by a loud knocking on my window (my bed was next to the front downstairs window). As I came out of a deep sleep, I saw the face of Alper urgently and determinedly peering in through the window at me.

Blimey, he was true to his word! Great.

I dressed quickly and rounded the others up. We were to go by train and boat to do the gig the following evening. But when we got to Birmingham New Street Station, it became clear that Alper had miscalculated his finances. He held out all the money he had in his palm. It was nowhere near enough to get us all to Paris.

OK ... I thought, *there should be enough money here for us to get the ferry from Dover to Calais; we can bunk the rest.*

There was a machine close to the ticket barriers that sold platform tickets for 2p each. We bought one for each member of the band, and one for Alper. We went through the ticket barriers separately, so as to not draw attention.

As Alper tried to pass through the barrier, the ticket inspector asked him a question. Alper couldn't speak a word of English and didn't understand what was being said. He was allowed to pass through, but one of the inspector's colleagues followed him down onto the platform and confronted him.

We were all standing nearby, pretending to be on separate journeys from each other (a bit like in the film *The Great Escape*). Poor Alper was standing there, in a foreign country, with a bewildered look on his face, innocently proffering his 2p platform ticket every time he was asked a question. I couldn't help but laugh almost hysterically.

Eventually I walked over, pretending to be Alper's friend, and also French, but with a small amount of English at my disposal. Luckily, the ticket inspectors didn't speak French, because I certainly couldn't.

In a French accent, I waffled that we didn't understand the system. He marched us back to the ticket office, where we bought tickets to the next local train station, to the value of about 30p. We joined the rest of the gang there and then all bunked the train to Paris.

We did an OK gig. It wasn't anything special. It was a mostly funk-jazz-rock audience and they were perhaps a little bewildered by us. Again, we knew it was all good experience. Another gig under our belts, and this one on foreign soil!

Alper had done a good job for us and, later, when Dexys started to get successful, I asked our management to involve him in our French live work. Sadly, that didn't happen.

On the way back, we again bunked the train from Paris to Calais. This time we did it in twos and threes and separated into different carriages. Big Jim, Kevin and I sat together in a big compartment near the middle of the train. We kept an eye out in both directions for the ticket inspector. Before long, we spotted him coming towards us from the front. We quickly made our way to the first available toilets. Kevin and Jim got into one cubicle, and I got into the opposite one. I waited in the toilet for what seemed like plenty of time. I came out to find that the ticket inspector had just passed. It was OK, we were safe.

I decided to play a joke. I'd learned the French word for ticket was *billet* (pronounced 'bi-yay') and I've pretty much always been able to mimic the basics of any accent after being around it for a few days. I crossed to the toilet where Jim and Kevin were hiding, knocked on the door loudly and, in my best, most forceful Maurice Chevalier accent, said: 'Billet, monsieur.'

No response. I knocked again, now harder, and said louder, 'Billet, monsieur; billet, monsieur!'

Still nothing.

I knocked much harder this time, and almost shouted: 'Billet, monsieur!'

Finally, the door opened very slowly, to reveal Kevin Archer leaning down over the sink, pretending to be sick, Big Jim's arm around him for comfort. They were both looking downward and hadn't even realised that it was me, so consumed were they in their acting roles.

I burst out laughing. They were relieved and took the prank in good spirits.

When we got back to Birmingham, we had run out of old city-centre warehouses to break into and were becoming regular fixtures at Steelhouse Lane Police Station. They had taken to arresting and holding us in an effort to deter us, and they were now getting seriously pissed off and were surely going to charge us with something or other soon if we didn't get out of their hair.

Geoff Blythe started talking about a local arts centre. I'd never heard of such a thing.

He attempted to explain the nature of it.

'What is it?' I said.

'It's an arts centre.'

'What's that? Isn't it somewhere people go to paint pictures?'

'No,' he said. 'Not necessarily. We should be able to rehearse there.'

'How much is it?'

'Nothing.'

'What?' I couldn't understand it. 'A rehearsal room, for free?'

'Yes. Free.'

'Why is it free?' I asked, suspiciously.

'I don't know. It's just free.'

'Completely free?'

'Yes!'

I couldn't get my head around it.

But we were desperate. We moved our gear into the arts centre and started playing. Even on the first day, I was expecting someone to walk in and tell us to shut up or get out. But that didn't happen.

The arts centre had recording facilities and all kinds of musical equipment, as well as other tools for creative pursuits. I couldn't believe it. It was culturally a million miles from anything most of us were used to. The women wore hippy dungarees, with hennaed hair and no make-up. The men had names like Ralph and Jeremy, and usually wore studenty-looking glasses and scruffy, loose, multi-coloured sweaters, with uncombed hair.

Many of us in the band hadn't really had any previous dealings with people like this. I kept probing Geoff. 'Who is paying for it?'

'They are!' Geoff said.

'Well who pays *them*? And why are they giving it to us?'

Exasperated, Geoff gave up trying to explain.

Then it dawned on me. *This place is run* by *middle-class fuckwits,* for *middle-class fuckwits*, went my thinking. It was bang-opposite Aston University, and was government-funded – for students, or the like.

We now understood. There was nothing like this in Smethwick or Handsworth. People in those areas didn't even know about these kinds of places, yet they would be paying for them, by way of their taxes.

We saw the situation as unjust, and responded with what we felt was the only appropriate action – rob the bastards.

Musical equipment, recording equipment, headphones, food. We made full use of the 'government facilities'. We saw it more as requisitioning than stealing. We had worked and paid taxes to pay for this stuff, we reasoned. Fuck them.

We also did a serious amount of piss-taking. There was a café there. They called it a 'refectory'. Mostly, they sold food with names that we had never heard of: 'Waldorf salad', 'lentil soup', 'chickpea casserole'. The only thing vaguely familiar to us were the flapjacks.

The staff were incredibly trusting. We'd laugh as we overheard them say, 'These flapjacks are going really well. We need to bake some more.' After we had got bored with just *stealing* the food, we'd then amuse ourselves by creeping up to the counter and changing the meal options on the menu blackboard. We crossed off all the hippy, veggie meals and replaced them with items found only in typical working-men's caffs. Puy lentil bake became 'sausage and tomato sandwich', nut roast was now 'tom dip' (a south Birmingham working-men's caff 'delicacy' – a piece of toast dipped in heated tinned tomatoes), and veggie lasagne became 'bacon, egg and tom'.

Early one morning, when a couple of us were hanging around and waiting for the others to turn up, the refectory phone rang. We looked around, but there were no staff to answer it. I grabbed the phone and in a broad Brummie accent, said:

''*Arow...*'

A posh male voice on the other end of the phone said, 'Who's this?'

'This is Tony's caff. Warra ya want?'

A pause. And then he said, disbelievingly, 'Is that the refectory?'

I continued in the same accent, 'Look, mate, this is Tony's Caff, warra ya fuckin' want? Do ya wanna tom dip, a sausage and tom, or an egg, bacon and tom? Mek yer fuckin' moind up!'

The fact that the arts centre staff couldn't see the joke made it all the more funny to us. I guess with them being so consciously egalitarian meant that they suffered us in silence for as long as they could, at least.

Finally, after identifying me as the leader, they brought me into their office for a 'conflab'. They challenged me about the disappearance of items of equipment, the theft of food, and our general disrespectful attitude. I sarcastically told them that I loved the place and would never steal from it. And how outraged I was that they accuse me, of all people!

They, of course, knew I was lying. And although I was full of bravado, deep down I knew – as I do clearly now – that I was out of order. These were very decent people who had been good to us.

Here's an example: we decided we needed a 'sky at night' backdrop for our live performances, and figured the best place to get a canvas would be a theatre.

We walked across the city to the Birmingham Repertory Theatre and went in the big storeroom in the back of the building, which happened to be open. And right there, on the floor, was a massive, 12ft-high and 20ft-wide, brand-spanking-new blank canvas! It really seemed like serendipity. There seemed to be a lot of that kind of fortune in those early days of Dexys.

The backstage area was deserted, so we rolled it up like a carpet, carried it out, and four of us (it was heavy) marched it on our shoulders across the city-centre streets of Birmingham and back to the arts centre.

Geoff Blythe told us the arts centre would give us paint, and even help us decorate it. Again, to my surprise, they did. They rolled the canvas out onto the floor of the main area, immediately produced some pots of paint, and taught us how to decorate it. It was like we were children and they were the teachers, but they weren't patronising. My view of them was really starting to change.

Then, to top it off, a few days later we were doing a show over on the other side of Birmingham at the Romulus (supported by Joy Division, incidentally – I missed their set because I was downstairs getting my hair done). Halfway through our set, I looked up from singing and playing my guitar, and saw two of the arts centre staff in the audience dancing away. We hadn't invited them. We hadn't even mentioned that we were playing there. They'd found out somehow and taken it upon themselves to come over.

They were good people. I wish I had a way to thank them now, and apologise to them, properly.

We wanted to be our own thing

The stakes in Dexys succeeding were very high. Certainly for me. It was all or nothing; there was no safety net. I was desperate to prove I wasn't useless.

Dad was less convinced of my career ambitions than ever. One summer's day, when he was up from London, he said to me: 'Face it, you're just a layabout, aren't ya? You're a hippy.'

On this occasion, it didn't hurt as much. I don't know why, maybe because I knew that what we were doing was really good.

I never told anyone in the band about my relationship with my dad, even though they were by now my quite close friends. I never told a soul about what happened with my ex, Jackie, either. I felt that if I mentioned any of this stuff, they would see it as my fault, because I suppose I *did* think everything was my fault. I did my best to present a picture of perfection, around my past, to everyone. I believed that if I told anyone some of the things that had happened to me, they would lose all respect for me. But one night, just outside Leeds, I came close to opening up.

It was snowing, and most of the others had gone back to Birmingham in a car after a gig at a university. Myself, Pete Williams, Jim Paterson and a temporary drummer went back in a Ford Escort van. We broke down in the snow, and we had to wait until morning before any mechanical services were open. We spent the night huddled together to keep warm in the back of the small van.

It was too cold to sleep, so we chatted about all kinds of things – the music business; our hopes; funny stories from childhood. After a couple of hours, the conversation started to turn serious. It was as if a confessional atmosphere descended upon us. First Pete Williams shared some intimate and heartfelt stuff, then Jim shared some personal stories about his life. Then it *really* felt like my turn.

I've no doubt that in that moment, there existed such an understanding atmosphere, that if I had shared something, it would have been received with sensitivity and understanding. My intuition strongly told me to speak and open up.

It was on the tip of my tongue … But somehow, I just couldn't do it. A terror overcame me and I blocked it.

A few seconds later, someone changed the subject, and the opportunity had passed.

. . .

During this time, Billy's and later the Blitz club were happening in London. A similar but smaller dressing-up scene was taking place at the Romulus in Birmingham. A few of the Romulus crowd came to a couple of our gigs and it got back to us that they liked us. I was delighted.

Although I would occasionally go to the Romulus, I didn't go to places like the Blitz. Not because I didn't want to. I *did* want to, but I stayed away because of my social anxiety. I had plenty of outward bravado but it was all bluff and bluster.

We were playing a weekly residency at a place called Mr Sam's in Birmingham city centre and building up a following. Dave Cork, the Clash promoter, came to see us. We were, of course, dressed up to the nines. Afterwards, he described the gig as 'phenomenal'. He subsequently invited Bernard Rhodes, who was having a break from managing the Clash. We were in awe of Bernard and his achievements. Here was a big chance for us, surely.

One of the first comments Bernard made after watching the show was that I looked better in the clothes I wore offstage than those I had worn on it. That should have been a warning. Offstage, I wore forties and fifties suits and shirts. Occasionally, I might wear a bolero jacket and some big trousers with a cummerbund, but I saved my best looks for the stage. On this occasion I was wearing a rose-pink, satin suit with a mandarin collar. Over it, I had a black crocheted jacket that had a train, like a bride. I was also making friends with my tight curly hair.

Previously I'd seen it as the enemy. It was done in braids at the top, in the style of Stevie Wonder in his *Talking Book* days. At the back, it stuck out in coiffured curls, while at the front, it was straightened and criss-crossed in quarter-inch strips, giving the impression of a 1940s women's veil hat coming down over my forehead to my eyebrows. All done by friend and sometimes girlfriend, Claire.

I told Bernard that I knew the dressing-up thing was soon going to be important to people and popular. He disagreed and said he thought that scene was over-hyped. I just thought, *OK. He's wrong about that. But no big deal.*

The Specials, who were from Coventry, also turned up to see us at Mr Sam's around the same time. They hadn't released a record at that point and were mostly unknown, but certainly they were further along than we were – they'd had plenty of good reviews and had supported the Clash on a tour.

They were playing at Aston University and invited us along. They were great; their stage show was strong, fresh and interesting. Jerry Dammers, their leader, was keen for us to be allies, as we were both drawing from the past to make something new. I felt they were more literal, hence more retro than us, particularly in their dress sense. We were a paradoxical mix of retro and futuristic and I wasn't sure about forging an alliance. But we liked the band – they were nice guys, and we were grateful for the interest.

A few weeks later, they asked us to support them at a club in Manchester called The Factory. 'Gangsters', their first single, was about to come out and they were starting to build an audience. We jumped at the chance.

The venue was reasonably packed as we trooped onstage, all dressed up in our bright colours. I was wearing the purple jacket I'd had made by Vicky at the college of fashion. Kevin Archer was in his bolero jacket and blue satin harem pants and boxing boots. His hair was cropped on top but with thin strands at the front. Geoff Blythe with his jodhpurs and asymmetric wedge haircut, later made famous by Phil Oakey in the

Human League. Pete Saunders wore a big 17th-century-style lace shirt, and also sported jodhpurs. Jim was dressed as a Mod and Pete Williams was dressed as a 1930s baseball player.

We used to have taped announcements instead of speaking between songs. For example, 'Burn It Down' was preceded by the sound of a comedian telling an Irish joke. Then I would say, 'For God's sake, burn it down!'

The Factory was a bit rough but no harder than clubs in Birmingham, Wolverhampton or London. It was situated on a council housing estate and there was a vociferous gang of about 12 local kids who were there just for a laugh and probably wouldn't have bothered to attend had it not been on their doorstep. From the off, the kids at the front of the stage were wolf-whistling and shouting derisory, homophobic comments. It continued throughout the first few songs. They were the dominant force in the audience and, as far as they were concerned, we were just there to be the butt of their jokes. The music was of no interest to them.

The stage was low and close to the audience, and soon the kids tried to take things further by attempting to grab my microphone lead.

I didn't want our first gig in Manchester to go like this. What bothered me most was the presumption that we would just suffer their abuse, no matter how much they gave us. *Fuck that*, I thought finally. I spotted the main heckler looking up at me, leering gleefully, surrounded by his mates. When he saw I was now making eye contact with him, he became even more animated.

'Oh, darling. Hello, sweetie.' All the time blowing me kisses.

I leaned down, with the microphone still in my right hand, and thumped the fucker in the face as hard as I could.

Thwack! went the sound of his nose breaking.

He held his face. Blood was streaming down onto his shirt. A space opened up around him at the front of the audience. An eerie silence descended. I stood my ground.

'Come on, you fuckin' cunts!' I shouted.

The band had stopped playing. His mates were going crazy, baying for blood and making like they were going to get on the stage. 'You are a fucking bastard. We're gonna kill ya!'

I just stood there and motioned: *Come on!*

Before anything could escalate further, the bouncers ran to the front of the stage and hemmed us in. We played another song, now feeling vindicated, while the bouncers held back the mob at the front.

After the gig, we were locked in the dressing room 'for our own safety' by the bouncers. They told us there was now a gang of about 30 kids in the club. A couple of them had left the venue to recruit all their hard mates, who were now patrolling the premises, looking for us.

We remained in that dressing room till about 3am, long after the Specials and everyone else had left. Finally, as the last workers were leaving the club, the chief bouncer came and told us that it was safe for us to go out to our van. The gang had got bored and gone home. I'm grateful to those bouncers. They saved us.

. . .

I decided to give up smoking. I'd tried before but I'd never lasted long. Now it was different. This was early summer 1979. The hot weather gave me optimism, and with Dexys I had a reason to be strong – a plan, a future.

I was never confident about my singing and I reasoned that fags was probably why my voice wasn't sounding as good as I thought it could. I started going to the gym and doing weight training too. I had always been skinny and acutely conscious of it. Any turmoil I felt from cutting out cigarettes was exhausted out of me by my rigorous weight-training schedule. The exercise gave me a feeling of warm contentment and peace – a release of endorphins, as I now understand it.

I felt bigger and more powerful. The way I moved as I went about my life became slower and calmer. A lot of my fear just left me. I would sometimes feel invincible – like a lion – and, for the first time, worthy of leading Dexys. The band responded to the new me, too. I took charge with authority and confidence.

Meanwhile, the Specials were signing to Chrysalis and were in the process of setting up their own label, Two Tone. Jerry phoned me at my mum's place and told me that when the deal was finalised, he wanted us to sign to Two Tone. I was flattered and happy to be able to tell my mum that we'd been offered a record deal, but I told Jerry that I didn't think it was right for us.

Certainly, myself and the main hardcore members of Dexys didn't want us to be part of anyone else's movement. We wanted to be our own thing.

Bernard Rhodes seemed to be taking more interest and we went down to his small studio in London to make some demos. The music sounded good, and everyone was pleased with it. But there were subtle innuendos from Bernard and his cohorts Mickey Foote and Dave Cork that our clothes were wrong. I ignored the comments again, just thinking they were good guys but not as in touch as I was.

Kevin Archer voiced his concern to me that Bernard might not be the right guy. I didn't even consider what Kevin was saying, so mesmerised was I by Bernard's power and success. *If not Bernard, then who?* I thought. *No one that I know!* I didn't have the faith to wait.

Dave Cork told us that Bernard wanted us for a new label he was launching and he, Dave, would manage us. He said that Bernard had a heart of gold and would look after us.

I met with Bernard for a chat about the situation at Marine Ices in Camden Town. It was midsummer 1979 and I was wearing a white 1930s shirt and big, baggy, light-grey trousers tucked into white football socks, just below the knee, to give the effect of 'plus fours'. I wore pink Mary Jane ballet shoes and my hair was swept back, Valentino-style.

After a few pleasantries, Bernard started talking about *now* being the right time for Dexys to make our move in music. He said that although conditions may not be 100 per cent perfect, they were certainly close, and if we were to defer making our move until everything was exactly right, it might be another five years, by which time we would be too old. I was pleased to hear him say that; I knew it to be the truth.

He made a small quip as he looked down at my Mary Janes. 'I'm sure you want to be known as more than someone who wears flashy shoes.'

I just thought: *He's getting on a bit.* I had no intention of changing the way I looked to suit him.

He then started talking about how we should record a single in a funky little studio nearby in Camden. He told me the studio had a good vibe, and we would be able to capture the essence of the group there. That sounded great!

He and Mickey Foote would produce it, he said. I wasn't sure about Bernard's prowess as a producer – I was aware that he didn't have any experience, and wondered how much of this was ego. I knew Mickey Foote was a good musical guy, though, and I was confident in the band's playing and in our arrangement of 'Burn It Down', the song we planned to record.

With regards to how we would operate in the music business, Bernard talked about him being a buffer between us and the record label. He talked at length about how the machinations of the music business could easily destroy a band and kill their spark of creativity. Even at that early stage, I knew that what he was saying was true.

'I will deal with all that shit, so you don't have to,' he said. 'I can protect you and you can get on with what you want to do. You can exist in your own little world. I can advise you if a jacket looks good on you or whatever.'

I said, 'That sounds fucking great!'

I was glad we were about to move forward. This was our time. I could almost smell it.

Meanwhile, 'Gangsters' had stormed up the charts and become a top-ten hit. The music press loved the Specials; they were the hottest band in the country. A big Two Tone tour was being planned for that autumn of 1979 and the band were in the studio, recording their first album. They sent a message through Dave Cork, saying they wanted to use our brass section on the record.

'Forget it. No way,' I said. I knew our brass section was a massive part of our distinctive sound. It would be stupid to give it away before we had a record out ourselves. If the Specials had hits with our brass sound before we did, our impact would be lessened.

The word came back to us that if we weren't going to let them use our brass section, then the Specials wouldn't let us put out a single on Two Tone.

I laughed and said, 'What? We don't want to put out a single on Two Tone!'

And we didn't! Signing to their label was of course by far the best offer we'd ever had, and it was tempting. Two Tone was now *the* happening label, and other local bands were queuing up to sign up. The Beat – an unknown Birmingham group at that point – jumped at it, but I knew that scene was wrong for us. We had our own vision.

The Specials were all about ska, late 1960s music, and – as good as they were and no matter how much of themselves they brought to that genre, which was plenty – the fact that they were dressing in late 1960s clothes made it, for me, too literal. Sixties clothes *and* sixties music – too much.

Yes, we were soul, but there was lots of other stuff mixed in. And in any case, we had the whole futuristic clothes vibe going on.

Some people around the band, and at least one *in* the band, thought I was mad for turning down Two Tone. But I was confident that if we stuck to our guns, in time we'd come through in our own way, much better, bigger and stronger.

I must admit, I was thinking: *Shit! What fucking bad luck that the Specials are from Coventry.* It was so close to Birmingham and we were being all lumped in together because of this regional thing. There had been mentions of us in the press, giving the impression that there was some kind of local West Midlands revival movement.

Fuck that! We weren't about revival, and fuck that Birmingham schtick! We were never about a place. We were grateful to Birmingham, and we liked it, but we didn't want to be about a city. Any city. We were dreamers. Roxy Music wasn't about a place either, and that's how we saw ourselves. There was only one guy in the band who was actually from Birmingham – Steve Spooner on sax. Kevin Archer and Pete Williams were both Black Country boys. And that's a different proposition entirely.

Billy Adams, who was a fan of early Dexys and would later become our guitarist and more, put it well: 'I don't know why you focused so much on soul in your early interviews. Yes, soul was part of it, but it was *everything*. A collage.' He was right.

. . .

Meanwhile, the Specials had their second big hit single with 'A Message to You, Rudy'. It sounded great, and their presence was everywhere. Word came back to us: 'Unless you let us use your brass, you can't come on the Two Tone tour.' I sent the message back: 'What? Tell them we don't want to go on the Two Tone tour!'

I knew it wouldn't work for us. Their audience was not only very singular, but massive, and would probably want to lynch us when they saw what we were wearing, as our gig supporting them at The Factory in Manchester had proved.

Then we got another message back from the Specials: 'It's OK. We don't have to use your brass section. We want you on the tour, regardless.'

I asked Dave Cork to send the message back: 'No thanks. We don't want to do the tour, but thanks for asking.'

A few days later, Dave Cork came into our café and 'hangout', the Saints and Sinners. He was looking serious and told us: 'Bernard says that this is the biggest tour of the year. You *have* to be on it! This is your big chance. Don't blow it!'

This was serious pressure from our record company and manager. They were absolutely convinced we needed to do the tour. It was put to me that if we didn't do it, our chance would pass us by. Was I being belligerent and stupid by refusing to go on the tour? The Specials were the biggest band in the country. Their music and scene was everywhere.

I was weakening. I don't know for sure why my resolve started to go at that moment. I think it was fear of our time passing us by and missing the opportunity. That's how it was being presented to us. *Maybe I'm wrong about my vision? If we don't do the Two Tone tour, maybe we'll lose Bernard and the opportunity to make the single?* He had already started working with lots of different bands.

I knew in my heart that going on that tour was the wrong move, but that wasn't the part I listened to.

I called a group meeting. We sat in the Saints and Sinners and talked for hours about what we should do. I laid it out for them. There were two options – completely change our look and go on the Two Tone tour, or stick to our guns and take our chances.

I was being a coward. I didn't want to take responsibility for the decision that I had pretty much already made. I wanted going on the tour to be a 'collective decision'. And unless there was staunch opposition from the band, that's the way I wanted it to go. I was even starting to get a little excited by the idea of it. I'd never been on a tour before.

As I was the leader and the guy who had been so insistent on the fashion concepts up to now, I was reasonably sure that most of the guys would support me in what I was now thinking. But Geoff Blythe said: 'I think it would be a real shame to change the look of the band. The whole thing was a vision from start to finish. We should stick to it.'

I knew he was right. But by now, I was in the grip of fear. I had become increasingly nervous about trying to hold the group together – there were murmurings of discontent and Kevin Archer confided in me that at least one member was getting restless and tired of living on promises. Dexys had been working hard for over a year. *How could I be sure we would come through later on our own terms?*

We wrapped up the band meeting with the decision that we would change the look and go on the Two Tone tour. On some level, I knew I was making a decision that I would regret in the long term.

But I went ahead anyway. The old feeling of compromising was almost comfortably familiar and a relief. I can see now that if I had been going to the Blitz or hanging around with the prototype New Romantics in Birmingham, I might have had some support and hence more strength and resolve.

Dexys' situation was weird. We were dressing up, and the handful of style heads in Birmingham came to our gigs, but we were still separate. None of us socialised with them. I was too nervous to approach them.

As the result of that decision to change our look, I feel we missed an opportunity to become the most culturally significant and coolest group of the 1980s. I have found it very hard to forgive myself for that decision. In fact, I've tortured myself about it over the years.

Looking back, I see that neither Corky nor Bernard really got us. It's obvious that they saw us as a 1960s soul revival band. I remember, about three months earlier, Corky was shocked when I told him that most of the songs in our live set had been written by us and weren't covers. He immediately went and phoned Bernard with the news. It's amazing that, although both had seen us live, they didn't know that.

• • •

We talked about what we should wear on the tour. We wanted to find something that would express at least some individuality, but not be too alien to the Mods and skinheads in the Specials' audience.

To be frank, I didn't like the blurred skinhead and Mod revival that was happening at the time. I don't doubt that the first guys to resurrect these looks in 1976 or 1977 were doing something that was cool and different, but no way did we want to be part of a revival scene. Many of these audience members had taken the lowest common denominator of Mod and exaggerated it. I'd watched the original Mods in Harrow when I was 11 or 12 and they looked seriously cool. Same with the skinhead revival. I'd been one, ten years earlier. How could I be a skinhead now? It was all wrong.

We put together a look that we hoped would appeal to the Specials' audience. I wore a leather trilby and a long leather coat. And, though it pains me to admit it, it was not un-Mod.

I had my hair cut short and I bought a V-neck jumper, some parallel trousers and big shoes, which was not too dissimilar to what I had worn in 1969. At the time, I thought I was just making a compromise, but what I was actually doing was killing the band, certainly as far as I was concerned. We became literal, instead of visionary. In that move, I side-lined Dexys. I had wanted us to be *influenced* by the past, but not *be* the past. I wanted us to be Roxy Music (referencing the past, but *not* the past), not Showaddywaddy (*the past*). Not that we *were* Showaddywaddy, but hopefully what I'm saying is clear.

That decision spiralled me into a negativity that would last decades and still affects me today.

In the end, Dexys' image in the media became one of us being outsiders. But it was never planned that way.

At someone else's party

Everyone was getting excited about the tour.

Dave Cork took me aside and told me it was important that we form a nucleus of maybe two to three members, four at most. He told me the idea had come from Bernard. Dave explained to me that as we were such a big group (eight), there wouldn't be enough money to go around, so some of the band would have to be on wages rather than a percentage of the profits.

Deep down I knew the idea was wrong, and I didn't like it at all, but it's funny that as soon as you make one compromise, it's very easy to make another. My principles were falling like a pack of cards.

I had already put all our eggs in Corky and Bernard's basket, and I was afraid that if I upset them they wouldn't help us be a success. I see now, I was on the wrong road and going further and further down it.

Corky asked me who I thought should be in the nucleus. I wasn't sure, so I invited Kevin Archer round to my place to speak about it. I was surprised when he said it should just be only himself and me, as we were the main two members. A part of me could understand his point of view; we had formed the group and wrote the songs, and certainly spent more time working on Dexys than any of the others. But I was shocked at how clear and forceful he was about it, and that scared me a little bit. I thought, *If he's like that with them, maybe he'd be like that with me.* I pretended to agree with him and told him that I would announce it to the group the next day.

Instead, when I called the band together, I threw it open to them. I told them we had been advised by Corky and Bernard that as it was such a big band, we would need to form a nucleus. Also that Kevin Archer and I, as main songwriters and having formed the group, were definitely going to be part of it. Then I said, 'Who else would like to be in it? It will mean extra work and responsibility. Working as hard as Kevin and myself do. You're all welcome to put yourself forward. Who fancies it?'

Kevin looked at me with a mixture of anger and disappointment. I had gone about it the wrong way. I should have been honest with him, told him that not inviting the others to be involved felt wrong. He didn't say anything. But his look said everything.

Only Geoff Blythe put himself forward as being prepared to do more. Geoff was well educated compared to us, and we decided his role would be to keep an eye on the books – the money.

I was disappointed when Jim Paterson didn't put his hand up. I knew what a talent he was and how committed he was to Dexys.

'Jim, are you up for it?' I said.

'I don't want any more responsibility,' he replied.

No one else raised a hand. They pretty much all said they didn't want any more responsibility. So the nucleus would be made up of myself, Kevin Archer and Geoff Blythe.

The idea was a betrayal of what we had built up together. It didn't truthfully reflect the camaraderie, the spirit that existed among us. Maybe it made sense to Bernard, on paper, sitting in London, and even Corky. But it didn't reflect our experience. I shouldn't have listened to them.

I hated telling the others about the idea and I don't doubt that I did it clumsily. But because I was the one who ended up doing the dirty work, I was later credited with devising the idea. I didn't. That was Bernard and Corky.

To this day, at least one member of the first Dexys still blames me for coming up with the nucleus concept. No matter how many times I have patiently explained to them that it was Corky and Bernard's idea, this guy continues to blame me. *C'est la vie.*

Some years ago, I allocated my third of the record royalties to the five band members who weren't signed to the label for the first album and surrounding tracks (i.e. those members who weren't in the nucleus). The record royalties never were and still aren't a fortune – it was a hideously bad deal.

Another suggestion from Corky was that Kevin Archer call himself 'Al' to avoid confusion with me. Kevin agreed.

From the time of making the decision to go on the Two Tone tour, I had started smoking again. From that point on, right through eighties Dexys and beyond, there was a draining tug of war with nicotine going on within me. It was a battle of self-esteem, where smoking was the measure. My thinking went: *If I'm not smoking, my singing is OK. If I smoke, it's shit! If I don't smoke, I'm clear-headed, creative, and I can trust my decision-making. If I smoke, I'm useless and I can't trust anything I think.*

I would try and get a couple of days off the fags before a recording session or an important gig so that my thinking and singing would be 'clear'. Sometimes I was successful and sometimes I wasn't.

Every morning, I'd be determined not to have a cigarette that day. Usually, I would weaken. As soon as I'd had that one, or even one drag, a feeling of negativity would engulf me. As far as I was concerned, everything was now fucked. There would be no point trying to sing or write or even talk to a woman.

As I look at it now, I'm not sure that one drag on a cigarette could have such a physical effect on me. Other people smoked and were clear-headed and creative. There must have been something psychological in it. But it seemed an absolute truth at the time.

I didn't tell *anyone* about this internal battle, though I'm quite sure that all who came in contact with me suffered the effects of my almost constant nicotine withdrawals in the form of my mood swings.

When I *wasn't* smoking, I would make a big deal about my fitness. But often, after a few days, I would sit in my room, curtains closed, watching bad TV, drinking tea and smoking – 25 or 30 a day – for a couple of days at a time. It was a sort of low-grade binge of depression. I tried not to let anyone see me during these periods. I would dread the phone ringing or doorbell going and often wouldn't answer.

· · ·

We talked about how we were going to blow the Specials off the stage. But we were wrong. We soon discovered we were at someone else's party and wearing the wrong clothes.

The Two Tone movement was now massive, the Specials and Selecter were selling out big gigs and the audiences were going crazy. In truth, we just weren't needed on that tour, and we didn't fit in. We were largely unknown, we didn't even have a single out and, because our music wasn't ska, it was greeted mostly with bemusement.

Going on the tour was a big mistake for Dexys. And the decision to not sign to their label, but to still go on the tour, ensured that we had the worst of both worlds. We had one foot in Two Tone, and one foot out.

It was like we had to start all over again. Certainly, I did. Up to that point, I had done most of the lead vocals but Kevin Archer also sang on most of the songs and did a couple of lead vocals himself. We both kept our guitars on all through the show and made up a front line of two guitarists/singers in the middle of the stage, with brass on either side of us.

Now it was different. Bernard said to me: 'Take off your guitar and lead that group, or I'll pull someone else forward.'

I didn't want someone else to lead the group. So I took off my guitar and became the out-and-out frontman on that Two Tone tour. I felt exposed and awkward. It was like a different band. I felt fucking miserable in the new look, but was in denial.

Bernard had given us an early warning sign that things would go wrong. I opened a music paper one day, shortly before the Two Tone tour, to see an announcement from him about his new record label, Oddball. Six acts were named, including 'a Northern Soul band from Birmingham called Dexys Midnight Runners'. We hadn't even discussed how we should be described, and we were *not* a fucking Northern Soul band. I have nothing against Northern Soul, but we studiously avoided that label. When I bought 'Seven Days Too Long' and 'Breaking Down the Walls of Heartache', on release in 1968, they were just soul records. Northern Soul didn't even exist.

I think because Bernard had been so heavily involved in punk, the last big thing, he had no serious interest in usurping that. He wasn't emotionally invested in us.

. . .

It had come back to me through Corky that Bernard had said, 'Dexys aren't the next thing, they are an in-between thing.' I definitely saw us as the *next* thing.

Our original plan was for Dexys to make as much impact as Roxy Music had with their first appearance on *Top of the Pops* in 1972. Had we stuck to the script, we would almost certainly have had a record out way before Spandau Ballet, who didn't release their first single until late 1980. Duran Duran were later still, so we could well have established ourselves as the first and possibly number-one band of the New Romantic scene.

Instead we consigned ourselves to be an afterthought of punk, later known as post-punk.

Our music wouldn't have sounded very different to how it ended up on our first album even if we had kept our original look – although we would have been open to a more avant-garde approach in terms of production. The sixties soul thing was always just a starting point for us.

The bizarre thing is that when the likes of Spandau did release records and the New Romantic scene exploded, I didn't even acknowledge to myself that I'd made a big mistake. It was all buried so deeply within me, and I was so committed to the stance I'd made for Dexys. I guess it was more than I could bear. I didn't become aware of how I really felt until 20 years later, when I woke up from denial. What I did do, instead, was get more and more bitter. I *hated* all the people who were doing what I had originally set out to do. That whole movement. 'Fuck 'em. They're shallow. Wankers,' I'd say.

I slagged off the likes of Blue Rondo à la Turk (who were actually very good) without acknowledging to myself why they sat so uncomfortably with me. I made it about them, but really it was about me. And I didn't even know it!

Some years later, I met Bernard in a social situation and we chatted. Referring to this time, he said: 'I had to slow you down. You were too far ahead.' He was making out that he'd done me some kind of favour. I see constant reminders of that decision all around. I see TV programmes about the eighties and realise culturally that we weren't part of it. We were on the outside. It irks.

In 1982, we wore dungarees, which was a cool statement at the time, but still a reaction against what I should have been. My old girlfriend from my teens, Jean, who had by now moved to Australia, wouldn't believe it was me when she saw the video for 'Come on Eileen'. 'That can't be him. He was always so smart,' she said.

Unfortunately, the *only* picture I have of the clothes we wore in 1978–79 is the one on page 191, which is a very early shot from January 1979. We developed the look a lot more after that was taken, and there were some later shots from that summer, but they are lost. The drawing below shows the hairstyle I wore.

Over the next few months, we would try different clothes, finally settling on the New York docker thing (woolly hats and leather or US Navy pea coats or donkey-type jackets), which we wore for 'Geno' and *Searching for the Young Soul Rebels*. It became known as the first and now classic Dexys look. It wasn't a *bad* look, by any means, but it wasn't a patch on what we sacrificed to go on that Two Tone tour.

And once we had appeared with the first well-known Dexys image, I couldn't go back. My ego wouldn't let me – I couldn't be part of something where I wasn't seen to be the first with the idea.

That attitude made things very difficult for me: Roxy, Bowie and soul music laid the groundwork for what would become known as early eighties culture – the New Romantics – and all of it was totally me, probably more than it was for the leading New Romantic bands.

. . .

'All good singers have distinctive vocal styles,' Bernard had said to me. At first I took it personally; I thought he was criticising me. Then I went away and thought about it. I realised he might have a point. It was certainly true in the case of Bryan Ferry.

I started thinking about how I could make my voice sound more distinctive. At first, I drew a blank; then after a couple of weeks, I came up with the idea of putting a cry into my voice. It ended up sounding a little like General Johnson, and Jackie Wilson before him, but that was never my intention. It was pure coincidence.

I went round to Big Jim's place, and we started running through the songs in higher keys to suit the new vocal style. If you had asked me about that style even a few years ago, I would have said that adopting it was a good thing. But now, I don't think it was. My voice had a quite unusual tone anyway, and I believe the heavily pronounced vocal style that I adopted for the first album probably stopped our music connecting with as many people as it could have. Plus, since I've started taking my singing more seriously in recent years, I've learned that I'm actually a baritone. Changing all the keys to a tenor pitch made doing gigs considerably harder on my voice. To this day, I wonder how I managed to perform in such high keys.

Bernard had also come up with the idea of Dexys talking about ourselves as a gang in interviews, and it made sense, given what we were now wearing and our 'Dexys against the world' attitude (which the mostly studenty Moseley musicians across the other side of Birmingham used to complain about).

The record deal Bernard presented us with was basically a short letter, not a contract. Kevin Archer and I found a music business lawyer who got Corky and Bernard to a meeting to discuss it. Bernard seemed to see the fact that we enlisted a lawyer as some kind of betrayal. I don't recall the exact details of what was in his contract, but there was plenty in it that I wasn't happy about. The meeting ended in an impasse. A few days later I told Corky that I wasn't going to sign Bernard's contract, but in the end we compromised and the deal was signed – not by me but forged with my consent.

The reality of working with Bernard had turned out to be very different to what he described to me that day in Marine Ices. In truth, it was a catalogue of disasters. An example of this was the first single, 'Burn It Down'. We recorded it, as planned, in that 'funky little studio in Camden', with Bernard and Mickey Foote producing. There was a great atmosphere as we recorded. Bernard and Mickey put us at our ease.

After the session had finished, I kept phoning Bernard and asking when the mixing would take place. I wanted to be there, with hopefully one or two other band members. But Bernard wasn't telling us anything and neither was Corky. Whenever I asked when the single was coming out, I would get cryptic answers like: 'At exactly the right time for your career.'

Finally, one morning Corky turned up at my place with a white label of 'Burn It Down' in his hand, saying: 'Bernard and Mickey got some time to go into the studio a couple of nights ago and there was no time to contact you.'

This was obviously a lie. As green as I was, I knew that getting the sound from a master tape to the test-pressing stage took at least a couple of weeks.

When I put the test pressing on my record player, it was a travesty. It didn't sound like us: my voice was swamped in a dodgy echo, as was the brass. Dexys had a tough sound, and this was nothing like it! An excellent recording had been ruined in the mix.

Steve Millward, my friend who was living in the next room, came in when he heard it. He didn't say a lot but, just as he was leaving, said, 'It's not as good as the live version.' And he was right.

Corky and Bernard also told me that the parent company, EMI Records (who were putting it out under Bernard's Oddball label), loved it and were confident about it doing well. We found out later that this was another lie.

A few weeks on, when I met EMI, they told me that they felt the same as we did. In fact, they had disliked the mix so much that they had got Dennis Bovell, the reggae record producer, to do another version, with Bernard's blessing. But EMI didn't like that mix either. All of this was taking place while I was asking Bernard when we were going to mix the song, and being told 'soon'! It was so frustrating. We could have made sure it sounded right if we'd been there. We were being treated like a know-nothing boy band.

The label wanted to get it out before the Two Tone tour ended. I tried to convince myself that it sounded OK. Eventually, I had to face up to the fact that, although it was a good song and a good performance, most of the power and uniqueness of the track was buried in this awful, amateurish mix.

The sleeve was another bone of contention. We were shown the finished article. We were given no involvement at all. Kevin Archer was highlighted in the picture, which I wasn't happy about. But the biggest thing was that we had been told we were going to be collaborating, yet after only a few months we were having less and less control over our own work. We had been bursting with ideas on how to make things great. And not only were our ideas not being heeded, they were being replaced with far inferior concepts. It was a painful situation.

I realised that we had to take stock and admit that these people were going to screw up any chance we had of success. No question. We had been sleepwalking too long. Certainly I had.

We didn't have an album deal, only an agreement for two singles, with an option from EMI if they wanted more. If the next single failed, we were out. Clearly, if we allowed Bernard and co to ruin another song, that would be the end of us. *Sorry, lads, you weren't good enough.*

But I knew we *were* good enough.

It was obvious that we were going to have to take control. And if we failed, it was better we go down by our own hand than someone else's. Bernard had to go. His record deal was through EMI, so our contract would automatically revert to them.

We had a band meeting and, on a day when I was off cigarettes and felt clear in my judgement, I said to the others, strongly, that if we stick with Bernard then we can say goodbye to any chance of doing well. Everyone agreed.

'Also, Corky is working for Bernard, not us,' I added. 'He hasn't been straight with us, and he's supposed to be our manager. I think he has to go, too.'

Everyone agreed, again.

We had a meeting with Corky and let him go. A couple of days later, I started smoking again and thought: *Shit. We don't even know another manager. We will be on our own without him.* I panicked. I also felt incredibly sorry for him for some reason. This was the wavering between clarity and guilt that was so characteristic of me. I spoke to the others and convinced them that we had made an error and should reinstate Dave. It was a panic move and another mistake.

I remember listening to 'Dance Stance' being reviewed on Radio 1's *Round Table*. (Bernard said we needed to change the name from 'Burn It Down' as people wouldn't want a title like that at Christmas.) It got a lukewarm response.

David 'Kid' Jensen, the host, said: 'Dexys Midnight Runners? Great name.'

That was heartening. As the panel talked about the record, Andy Peebles said, 'It's not as good as the Two Tone stuff.'

I was so disappointed. It felt like life was draining out of me. I was jaded, and we were only just releasing our first single!

We had cut off our wings and at least halved our potential by changing our look. The only thing we had left was the music, and now they'd messed *that* up. We'd been well and truly shafted. Of course, neither Corky nor Bernard were in any way apologetic. Corky said, 'Just write some more songs.'

I saw Mickey Foote, Bernard's co-producer, in a café. We stopped and talked. I told him that I felt the song was ruined. He said, 'That's the best you could do at the time. Maybe you could do better now. But that was the best we could do with you as you were then.' I knew that was bullshit. It felt like he was taunting me.

The blood rose to my head, and I thumped him in the face, hard. I shouldn't have done that. Mickey didn't fight back.

. . .

We signed officially to EMI Records at their Manchester Square offices. The legal affairs guy handed us a 60-page contract. I read the first page. It was full of cumbersome terms like 'wherefore', 'shall hitherto', etc. I knew I wouldn't be able to understand it and we didn't have any money for a lawyer.

'Have you got a pen?' I said.

The EMI lawyer said, 'Aren't you going to read it?'

'No.'

I signed it there and then, as did Kevin and Geoff.

It wasn't just about the cumbersome language or the fact that we were broke and couldn't afford a lawyer. The truth is, I was just weary. I didn't care any more. I was pretending to, but really I didn't. It didn't feel like a happy day. All of the enthusiasm of a few months ago had gone. After only a couple of months in the music business, I was beaten.

That said, two months later, January 1980 – our first *Top of the Pops* appearance with 'Dance Stance'. I couldn't believe it – I was going to be on the programme I'd watched all my life.

I barely slept the night before. We'd drilled the band that evening. I'd given some of them suggestions for stage moves. But what about *my* act? I see now that a lot of my obsessive focus on the band's preparation throughout Dexys was often about my own fear of not performing well.

When we walked into the studio the next morning and saw all the lights and the cameramen doing their run-throughs, it was daunting but exciting.

This is it. The boy who was going nowhere, on *Top of the Pops* (I feel tearful even as I write this). This was where it all happened, where all my heroes had performed. *Now I'm here.*

Then, a sobering thought. I didn't want to think of the impact Roxy Music made when they did their first *Top of the Pops*, or Rod Stewart when he sang 'Maggie May', or Slade when they tore the place up with 'Cum on Feel the Noize'. In my heart of hearts I knew we weren't going to make that kind of impact. I was wearing a fucking donkey jacket, and I believed it was too late to change now that we'd publicly nailed our colours to the mast with our New York dockers look. Perhaps I was too singular about that.

Bernard Rhodes was there too (even though the song would be the first and last on his label). At the rehearsal he suggested, via Corky, that we have a young kid, Bernard's son, on the stage with a measuring ruler pointing to a blackboard signalling the lyrics: 'Oscar Wilde and Brendan Behan, Sean O'Casey, George Bernard Shaw …'

I refused. It wasn't a bad idea at all, and if we had been a boring band with no visual ideas of our own, which is kind of what we'd become, it would have been useful. But although deep down I knew that we weren't going to look strong enough to make a big impact on our own, I was through listening to ideas from Bernard.

We did the rehearsals and it felt good. I looked at the monitor and I could see that I was looking all right. I felt strangely relaxed. But when it came to the actual recording of the show, it was a different story. The nerves had been creeping up as the day wore on.

Simon Bates introduced us: 'Come over here and I'll introduce you to some people from Birmingham.' Obviously, I wasn't crazy about that Birmingham thing. But the song started and we began our performance. I was doing my swim dance (front crawl in the air) on the intro. So far so good. I wasn't feeling as comfortable and fluid as in the rehearsal, but I was keeping it together. Then the opening verse started, and I sang, 'I'll only ask you once more.'

That was OK. Then it hit me. *Fuck! The red-light camera is on me, which means I'm on screen. There's ten million people watching me! Ten fucking million!*

I started to feel tense, self-conscious. So many thoughts running through my head. My jaw became tight.

Then, in a flash, it was over.

In those days, *Top of the Pops* was recorded on a Wednesday and broadcast the following evening. Geoff Blythe and I stayed over in London and went out to my parents' place in Harrow to watch it. I was nervous seeing myself on TV, especially in front of the family.

I didn't like my performance. I looked ugly. 'I'll do better next time,' I told them.

As the programme ended, I could tell that my mum was happy and proud of me. I followed her out to the kitchen. She grabbed the kettle to make some tea. As she did, I decided to speak up: 'Mum, whenever I go to hug you, you always pull away.'

That had been happening since I was about 15.

'Do I?' she said. 'Come here, love.' And gave me a warm hug.

The stars were aligned

As a band, we somehow got past the nucleus issue. We weren't making any money anyway so were all on the same wage. I even started to become a little more comfortable with the clothes, as we moved closer to the New York stevedore look.

That Straight to the Heart tour of 30 dates, early in 1980, was good! These were our first headlining shows. I'd started to grow into the solo frontman thing and we were now a strong live band.

A great suggestion of Kevin Archer's was that just before every gig, as we arrived at the venue, instead of going straight to the dressing room via a backstage door, we would purposely come in through the main entrance and walk through the crowd like a gang, carrying our 'holdalls', often over our shoulders. It set us apart and built excitement.

I had a negative attitude towards the audiences, which I wasn't even conscious of at the time. A big part of me didn't want to be playing to skinhead/Mod types, or alternatives/students in the colleges. I wanted to be playing to cool, fashion types. In a 1980 *NME* review, Gavin Martin said I performed like a caged animal. He was exactly right. That's how I felt, within that look and within that world, penned in. I would often start each performance in a bad mood (nicotine withdrawal symptoms didn't help). I would arrogantly judge the audiences, but by the end of the show, I would be bang into my performance and feeling heartened and humbled by the fact that the crowd were loving us. I could see that they were genuinely moved by the music, and *I* was moved by *that*. We were going somewhere and everyone knew it.

One night, I arrived at a college gig, late and alone. I passed through the bar, just before the show. 'Dance Stance', our first single, was playing. I heard a girl with her back to me, singing passionately along with some of the lyrics. *Oscar Wilde and Brendan Behan, Sean O'Casey, George Bernard Shaw.*

She had no idea I was behind her (and probably wouldn't have known me anyway). That was the first time it had happened. It was such a buzz.

. . .

For the recording of 'Geno', our next single, Roger Ames, our A&R guy at EMI, suggested Pete Wingfield to produce. I had adored his 1975 hit, 'Eighteen with a Bullet', and agreed that he was a perfect choice.

The recording went well. Obviously, after the experience with 'Dance Stance', I was determined to make sure the mix was right. This was our second and last single of the deal and if it didn't go well, that was the end of our contract.

Pete and I clashed on the mix. I wanted the horns much louder and more raw, as well as less echo on the drums and voice. Pete wanted the brass lower and sweeter, which to me made it sound more ordinary.

We finally agreed that there would be two mixes, the one Pete favoured and mine. Pete made it clear that he profoundly disagreed with the approach on my mix. I left the studio, wondering how I was going to get my version used. I phoned up Roger Ames.

'Roger, it's really important we use the right mix. That one that Pete likes doesn't sound like us. It's too ordinary. It won't stand out.'

'We will use whichever mix sounds best at the mastering session,' he replied, referring to the process that transfers the tape to disc.

'Roger, honestly, the other mix is boring. It's no good.'

'Well, I'm sure we'll choose the right one. There is a small mastering place that I've heard about in Tottenham that boosts the volume way louder than other records. That should give us an advantage.'

Clearly, I wasn't being invited to the mastering session.

Roger went on holiday and I didn't hear anything for a couple of weeks. Then one morning I got a phone call from John Preston, our label manager at EMI.

'Hi, Kevin. We have a problem. We've just received a test pressing of the single, "Geno", and it's jumping. Roger is on holiday and we can't contact Pete Wingfield. Any chance you could come down to London and oversee a mastering session? We need to get it done at our regular place in the West End.'

Absolutely no problem at all, John!

Myself, Kevin Archer, Steve Spooner, and I think one other band member went down to the mastering house, and of course we used the correct mix.

A few weeks later, I got a call from Roger.

'I've just heard "Geno" on the radio and it sounds fucking rough! You used *your* mix, didn't you?'

'I did, Roger.'

Who knows, if we had used Pete's mix, it may have done even better. I must confess that, although I loved it at the time, the version of 'Geno' that went out now sounds too small and compressed to my ears. Perhaps I was still reacting from the messed-up mix of our previous single and went over the top with the raw brass sound. But in any event, it worked, lots of people loved it and it went to number one for two weeks.

On the morning of the first *Top of the Pops* appearance for 'Geno', on the spur of the moment I had the idea to revert to the hairstyle I'd had the year before – in braids at the sides, but with a quiff at the front, similar to how I had it when we were wearing all the interesting radical clothes. I went to the Ricci Burns salon in the West End and told Ricci that we were doing *TOTP* that night and how I wanted my hair. He was completely blocked out with clients, but he got his top stylist to do it. My hair was only just long enough, but the guy did it and it looked good. From there I went straight to the *Top of the Pops* studios in Shepherd's Bush.

At lunchtime, Mum and Dad drove up from Harrow and dropped off my young cousin Gerry so that he could hang out with us and watch the show. We all had lunch in the canteen. Just as my parents were saying goodbye, Mum said, in an almost pleading, concerned tone, 'Kevin, please don't go on television with your hair like that.'

I didn't respond. I recognise now that I experienced that old, familiar, confused and guilty feeling.

But more than that, having been enjoying the good vibes that now existed in the family due to Dexys' success, and being pleased that my parents seemed to be proud of me, the dominant thought in my mind was to keep the good vibe going. *And maybe this hairstyle was making me look too foreign, anyway.*

I went back to the make-up room. Kevin Archer was there. I told him that I was going to wash my hair out and blow-dry it in the normal way (a pleasant, but inoffensive, traditional hairstyle – parted over the side, à la *The Six Million Dollar Man*).

'Oh, I think it looks really good now,' Kevin said.

'Nah,' I said. 'I'm changing it back.'

I didn't possess the mental clarity to realise that I wasn't there to do what Mum wanted. I was there for my band. I couldn't make the distinction between loving my mum and not doing what she wanted.

At the same *Top of the Pops* appearance, a 40-year-old square-looking TV plugger, who worked for EMI, said to me, 'Kevin, if you get on this show again in a couple of weeks' time, how about we add a few different-coloured T-shirts to brighten it up a bit?'

Fucking hell! Even this old square guy is saying that we look dull. I responded with hostility, but deep down I knew that we had painted ourselves into a corner with our dark clothes.

. . .

While 'Geno' was going *up* the charts, it was damned exciting. And I can clearly remember walking up Bearwood High Street in Birmingham when four or five female employees ran out of a women's clothes shop, practically screaming with excitement. It was embarrassing but fun.

Very soon, the success turned into pressure. I began to see only the negatives. *I only wrote the words for 'Geno'. It was all Kevin Archer,*

I thought. Kevin remembers it differently. He says that I arranged the music for 'Geno', but I don't remember that.

Stoker, now our drummer, asked me at *Top of the Pops*, 'Do you feel like a star?'

'Fuck off!' I said. 'Don't be stupid.'

A star was the last thing I felt like, especially the way I was dressed. That didn't stop me scrambling for as much credit as I could get, though. As the lead singer, the media picked me out, and I didn't need any encouragement.

We recorded the album *Searching for the Young Soul Rebels* that June, 1980, over a 12-day period at a residential studio in the Oxfordshire countryside. I enjoyed the restful vibe of the place and, although we had a few tense moments with producer Pete Wingfield, he did a great job and the recording went very well, barring my silly and, in the case of the Specials, ungrateful idea of including clips from a Deep Purple, Sex Pistols and Specials song at the start of the album, then shouting, 'Burn it down.' Sorry, guys. I behaved like an idiot.

We listened back to the album. Wow! It sounded amazing. I was happy. I knew we'd done our best, and it had worked out. The stars were aligned.

All we had to do now was release it. But I decided that our record deal wasn't good enough. In fairness, it *was* a spectacularly unfair deal – the original contract from Bernard that EMI took over was shocking. Plus, it was one of those deals where they take deductions off for this or that at every turn and you end up with very little. When we signed direct to EMI, they gave us only the tiniest increase.

While making the album, we decided that a couple of group members should go down to the record label and ask for a better deal. They did, but drew a blank. Now was the time to strike, right after a number-one single. Fuck it!

I decided we should hold back the tapes of our album and keep them until EMI significantly improved the contract. I told Pete Wingfield what we were planning and he agreed, saying, 'Yes, good idea. Hold back the tapes; renegotiate.' But as it came closer to the time, he changed his mind.

Nevertheless, at the end of the last day of recording, at a pre-arranged signal, we meticulously scooped up all the tapes, much to the protests of Pete and the engineer, Barry. We had used the element of surprise.

We all quickly piled into the van. Trevor, our road manager, was driving. I was sitting next to him. As we approached the exit, Pete Wingfield suddenly appeared from nowhere and threw himself in front of the van, arms outstretched. He was basically saying, *You'll have to run me over if you want to get past.*

Trevor braked and the van came to a stop.

'Fucking drive!' I shouted.

He hesitated.

'Fucking drive, Trevor!' I shouted again.

He accelerated. Pete jumped out of the way at the last second and off we went.

We figured that if we took the road to Birmingham, there might be problems, so we headed a few miles in the other direction to the house of some girls we had met during the recording. After a couple of hours, we headed back to Brum. That turned out to be the right decision. We later learned that the police had been called and had been looking for the van on the road to Birmingham.

I can understand Pete's point of view now. He was being paid by EMI to deliver the album. He had done a fantastic job on the production, coming down into the recording room with us, creating a vibe and dancing around the room while we played. He helped us so much.

It's also crystal clear to me now that my plan to hold back our album tapes wasn't really about the money. I just wanted to have a fight. Deep down I was afraid that I was losing control of the group. I didn't have any new ideas. And all of the things I'd promised them, at the start, had come to pass, and maybe those things weren't that great. What did I have to hold the band together now? Practically nothing.

I started to become much more afraid of being found out as lacking in the talent department. I'd run out of songs and I always felt that Kevin Archer was a better songwriter than me. I didn't know where we could go from here. The album was such a complete statement. Maybe the others could come up with a different direction, but if that was to be the case, I didn't fancy not being the leader.

Taking on EMI felt like the early days, when we had something to fight for again.

I took the tapes to Mum and Dad's place in Harrow.

'Why didn't you just do it?'

When 'Geno' got to number one, I said to Corky, 'What we wanna do now is work hard playing live for the next three months, to break through to as many people as possible.'

I was referring to going to places like France or Italy. Corky misinterpreted my words and booked us on a gruelling seven-week Transit-van tour of the UK! It was geographically ill-thought-out, 40-plus dates long, with hardly any days off, playing in Locarnos and Top Rank dance halls around the country, just like the Specials had done six or seven months earlier, but on a shoestring. We called it the Intense Emotions Review.

Because things still hadn't been resolved with EMI, we were doing the tour with no album available in the shops. We now had a much bigger audience down to 'Geno', but the crowds didn't know what to make of us – most of them had turned up expecting to hear ten 'Genos', and were confronted with a varied set. There were subtle and quiet moments in our show that a few months earlier, on the Straight to the Heart Tour, had worked well. During those quiet spells, you could hear a pin drop. Now, when we brought down the volume, we would often hear roars of 'Geno'. In fairness, that was of course all most people knew. But I didn't like the situation. I knew we were worth a lot more than that.

Plus, there were tensions building within the band. I withdrew into myself. Most of the other guys just smoked dope after the shows. I joined them once or twice but didn't enjoy it that much.

I was uptight and permanently stressed, and even when I went onstage my mind was racing. Looking back, I'd say I was having some kind of anxious reaction to what was happening.

A couple of people on that tour – Archie, the lead singer of the Upset, who were supporting us, and Bernard Rhodes, who was managing our other support band, the Black Arabs – were seeing my hesitancy and urged me to enjoy it. They both said to me, at different times, 'Take it. It's yours.' *It* being success and the connection with the audience. But I felt estranged from the crowds. And not just from them, from everyone. If this was *it*, it just didn't seem right. I wish now that I'd been able to let go a little. But I had no idea how to.

Also, a big concern to me was that the money from the shows wasn't being taken care of. There were large amounts of cash being paid over each night and we weren't shown records, books or anything. For example, my brother-in-law Phil promoted one of our shows in Hatfield. At the end of the night, he presented the band's money, plus a neatly put-together register of all expenses, but where all that went is anybody's guess.

Simultaneously, we were trying to sort out the negotiations with EMI. Occasionally someone from the label would come to a show and we'd 'negotiate'. I had turned the record company into the enemy and, in the process, backed us into a corner. Finally, they gave us a minuscule increase. But this was no victory: record companies don't forget things like that. It was, and still is, a hideous financial arrangement, one that would probably be illegal today.

I got more and more serious and alienated from pretty much everyone in the band. Previously I'd led. Now I thought no one was listening to me, and I resented them for it. In response, I tried to dominate. The more I believed I wasn't being listened to, the harder I pushed. The harder I pushed, the less people would listen to me. I didn't even trust the fans who would come to wish us well after a gig. I thought they might have agendas, having spoken to other band members about me.

And we were under-rehearsed on that tour. We had been so busy that we'd finished the album and practically went straight into the shows. On the first night, in Portsmouth, when we started the first song (always an instrumental, either 'The Horse' or 'Soul Finger'), half the band went into 'The Horse', the other half into 'Soul Finger'. We had to start the song again.

When we played Newcastle, Paul Burton, my old boss and owner of Brown's hairdresser's, came to the gig and hung out with us afterwards. It was nice to see him. He had always treated me fairly, and he was a successful businessman.

It occurred to me to get him involved, to help sort out what was clearly a mess. I mentioned it to him, and he was willing. After speaking with Corky, who was agreeable, Paul Burton joined the tour for a few days, basically on a trial to see how everyone got on. All the band liked him, so we agreed he would work with Corky – although after a few months, he ended up replacing him.

During that hot summer of 1980, we would rise early and set off in the cramped Ford Transit minivan, often on a long journey to the next gig. We had a group rule, or rather *I* had a group rule: 'No girlfriends to travel with us.'

It was a kind of light-hearted rule that pretty much everyone was cool with on the previous tour. But now, we were in a different place entirely. On one occasion, when two of the band's girlfriends got in the van – a 12-seater minibus – to get a lift to the next gig, I got the driver to stop at the nearest railway station and told the girls to get out.

What a dick I was. I had no thought or regard for them. I watched the girls sheepishly get out of the van. If you happen to be reading this, girls, I'm so sorry. I was an absolute idiot and you deserved much better.

There was a lot of this kind of bullshit control-freakery coming from me, and it rightly pissed off members of the band. It also alienated me further from them.

At the beginning of that tour, I did another silly thing. I convinced the band that we should stop doing interviews with the music press and, instead, use the record-company-funded adverts in the music papers to communicate directly with the audience – often making sure to slag the music press off in the process. On some level, I was afraid of a backlash and wanted to get my retaliation in first. In a few short weeks, I had alienated the record company, the music press and, most importantly, the band!

Nine or ten years later, I'm out of my head in the Wag Club. My pal Chris Sullivan introduced me to a guy who was *also* off his nut. The bloke said, in a druggy haze, 'All right, mate … You were in Dexys, weren't you?'

'I was,' I said.

'Great group,' he said.

'Thanks, man.'

'One question,' he said.

'Yeah. What's that?'

'Why didn't you just *do* it?'

'What? What do you mean?'

'Well, why didn't you just … *do* it?'

Even through my druggy haze, I knew exactly what he meant. It was a fucking good question. And one I couldn't answer. Why didn't I just *do* it?

The truth is that I couldn't. I was incapable of keeping it simple and just getting on with the job of music.

I must also say, in fairness, that we didn't have anybody around us with experience. We were on a tour where the finances were chaotic, we were trying to deal with the record company, and the tour itself was gruelling. I don't know if I would have listened to any good advice at that time but, for sure, there were no calming voices around.

My resentment towards some of the band members was growing. We were so distant now. I started thinking about replacing some of them.

. . .

We had a day off from the tour in Birmingham to film the video for 'There, There, My Dear', the next single.

I was enthusiastic about the video. I had what I felt was a strong idea for it – alienation. I wanted to feature a lonely tramp. I set off through the city-centre streets to try and find one.

It was about six or seven o'clock on a Saturday evening. As I walked across the green on Colmore Row, I recognised an unknown part-time band who used to rehearse in the same studios as us, walking in my direction. I didn't think anything of it, but they seemed like they were on a night out – they had a boisterous swagger about them, which told me they'd had a few drinks.

They went past me and made some sarcastic comment under their breath. I didn't heed them. I wasn't interested. I was on a mission.

About a minute later, I could hear them walking excitedly back in my direction and getting closer. There were five of them. The guy who seemed to be leading the gang started to kick my ankles. The others were now pushing and jostling me. They were firing insults too. I realised that if I didn't do something, it was going to get worse.

I turned around, punched the leader in the face and kicked another one in the groin. Seconds later, I was on the ground, getting a hiding. It wasn't the worst kicking I've ever had, but it wasn't pleasant. After about a minute, they walked away laughing, looking very pleased with themselves. Their laughter made my blood boil.

Fuck it! I'm not taking this off them cunts!

There was a building site maybe 20 yards away. Having grown up around building sites, I knew there would be something in there I could use. The guys were now walking happily in that direction. I ran past them and into the building site. I saw a scaffold pole – about four feet long and three inches wide. I grabbed it and ran at them.

'Come on, you fucking cunts!'

They ran. I chased them and whacked the biggest one across the back.

Thwack! He fell.

I was running towards the leader and making good ground on him. I was just getting ready to hit him when, from nowhere, a copper appeared. He was on his own. I looked at him. He looked at me.

I dropped the scaffold pole and ran towards Needless Alley, a narrow walkway that led down to busy Birmingham New Street. The copper blew his whistle loudly. I knew that if I could get among the shoppers, I would be safe.

I continued running as fast as I could.

I couldn't hear anyone coming behind me, but I wasn't going to slow myself down by looking round. By now, I was close to the end of the alley and safety. Then, just as I approached the bottom of the narrow strip, a big fat copper stepped out from a doorway.

He outstretched his arms, taking up the complete width of the alley, and shouted, 'Stop! Police!'

To get past him, I would have to have hit him or, at the very least, shove his arm out of the way. I was aware enough to know that 'assaulting a police officer' would mean a lengthy prison term, especially with *my* record. I stopped and surrendered.

I was arrested and taken to Steelhouse Lane Police Station where, after a period in the cell, I was charged with assault. The policeman had only seen me going at the other guys. He hadn't seen them beating me up.

The other guys gave some bullshit statements about there having been a rivalry between our two bands. There was no rivalry – we barely knew them, but they saw my arrest as an opportunity to get some publicity for themselves.

I wanted to plead not guilty. I felt I had done nothing but defend myself. But the copper had seen me hitting one of them with a scaffold pole and about to hit another. Paul Burton, by now our manager, got me a good, expensive barrister, who did a deal with the prosecution: for a guilty plea, they would settle for a suspended sentence. The lawyer strongly advised me to take the deal. If I pleaded not guilty and lost, with my previous form – 13 convictions by that time, including two for violence – I would surely have gone to prison. I took the deal.

I was given a nine-month prison sentence, suspended for two years.

· · ·

Towards the end of that tour, we found ourselves booked into the Oxford Apollo Theatre. I'd never previously heard of it. I noticed that we had an early showtime of 8.30pm instead of the usual midnight.

When we went onstage, the audience were all seated. It was a proper sit-down theatre. I immediately felt uncomfortable. I ran to the front of the stage as I usually would and started belting out the first song with as much conviction as I could. I was trying to get the audience going, but there was no noticeable reaction. As the song ended, they applauded, but it wasn't frenzied like we had been used to in dance halls.

We did another song. Again, I stormed to the front and tried to get a reaction, but they remained seated. The front row were maybe 15 feet away from me, which seemed a long way. When we'd finished the song, the same thing happened – enthusiastic applause, but not hysteria.

The stage was big and I was acutely conscious that everyone in the audience, including the upper tiers, could see all of my body, not just my upper torso, as in clubs/dance halls. I became more and more rigid and self-conscious about my stage movements.

Then, about six songs in, something changed. I realised that to 'come over' in this environment, I would have to approach things differently. Merely attacking the audience, as pretty much everyone had since punk and even before, wouldn't work. I would have to perform *for* the audience, as opposed to *at* them.

Once I started to make that adjustment, I began to enjoy it. The fact that they were seated gave me a starting point. And more than that, they weren't drunk! We weren't coming on to pandemonium and then feeling a pressure to sustain that intensity, which of course was impossible, given that our set included slow and softer songs. Instead, we had an opportunity to build the show and then take it down a few side alleys, then build it back up again. *They* were the audience, and *we* were there to entertain them. It was simple, but a revelation to me.

I saw that this way of performing suited me much better. When I got down on my knees and belted out a refrain, the whole audience could actually *see* me and understand what I was getting at, instead of only the first 15 rows or so. Dexys had always wanted to be a visual group; now we were having a chance to be seen!

By the end of the show, we had completely won the crowd over. I felt I had done my job – whereas in dancehalls, I felt I was faking it, as the result of being dragged along by the audience's frantic energy.

I don't know how the rest of the band felt about it, as we weren't really speaking at that point, but I loved this. Obviously, the venues on the rest of the tour were already booked, but I resolved that in the future Dexys would play only theatres. Something we have just about stuck to.

As the tour ended, we replaced Pete Saunders with Mick Talbot on organ. That was a mean thing to do to Pete, who had ditched his university course to rejoin Dexys, but I think everybody agreed that Mick's playing and the fact that he could sing well was what was needed.

After a couple of weeks at home, we were due to set off on a European tour. I missed the plane to the first date, a German TV show. I'd been up all night, overseeing the mix of our next single, 'Keep It, Pt. 2', and got to Heathrow just after the plane took off. The band had to do the TV show without me – Kevin Archer stood in and mimed my pre-recorded vocal. I saw a clip of it later, and he looked great.

I had long since felt intimidated by Kevin Archer's talent. Now he even *looked* better than me. I felt old, and I knew I looked it. It seemed the band didn't even need me.

It was a dark period. Everything was an effort. My vitality and any sense of enjoyment had completely gone.

We had re-recorded 'Keep It' from the album, in London, and called it 'Keep It, Pt.2 (Inferiority, Pt.1)', but weren't happy with the performance, so recorded it again, in Hamburg, during a day off.

In the lyric, I wrote down exactly how I was feeling and poured it into that vocal performance. It was a much slower, darker version, and my vocal was manic, raw and very much on the edge.

The record label didn't want to release it. They wanted 'Tell Me When My Light Turns Green', which, with hindsight, would have been a great single. It was so catchy. But I had written it alone and, by then, didn't have confidence in my own tunes. I thought it much better to go with music that Kevin Archer had written. Plus I was on a mission.

I thought 'Keep It, Pt. 2' was so much more pure and powerful than anything we'd done previously, and would completely blow people away, as did Kevin Archer. *If you liked 'Geno', you're going to fucking love this!* I thought.

I recognise now that the performance was too raw, and these days I can't listen to it, but it totally reflected how I felt at the time.

'I'm coming with you!'

The way the first Dexys broke up was weird. I was told on the last date of the European tour, three hours before the gig in Zurich. Funnily enough, as we arrived in the city, I remember thinking Zurich would be a good place for a band to spilt up. I don't know why, but that was the thought in my head.

Kevin Archer phoned me in my room and said, 'Can you come down to reception?' We met in the hotel lobby and ordered some tea.

He delicately told me, 'They wanna carry on without ya, Kev.'

They had also asked him to join as lead singer, but he wasn't interested.

About an hour later, Geoff Blythe phoned my room and asked me to meet him downstairs. We sat in the lounge as he told me that they wanted to get another singer, and asked me would I be OK with them taking the name, Dexys Midnight Runners? I breathed a sigh of relief and said, 'Yeah. OK.'

They were putting me out of my misery. I immediately felt much lighter. It was over. Thank God. I felt at peace again. I was also grateful for the sympathetic and caring way Kevin Archer had given me the news. And I regretted that I'd been controlling and cold with him, often shutting him out. This man was clearly of impeccable character.

I went back to my room and reflected briefly on how I hadn't realised things were as serious as they had become, for the others. I started to see their point of view, although I felt some anger at their cheek – wanting to kick me out of Dexys.

I started to think about that night's show. I realised it would be my last. *I'm going to put everything into it, but thank heavens this is all over. No more struggling.*

I could think clearly again. I could breathe.

Maybe I'll do something musical on my own.

I walked to Jim Paterson's room. He told me he had already been approached by the others. I asked him if he would work with me.

'I'm not sure. Let me think about it,' he said.

I didn't even feel particularly afraid or wary of facing the others as we met in the hotel lobby for the last time, to be taken to the gig by bus. In the previous few weeks, I'd felt on edge about seeing them.

That night, I sang my heart out. I put everything into the show. I connected with the songs for the first time in what felt like ages.

In our version of Otis Redding's 'Respect', I got down on my knees. The refrain always continued for an unspecific length of time, depending on how I felt. That night, I must have let it go on for five minutes.

'*Give it to me, give it to me, give it to me, give it to me, give it to me,*' I repeated over and over, almost crying, howling from my heart.

I ran over to Jimmy. I was directing the line to him, as I often did. Jimmy motioned to me to come closer and, during a break in his playing, he made it clear that he wanted me to put my ear close to his mouth. I did.

'I'm coming with you!' he shouted in my ear.

'Fucking great!' I shouted back.

Maybe it was the performance that convinced him. Jim was always all about the music – the soul.

. . .

The next morning, I still felt the peaceful relief of surrender. I had slept better than in months.

Kevin Archer and I had to stay on in Zurich to do some pre-arranged media interviews, while the rest of the band went home in the minibus.

My brother Joe, who had been working with us, assisting in the selling of the merchandise, travelled back with the band. He later told me that it was a very uncomfortable journey for him – sitting with the rest of them going across Europe in a minibus while they talked about what sort of lead singer they would like to enlist to replace his brother.

As I wrote earlier, Joe has very little confidence in himself and rarely speaks unless first spoken to. Because of that, some people ignore him and act as if he isn't there. I feel that those guys let themselves down in treating Joe like that. Without doubt, I had been *more* than difficult to deal with in the preceding months, but what did that have to do with my lovely brother, Joe? Absolutely nothing.

Meanwhile, Kevin Archer and I did a lengthy interview with French journalist Alain Weiss. He wrote for *Le Monde*, the French daily newspaper, and had travelled from Paris for the Zurich gig, as we didn't play France on that tour. Alain was a sophisticated and cool guy, and had just discovered Dexys. He told us that he had written the most convincing testimony for an album since his review of the first Roxy Music album. This pleased us greatly. And we were absolutely delighted that someone as cool as Alain really liked Dexys.

As the day went on, and bolstered by Alain's enthusiasm, I started to think: *Dexys means something. We have done some good work. Kevin Archer, Jim and I have written some good songs and done something quite original.*

Fuck! I'm not letting them take Dexys! How fucking dare they?

I said to Kevin Archer, 'Fuck 'em. Let's form a better Dexys. Jim's with us.'

'OK,' he said.

By the time I got back to London a couple of days later, I was adamant. I told Paul Burton of my plans. I also mentioned that I'd said to Geoff Blythe that they could have the name and carry on without me.

He said: 'Look, nobody could blame you for anything you said at that point. You were probably in shock.' That was true. I found out later that as well as telling Kevin Archer, Jim and myself that he was in our corner, Paul Burton was saying the same thing to the other five. I guess he was keeping his options open.

I went home. I was broke and in debt. Although the UK tour sold really well, and we were incurring very little outgoing expenses (we were travelling in a minivan and staying in cheap bed-and-breakfast places rather than hotels), we had not been able to make ends meet, much less turn a profit. Halfway through the UK tour, Kevin Archer and I had to get a publishing advance on our songwriting royalties to keep the tour afloat! We were never shown records or accounts.

. . .

It's November 1980, we have no money, no band, and an overwhelming feeling of *what the fuck happened?*

To top it all, Spandau Ballet were coming through with their style-orientated thing. The dressing-up idea was exploding. The press were loving it. Everything was changing, and we were looking old-fashioned. One of Duran Duran, I think it was Nick Rhodes, said in an early interview: 'Kevin Rowland shouldn't have said all that stuff about soul. Everyone in Birmingham knew he was into Roxy and Bowie.'

He was right; I loved soul, and soul was always going to be a big reference point in Dexys' early sound, but for sure, I had abandoned that Roxy/Bowie-inspired part of myself. I used to see Nick Rhodes and John Taylor at the Romulus club a couple of years earlier. They were at the younger end of that scene.

. . .

We started to form the second Dexys. The guys who had left went to EMI Records and told them of their plans to find a new singer, guitarist and trombone player, and call themselves Dexys Midnight Runners. EMI didn't take them seriously.

Meanwhile, I hurriedly registered the band name, before anyone else could. After all, I had thought of it. I assured the record company that the new Dexys would be based around Big Jim, Kevin Archer and myself. They seemed up for it.

I have subsequently wondered how it would have been if I'd just allowed the other five guys to take the name and carry on without me. Maybe it would have been the right thing to just take my time and trust that things would be OK, but I was incapable of that.

I didn't stop and contemplate. I just reacted and immediately formed Dexys Mark Two. I was vaguely aware that I hadn't allowed myself space to pause and consider if this was what I really wanted, but my Dexys obsession was reignited by the quest of forming a new, better group.

Clothes-wise, it was hard. Although this was a good opportunity to change the look, the New Romantics were claiming so many ideas. I felt backed into a corner, with only a few scraps of post-punk standard shapes and the like left to choose from. We couldn't dress up too much – that would have looked like jumping on the bandwagon – but I didn't want us to be too scruffy either.

Then, all of a sudden, clarity! During a visit to Liverpool, I saw some scallies wearing boating anoraks. I didn't want to do the boating thing, but I liked the idea of anoraks. It looked radical. I explained the idea to Vicky, who had designed many of our prototype New Romantic clothes in 1978 and '79.

She liked it and suggested a great idea for the trousers. They should be neither tight nor baggy and have a sewn-in crease, which would work well when tucked into boxing boots. The look would be topped off with hair that was shortish at the front and sides, but pony-tailed at the back. We now had our own style!

Equally, after wondering if I would be able to write anything of value, my lyrics suddenly started coming thick and fast, as did the musical direction. The muse seemed to arise out of the mood we were in – melancholy and more inward-looking. Down but not out, and seeking something pure and perhaps spiritual. Big Jim Paterson's musical ideas were a massive part of that.

During sound checks on the European tour, Jim had been warming up with a brass riff that sounded amazing to me and would end up as the main instrumental melody on 'Until I Believe in My Soul'. It was a genius, epic riff – so beautiful. It came to signal a new direction for Dexys.

Jim and I connected deeply as songwriters. Our religious backgrounds seemed to bring us together – Jim's Presbyterian Scottish upbringing and my Irish Catholic roots. Over the next few months we would come up with 'Plan B', 'Until I Believe in My Soul', 'Show Me' and more. I now felt I had something to say again.

Kevin Archer had wanted to form his own band in 1978, but instead got involved in helping me form, lead and write for Dexys. And what a job he did. We wouldn't have had that level of success without him. He wrote the music for 'Geno', 'There, There, My Dear' and 'Keep It'. But I knew we'd be OK from here. I knew he had felt stifled by me. The guy had been nothing but 100 per cent classy and loyal.

As soon as the new band started to come together, and before I had properly started writing with Jim, I said to Kevin: 'I don't know how you're feeling, but if you wanted to go and do your own thing, Kev, now would be the right time ...'

He said he would, but not before teaching the songs to new guitarist, Billy Adams, an early fan and friend.

Seb Shelton, an amazing drummer who had played with Secret Affair, also joined and was totally committed to the new team. He brought with him much-needed experience and stability. The other new guys were pretty much all raw recruits.

The live performances of that year, 1981, were called the Projected Passion Revue. Inspired by that show at Oxford, we went for something that was more subtle and pure. This was a completely different approach to the first Dexys. We now ceased playing to the front stalls; we projected to the whole auditorium. Our show was something to *watch*, not be part of. We choreographed our stage movements so that there would always be something interesting going on. Every band member knew where they should be standing and what they should be doing at any given point in the set. I now had a lot of control: I guess these new guys were impressed by Dexys' success, and were prepared to listen to me.

There is a state of grace that sometimes happens in a live performance, if you are well prepared and on top of your craft. Everything falls into place and becomes effortless. You, and everyone in the room, are in the moment. We achieved that a fair few times on those Projected Passion Revues. Even when we took the volume right down, the audience would still be completely with us.

I was kind of self-righteous, and took everything we did very seriously. Some people thought we were pompous and even one or two in the band would sneer, but I meant every word, as did Jim, Seb and Billy.

A downside to this very insular approach was that it allowed me to justify all sorts of crazy stuff to myself. For example, rationalising that I shouldn't be friendly with other musicians, as it would impair my musical purity. With hindsight, of course, it's clear that I was avoiding people out of social anxiety and spending more and more time on my own. Initially, some solitude can be good for music, but ultimately, too much is not conducive to a healthy life or creativity. You end up going too deeply into your mind.

Plus, my alienated, loner way of being was further bolstered by the Dexys audience at that time. They were very intense, a lot like the Smiths' audience a couple of years later. We would get the most serious letters, and I would use their mail to console myself and bolster my belief that I was on the right track, feeling understood by these people who also found life difficult. To be fair, I guess some of them did understand me, but I don't think that was healthy for me.

Sometimes I'd meet up and hang out with these Dexys superfans. I'm sure they genuinely *did* like the music, but it was an uneven relationship, where I had the power. I see now that I was bathing in their adoration. And eventually I began to feel trapped and hemmed in by it.

At this point, I didn't have a massive interest in music but I had an *obsessive* interest in Dexys. I wasn't listening to loads of music for pleasure. I probably wasn't listening to *enough* music. I had loads of rules about what music should and shouldn't be, and so many reasons or excuses for not liking other artists, that sometimes I would get confused about what fitted my rule book and what didn't.

But for all of that, and to some extent *because* of it, the 1981 Dexys were brilliant and in a different class to the 1980 firm. Way more intense, tight and powerful. Sadly, this Dexys didn't make an album.

In 2008, a record label cobbled together a few tracks and called it *The Projected Passion Revue*. They warned me that they were doing it with or without me, so I went along with it against my better judgement. It was a hodgepodge of radio sessions and singles from around that time, with a few live tracks thrown in, none of them from the London Old Vic three-night run that were the pinnacle performances of that Dexys incarnation.

In the run-up to the Old Vic shows, I had the feeling that these gigs would be special, and that I should ask Roger (our A&R man) to get a mobile studio down there. But our stock was low – our latest single, 'Liars A to E', had just flopped, and I was too nervous of getting shouted down.

We were in trouble financially and lived from week to week. In the summer of 1981, our single 'Show Me' had stalled at number 16, and when 'Liars A to E' didn't make the charts in November of that year, the record label started to make it clear that we weren't giving them what was required.

Adam Ant had recently come through in a big way. He was the first artist of our generation who had the balls to stand up and say, 'I want to be really successful.' Up to that point, there was a sense, largely emanating from the music press, where you felt obliged to say, 'Oh, I didn't really want to be successful. It just sort of happened.'

Adam Ant and bands like Haircut 100 who were doing well in the charts seemed to be having a great time. By comparison, we seemed miserable.

I made the decision to go all out for that pop-star thing. I had a vague sense that a part of me would later regret it, but I felt resentful about where Dexys were positioned – respected but not really part of the conversation; marginalised; sidelined. Of our own making, of course.

I remember saying to one or two of the band, 'I would trade all of this credibility for the kind of pop success that Adam and the Ants have.'

For a year, I had been passionate about Mark Two Dexys, but now I'd had enough.

. . .

Meanwhile, my parents had just left Harrow and moved to Birmingham. One evening, when I was with them in Dad's car, we drove past a big old house in Bearwood with a sign outside. It was up for auction a few days later. I hadn't been thinking about a new home, but for some reason, I was drawn to this place and decided to knock on the door. The guy let us in and we looked around. It was old and in need of some work, but I liked it a lot and made the decision there and then to try to get the money to bid for it. My dad didn't like the idea and said buying it would be a bad move.

But I was obsessed. I went to the bank and got a loan that would cover about half the bid. I also went to the music publishers and asked for an advance for the rest, which, surprisingly, they gave me. I found myself with enough money to make a bid on the house.

I attended the auction a few days later and was surprised to see my dad turn up, looking serious. We said hello but I don't remember much more than that.

Undeterred, I bought the house. I paid £32,000, which was a good price given the size of it. Later that day, I met up with my cousin Barry who had been doing some building work for Dad. Barry told me that Dad had said to him, 'I'm going to the auction to stop Kevin making a fool of himself.'

Barry began doing some work for me in the old house. Dad also started to come round and kept trying to insist that one or two walls needed knocking down. I was resistant: I just wanted to be settled, so that I could write. I didn't want to live in a building site. Though I didn't confront Dad directly on what felt to me like him trying to completely take over, I did have some snappy moments with him. Eventually, he backed off.

'You're treading new ground'

Kevin Archer had left Dexys in late 1980 to form his band – the Blue Ox Babes. In the summer of that year, we had both read an interview with Bernard Rhodes where he talked about how folk music could be the next big thing. We thought that sounded like a great idea, just as soul did in 1978.

With the relative failure of 'Show Me', I deduced that people didn't want to hear brass any more and that Dexys needed to move on. We started to experiment with strings.

We recorded a version of 'Liars A to E' (only released on single) with a string quartet. It didn't sound as good or as different as I had hoped. Next, I asked the Dexys brass section to learn to play stringed instruments (a cello, a violin and a viola), but after a while I saw that that wasn't going to work either, so we started experimenting with some sixth-form college students that our tenor sax player, Paul Speare, knew. We tried a few combinations with a bit of trombone or brass behind them. It wasn't bad, but it wasn't amazing.

Kevin Archer's band had done some demos, and late in '81 he phoned up and said he'd like to play them to me. The three songs sounded really fresh and light, and, as well as the unique sound, I was impressed with his passionate singing and heartfelt, intelligent lyrics.

If Dexys Mark One often had a Stax/Atlantic soul influence, these songs sounded nearer to the Tamla end of things. The lightness about them was mainly coming from the piano and the solo violin he was using, which was paired with a melodica covering the same line. I told Kevin I thought his songs sounded great. I also commented on how good the violin playing was.

'It's a girl called Helen Bevington at the music college in town. Maybe she'd be good for you,' he said. He had heard our demos and Helen's playing was a way higher standard than the players we were using.

I asked Kevin if I could hang on to the cassette, purely because I wanted to play it to Jim, to see what he thought. Kevin agreed.

Jim and Paul Speare went to the music college and enlisted Helen. She was amiable, good-looking and a great musician. She found us another violinist, a viola and cellist, and we used that string-quartet combo together with Jim's trombone on some demos of new songs like 'The Celtic Soul Brothers'. I played them to my friend Steve Torch, who was now also doing music full-time. He said: 'You're treading new ground there, Kev.' And we were. The combination of a string quartet with Jim's trombone sounded different – funky and edgy. It was unique, and different enough from Kevin Archer's sound.

If we had stopped there, I would have saved everybody a load of grief. But I started to obsess about this heavy versus light thing, and the string quartet and trombone combo sounded good but still quite weighty.

Simultaneously, some tension developed between Kevin Archer and me. Over a chat in a café one day, he told me that he had purposely formed a *young* band. Rightly or wrongly, I imagined he was digging me out about my age. I was by then 28, which at that time was old for a lead singer trying to break through. Kevin was in his early twenties. Of even more concern was that during the same conversation, he said to me, 'When I do interviews, I'm going to slag you off. Don't take it personally.'

I didn't say anything at the time, but thought, *Fuck that*.

Plus, Kevin had approached Dexys' manager, Paul Burton, to take his demos to record labels. With hindsight, of course, why shouldn't he? Paul Burton had managed the first line-up of Dexys, which of course included Kevin Archer. He had as much right as I did to use Paul Burton.

But at the time, my shackles were up and I felt that I was being challenged. I resolved to try three violins playing the top-line melodies in our songs, despite the danger that it would sound similar to what Kevin was doing.

Helen obliged by bringing in Steve Shaw and Roger McDuff. I liked the effect from the trio of fiddles, but realised that the end result sounded too close to Kevin's. Justifying my choice by thinking about his warning that he would slag me off in interviews, I thought: *Fuck it. Let's fight it out.*

The main similarity was the combination of the light top lines (our three violins versus Kevin's pairing of a violin and a melodica), plus a Tamla Motown-style piano. It was too similar, particularly on 'The Celtic Soul Brothers', which we recorded in February '82. I later heard that Kevin was pissed off on hearing it, rightly.

It also dawned on me that now was a great time to add some Irishness into the mix. In the past we had used imagery: the cover of the first album showed a Catholic boy being burned out of his home in Belfast. Also, the song 'Burn It Down' was about anti-Irish jokes. Plus, we had made a point of playing Irish dance halls, like the National in Kilburn, which were at the time only used by Irish show bands.

I realised that as well as the violins, other traditional Irish instruments could be brought into the music. I asked Billy to learn the banjo, Mickey Billingham, the keyboard player, to play the accordion, and Paul Speare, saxophonist, to play the tin whistle. Adding these influences felt subversive, especially around Birmingham. You weren't supposed to talk about Ireland. This was the height of the conflict in the North. I was sick of being expected to keep quiet about being Irish and keeping the lid on Irish culture. I really felt it was that restrictive.

When I told manager Paul Burton that I was planning to put some Irishness into our music, he said, 'No, people here don't like the Irish.' Obviously, I ignored him.

By the time we had written more songs, for what would become the album *Too Rye Ay*, I decided to use brass behind many of the string lines, to give them more oomph. It worked well, and the sound was better than on 'Celtics'. Plus, although it still had a lightness, it was a broader sound. Not as close to Kevin's sound as on 'Celtics'.

One of the songs on Kevin's demo tape was called 'What Does Anyone Ever Think About?' It was a great song and had a break-down-and-speed-up section. I thought that was a brilliant idea. Though not completely unique – 'Hold Tight' by Dave Dee, Dozy, Beaky etc., the

Jewish folk song 'Hava Nagila', also 'Special Brew' by Bad Manners all used the speeding-up idea – it was very unusual. I realised that going to a breakdown and then building up would work really well on a song we were writing, 'Come on Eileen'.

Again, that was too much of an influence. The very least I could have done was spoken to Kevin about it. But I was in competition mode, and believed he was too. I knew he was planning for his band to release a single, so I thought, *OK, let's slug this out, publicly.*

There is one very important point that I need to make: I didn't steal one note, one melody, one chord sequence or lyric from Kevin Archer's music! Not one. All of the music was written by me, Jim and one or two others in the band. What I *did* steal was the sound and style of the music, mainly on 'Celtic Soul Brothers', and also the idea of breaking down and speeding up, which I used on 'Come on Eileen'.

What I did was wrong, and Kevin Archer deserved much better. Furthermore, we would not have had the success we did without Kevin's input. There is no question about that.

Also, some years later, in 1988, and well after the success of 'Come on Eileen' and *Too Rye Ay*, I did something equally mean-spirited. Kevin's band finally did release a single, which used something akin to his original sound. On being asked what I thought about it in a music paper interview, I replied: 'Oh, it's just Dexys, isn't it.'

That was really cheap. Here was an opportunity to maybe go some way to making an amend and possibly help Kevin's band along a little. I couldn't even do that. Very sad. Kevin, now, rightly receives a significant percentage of the songwriting royalties from 'Come on Eileen' and the *Too Rye Ay* project, and has done for many years.

In 2020, a big resolution came for Kevin and me in the form of one of Tim Burgess's 'Listening Parties'. Tim, who is best known for his role as lead singer in the Charlatans, had devised a format during the Covid lockdown in which people would listen to albums communally, with the artists expressing in real time on Twitter how they felt about each song, and maybe what was going on in the studio or around the band at the time. Fans would also chime in with comments. It was a great idea.

Kevin and I had recently started chatting again, after losing touch for a few years. We hadn't officially fallen out, we just hadn't spoken much in the preceding years. It was great to reconnect with my old mate – the genius that is Kevin Archer.

We'd both had our struggles with the *Too Rye Ay* album. Although it was impossible to avoid hearing 'Come on Eileen' on the radio in 1982, Kevin had never actually listened to the album itself – he had avoided it because he was convinced he would hear lots of his own music on it. Meanwhile, I had been torturing myself for years, thinking the talent was all Kevin, and that I had contributed very little, and for that reason had also avoided hearing the album. Now we decided to take part in the Listening Party.

For me, it was a revelation. As I listened, a cloud lifted. I remembered that I had co-written all of the songs on the album with Big Jim, and they were actually really good. There was so much originality there. I had dismissed it in my mind as being worthless without Kevin's input. I'd forgotten about all the well-crafted and original songs we'd written and arranged, as well as the strong performances.

It was also a really positive experience for Kevin. He thought he would hear his own musical ideas, and much more of his musical sound, but he too was surprised.

We spoke on the phone right afterwards. Kevin said: 'So, my contribution was the sound of "Celtic Soul Brothers" and the breakdown and speed up on "Eileen"?'

I said, 'Yes, Kevin. That was it!'

The Listening Party was a healing and positive experience for the both of us.

I also realised then that while Kevin and I weren't in contact, I had felt like a part of me had been missing. I think he felt the same. We remain good friends, and there is no one more enthusiastic about the current Dexys than Kevin.

We were happening!

During the writing of 'Come on Eileen', we had worked meticulously every step of the way, finding the best rhythm, chord sequence and melodies. I could see the potential in the song, so wanted to get it the best it could possibly be.

The group got understandably fed up with me coming into the rehearsal room with a different arrangement every day, having worked on it the night before. I would continually be asking them to try the chorus in this or that key. We literally tried every key. I would tape each version on my beat box, take it home, listen, and come back the following day with another batch of changes.

In fact, it was on the day that I showed the band the first rough arrangement of 'Come on Eileen' that Jim Paterson left Dexys.

To put it mildly, there was an unsupportive atmosphere within the group. We weren't doing well, the record company was losing faith in us, Paul Burton was giving up hope, and everyone was broke. Some people had gone weeks without getting paid. It was on my shoulders, and some of the band were starting to feel resentful towards me. We hadn't achieved the success we were hoping for and that I had promised them.

Whenever I showed the band a new song, I was always nervous. In the back of my mind, I would be thinking: *Is this song shit?*

On this occasion I was trying to get Brian Maurice, our sax player, and a couple of others to sing the backing vocals on the breakdown section that would later become 'Come on, Eileen, ta loo rye ay, come on, Eileen, ta loo rye ay'. At that point, I didn't have any words for the section, so I tried to get the guys to just chant the melody, using the words, 'bop bop, bop bop a lula, bop bop, bop bop a lula' to give an idea of how it was going to sound.

Nobody in the band was saying anything positive about the song. There were a lot of telling silences. I was nervous, and strongly sensed there was negativity towards the tune. Brian was making it clear that he was struggling to comprehend what I wanted him to do and was letting everyone know that he was uncomfortable with it. Not with his words, but in his attitude. I felt Brian was playing to the room, at my expense and at the expense of the song.

I started to get frustrated. In an exasperated effort to better explain what I wanted, I said, 'Look, it's like a chant.'

Brain said, in his strong Geordie accent, 'I know what it is, but I don't like it.'

At that point, I snapped: 'Well, if you don't like it, you can fuck off!'

Brian immediately walked out. It almost seemed that's what he had wanted.

Jim said, 'You can't talk to him like that. If he's going, I'm going.'

What? I thought. I didn't realise things had gone so far.

He followed Brian out of the door. I didn't try to stop either of them.

And that's how Jim left Dexys.

Clearly there were other underlying issues that had maybe been building up for some time, mainly lack of funds. In the preceding months, I had expected Jim to come round to my place after long daily rehearsals and write with me, which he often did. I didn't consider that people like Jim had partners or other interests. I saw such things as a hindrance. Dexys were everything. I really couldn't understand why the others didn't feel the same way.

I finished the song, first with the help of Billy as a sounding board, and then alone, changing and simplifying the chords under the verse melody. As I did so, what had appeared so puzzling in previous weeks suddenly became obvious and simple. The song seemed to be finishing itself!

I've always liked songs that sound like they've come out of the air. The kind of songs that I can't possibly imagine how anybody could've written them. A great example is the Tamla song 'You Can't Hurry Love', recorded by the Supremes. I found that melody and groove so infectious, and I couldn't figure out how they could come up with something as incredible as that.

I generally don't like songs that sound like they've been written on the guitar, the exception being those that are based on a really good strong guitar riff, like the Rolling Stones'. I find a lot of tunes that are written on guitar (I can usually tell which) seem limited. Often, people who write that way end up using melodies that sound very similar to the chords they are playing. That can be uninspiring.

In Dexys, we never once jammed. Not once. I have never in my life taken part in a jam session, which is how a lot of bands write songs. With us it was, and still is, always a question of writing the song at home, then bringing something as close to the finished article as possible into the band. It occurs to me now that my approach was more of a Tamla way of writing songs than the usual rock band method. Similarly, I've lost count of the times I've been asked in interviews why I often speak in our songs. To me, it's not unusual at all. It's unusual in *rock* records, but in soul music, talking over a track is commonplace.

Jim and Brian returned to perform on the album *Too Rye Ay* on a session basis.

As well as those two, I could feel an atmosphere of discontent and lack of belief in what we were doing from other members, and it was no surprise when immediately after recording had finished, Paul Speare and Mickey Billingham also left. Despite everything, producers Clive Langer and Alan Winstanley ultimately managed to get the best performances out of us.

We managed to come up with a new look. After much discussion and a few failed efforts, friend and stylist Debbie Baxter suggested the idea of dungarees, which we customised with accessories from different cultures. Other bands were still dressing up, New Romantic style. The fact that we were setting ourselves apart felt good.

We needed to decide on the first single from the new album. Roger Ames – our A&R man – was a great guy and a big part of Dexys' success. He had first worked with us at EMI Records, then brought us over to

Mercury after the first album. But he actually wanted our version of Van Morrison's 'Jackie Wilson Said' released before 'Come on Eileen'.

We had a meeting about it. I was determined that 'Eileen' should be the one, but my stock was low, as the last couple of singles hadn't done well, and Roger didn't want to listen to me. It got heated.

'OK,' said Roger. 'We'll ask Brad [Misell, our record label radio plugger]. He'll be taking it to radio, so he will know which is the best song.' Roger called Brad down from the radio department.

I knew that Roger and Brad were old friends, so I didn't hold out much hope. I was further disheartened when Roger played 'Eileen' first, then 'Jackie Wilson Said', meaning the latter would be freshest in Brad's mind.

But at the end of 'Jackie Wilson Said', Brad paused and said, 'Play that first one again.'

'You want the first one again?' Roger said.

'Yeah, please.'

Halfway through it, Brad said, 'That one.'

'Are you sure?' Roger asked.

'Yeah. That one,' Brad said again.

And that's how 'Come on Eileen' came to be released.

Now, I know that Roger also liked 'Come on Eileen', and if 'Jackie Wilson Said' had been released first and 'Eileen' second, maybe it would have worked out just as well, or even better, who knows? In any event, thank you, Brad! And also, thank you Roger for believing in us.

But a few weeks later, 'Eileen' was struggling to move up the charts. David Jensen initially championed it, but few others at the all-important Radio 1 were playing it.

It went into the charts at number 63 in the first week of release but, without daytime play, it looked like it was going to stall and drop down. Brad to the rescue again.

I phoned our manager Paul Burton and said, 'I'm worried. If this goes down, we're in trouble and I don't think we can write a better song than that. Do you think it would be worth me saying that to Brad?'

He said, 'Yeah, why not?

I got the train down from Birmingham and just managed to catch Brad as he was putting on his jacket to go home for the day. From my heart I told Brad that I thought it was curtains for me and the band if this song didn't do well. More than that, I thought this was the best song we'd written.

He said calmly: 'Don't worry. One of the daytime show's producers owes me a favour. We'll get a play this week and that will knock it up the charts a bit.'

He got the play, and he was right. It moved up to number 41. Then with another play or two the following week, it reached 31, which meant we got *Top of the Pops*. That drove it up to number nine in the charts the following week. Then it was number two. Then number one … for four weeks. I felt great, vindicated and excited. It was two fingers to all the doubters, some of them very close.

All of a sudden, because of the interest in 'Eileen', we started to get busy. As we didn't have a keyboard player, we asked Mickey Billingham to carry on, on a session basis, until we could find someone else.

While all this was going on, I was expecting Kevin Archer to put a record out. I was anticipating the battle between my band and his. I heard at that time that Kevin's band were due to release a single on Stiff Records, a big independent label that had had success with Madness, Ian Dury and others. I'd been told that the label boss Dave Robinson had said to Kevin Archer: 'Come on! Let's take Dexys on!' It never happened.

A few years ago, Kevin told me that he didn't take the Stiff Records deal he'd been offered because it was only a two-singles contract, with options for albums, rather than the albums deal that he wanted.

I couldn't believe it! I explained to him that even the second Dexys hadn't had an album deal – only a singles agreement, and an option of an album on the record company's side. That was standard practice. But although he didn't say it to me, I believe a lot of his reluctance to sign a deal was a result of me having stolen his thunder.

Kevin's band, the Blue Ox Babes, was brilliant and unique. I don't like the word star because it's overused, but Kevin really was one. He looked great and was full of talent and ideas.

At that point in my life, I was so single-minded that I believed that anyone talented would definitely be successful. Nothing would stop you. I realise now, there are many other factors involved. Far from every talented person gets recognition.

· · ·

I was pleased that Dexys had that Beach Boys thing of making records that would sound good in the summer. To me, summer songs are the best – 'Concrete and Clay' by Unit 4 + 2 in '65, 'A Whiter Shade of Pale' in '67, 'Hold Me Tight' by Johnny Nash in '68, the Beach Boys' 'Do It Again' in the same year, 'Young Hearts Run Free' in '76, and 'Do Anything You Wanna Do' by Eddie and the Hot Rods in '77. I'm glad to say that 'Come on Eileen' fulfilled the same function in '82.

Paul Burton explained to me that we needed to arrange a tour quickly. I couldn't see the logic of it. We had just had a number-one single without the stress of a tour and I told him so, but I think the idea was to strike while the iron was hot to get the album to as many people as possible. We couldn't really say no: we were in debt to Paul Burton and, of course, the record label, plus the idea of touring held appeal. We had a new pop audience. We were happening! And it would be nice to take the praise, enjoy it – and also enjoy some of the available sex.

I hadn't been sex-starved, I had been meeting women here and there, but when you go on tour at that level, it's another thing entirely. I wanted to experience success again, and hopefully enjoy it this time.

But there was a problem: we didn't have a band! Jim and co had left. Also, Giorgio Kilkenny, the bass player, had disappeared without a trace shortly after we'd finished the 'Eileen' video, so now it was just me, Seb (drums) and Billy (guitar). There were three of us. Five had left!

The violinists Helen and Steve Shaw (whom we named Steve Brennan) had played on the album and were up for whatever we were doing. We enlisted some session musicians to fill the other roles, although John Edwards (bass) soon came to feel like much more.

Paul explained that with such a big band (11), to make it pay financially, we'd need to do two shows a night.

'Blimey! That's a lot, but OK, let's try it,' I said.

It was too much.

After some intense rehearsal, the new band were pretty good, initially at least. We had Seb keeping immaculate time on the drums, so nobody could go too far wrong. Plus, the set-up around us seemed to be far more professional than previously – we had a proper road crew, we were travelling on a coach as opposed to a minibus and, for those few weeks or couple of months, the sunlight of success was shining on us and I felt blessed.

Screaming, hysterical fans meant that we would sometimes have to fight our way into venues. I loved it – it made me feel like I was in the Beatles. Glasgow got a bit scary, though. Those 'Glasgee' gals were strong and relentless in their pursuit – some were kicking their way to the front of the scrum and, for a moment or two, I wondered if we were going to get torn to pieces. It was fun, though.

The sex thing was ridiculous. We had a system. After every show, we'd do a signing session, which was basically an excuse to meet girls.

The band would be on one side of the counter, the autograph seekers on the other. The women would usually be about ten deep. Paul Burton would be on the same side of the desk as the fans, but behind them. His eyes would be on me.

He would point down at a girl's head, to suggest 'her'?

I would nod my head, as if to say, 'Yes, that one.'

I would then nod in the direction of another one that I'd spotted. He would invite each chosen one back to the hotel for a party. The philosophy was, get as many girls back as possible and then choose.

On occasion, there would be 20 good-looking girls in the hotel bar. I would often feel embarrassed at the lack of men as I walked in. Sometimes I'd walk up and down the bar, choose one, and we'd go straight to my room.

It got so that I didn't appreciate the women fans on that tour. I think it was Cardiff where, post-show, I'd made my selection in the bar and we had gone upstairs. She was beautiful and I made moves to get into bed. But she said, 'Can we at least talk first?'

I said, 'Listen, I'm tired. I've done two shows today. It's one o'clock. I have to be up at seven for a long journey and I've got two shows to do tomorrow night. I'm getting into bed now. If you want to get in with me, great. If not, no problem, I'll go to sleep.'

She got in.

Bad behaviour on my part, I know. Acting like this made me value women less and therefore value humanity (including myself) less. I knew it wasn't really *me* they wanted. They didn't even know me. It was the *idea* of me, or because I was a bit famous.

That said, I made a great, genuine connection with two beautiful girls from Bournemouth, Sarah and Louise. I met them at our hotel after a gig. They seemed giggly and fun, so I said to Sarah, 'Why don't you and your pal come up to room 218?'

They did. I really loved sex with two women, but the thing I enjoyed most was the closeness – being lost in the warmth of their bodies, the three of us squeezed tightly together, feeling safe, at peace and at ease. I would ask one of them to lay on top of me while I lay on top of the other. I wanted to get lost in their warmth.

I enjoyed it so much that I asked them to come to the London show the following week.

· · ·

When we played at the Coventry Apollo on that tour, Mum and Dad and several other relatives came. It was an expansive, old, proper theatre.

Because it was a big venue, I had my own dressing room. It was a lovely big space, complete with a bowl of fruit and some flowers. My family were ushered in pre-show by a theatre staff member as I sat in my comfy armchair.

I felt truly successful and looked it as I sat in this beautiful dressing room before going out to perform to a sold-out theatre.

Dad walked in first. Barely acknowledging me, he walked past where I was sitting to the back of the room, despite there being several other chairs close to me. Still standing, he started knocking on the wall with his fist and said: 'These walls are not built properly.'

I felt vaguely irritated and said, 'Sit down, Dad!'

With hindsight, it seemed Dad was uncomfortable, seeing me so successful.

My family also came along to the London gig of that tour at the Shaftesbury Theatre. We did two shows. I was very nervous, as the second show was being filmed, and while I'm sure I could have performed better if I had been more relaxed, the band was such that it was never going to fall below a certain standard and it was actually a pretty good gig.

As well as a post-show drink in the theatre bar, there was an end-of-tour meal and party planned at a Mexican restaurant in Covent Garden.

Sarah and Louise from Bournemouth had come along and, because I didn't want my family to see me with two girls, I asked them to wait in the theatre stalls while I went into the bar for the post-gig drink. That was mean to them in itself but, worse, while in the bar I told my family there was no room at the restaurant. I very much wanted sex with those two girls, but I didn't want my family – as in, my parents – to know that I was with two women. Facing that kind of discomfort was inconceivable.

There was a coach outside the theatre to take us from the gig to the restaurant. I sat on the coach and looked out of the window and saw some of my family members. I felt ashamed.

· · ·

David 'Kid' Jensen, who had championed 'Eileen', had us on his radio show while 'Eileen' was at number one. He suggested 'All in All' should be the next single. I excitedly went back to the record company and told Roger. I thought David Jensen's backing would seal the deal for him – as well as being a great choice, it meant we would have David Jensen's backing.

He said, 'No. It's "Jackie Wilson Said".'

I felt deflated. Surely the fact that we were having such a big hit with one of our songs, with our own sound, meant we should follow it with something original?

He disagreed, but I knew that was the deal. I'd had my choice with 'Eileen'.

We had another meeting about it. Both Roger and manager Paul Burton wanted 'Jackie Wilson Said', and I didn't speak up strongly enough. Bizarrely, I thought I needed to keep the momentum and happy buzz going.

I even started asking loads of people that I didn't even respect for their opinion. I was in panic mode. When I made the point to Roger that 'Eileen' was string-led, while 'Jackie Wilson' was brass-led with quite a different sound, Roger suggested we replace the brass with strings. We ended up with the worst of all worlds. The new version didn't have the power of the brass-led album track.

Strangely, rather than feeling more confident in my own judgement, the success of 'Eileen' made me less so and more out of my depth.

Van Morrison was and is an artistic genius, but 'Jackie Wilson Said' was a lousy choice for a follow-up to 'Eileen', which was perhaps the most interesting and original pop song of the year, and we had more like that on the album. But we followed up 'Eileen' with a bloody cover version! Roger Ames did many great things for us, but this wasn't one of them.

· · ·

We developed pet or jokey names for many of our songs. 'Precious' became 'Precocious', 'Geno' was 'Beano' and our pet name for 'Jackie Wilson Said' was 'Jocky Wilson Said', after the famous darts player.

While on the 'Jackie Wilson' promotion trail, we did *Top of the Pops*. We were well into the touring/interview treadmill and I was getting bored and looking for ways to amuse myself.

On arrival at the *Top of the Pops* studio, I asked the producer if he would put up a great big picture of Jocky Wilson on the stage. He said, 'But surely some people will think it's a mistake?'

'Yeah, but only those with no sense of humour!' I replied.

He agreed. And I was delighted to see a big picture of Jocky Wilson being mounted at the back of our stage as we performed the song in front of millions of people. We all thought it was hilarious.

The prank received no attention, until three weeks later when Mike Read mentioned it on his breakfast show, presuming it to be a BBC error. When we next went back to *Top of the Pops*, a couple of months later, the same producer said, 'That Mike Read. He didn't get it, did he?'

'Nah,' I said.

Bizarrely, apart from that Mike Read mention, it went largely unnoticed until about 15 years later, when *Never Mind the Buzzcocks* (the satirical music TV programme) screened it. From that point, the story did the rounds of TV shows and had many mentions in the monthly rock magazines. One of them asked me to comment. I explained it was intentional, but they didn't believe me. 'Kevin Rowland claims it was intentional,' they said. As if neither me nor any of the other ten band members wouldn't have noticed a 20-foot picture of a big Scottish darts player on the stage with us!

'Jackie Wilson Said' peaked at number five in the UK charts. Which wasn't bad, of course, but following up 'Eileen', which had been number one for four weeks, it was a disappointment. I had hoped for another number one or top three to seal our reputation as a big group.

When it came to the next single, I took control, and instead of releasing 'All in All' or another ballad, I opted for a new song, 'Let's Get This Straight', which wasn't even on the album.

Basically, I went from one extreme to the other, in an angry reaction to Roger choosing 'Jackie Wilson Said'. I believed we had to show some kind of progression from 'Eileen', but I was actually overthinking it. All we needed to do was release a good song from the album, one that showed another side of us. But of course, hindsight is 20/20 vision. 'Let's Get This Straight' would peak at 17.

1985

1988

1991

1999

Performing at
Reading Festival
in 1999.

2003

2012

2013

Royal Festival Hall, 2016.

2016

Mum, aged 93.

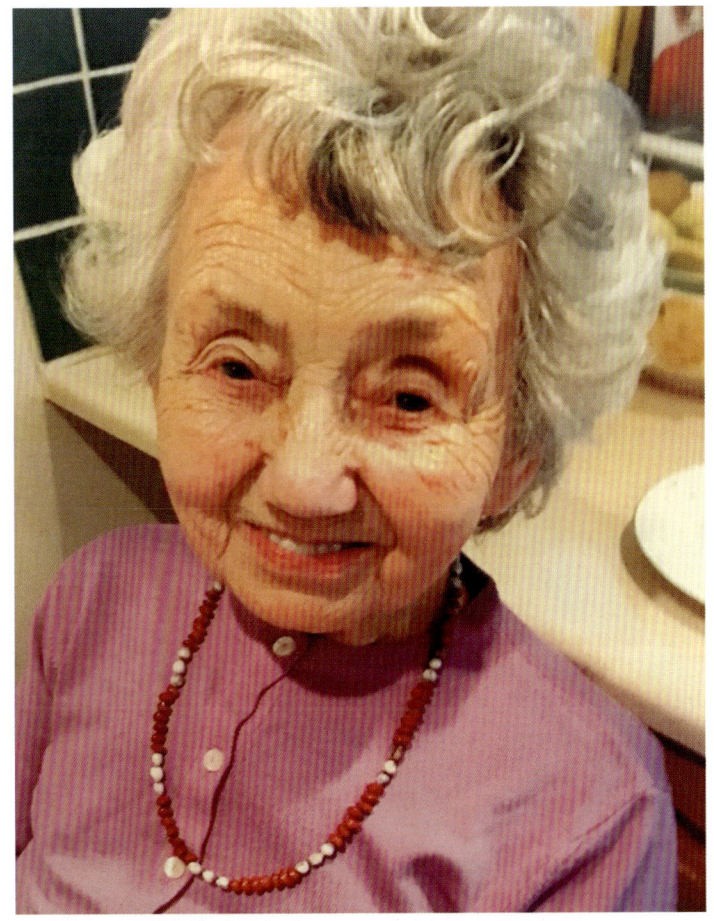

With Dad, aged 101.

2023

Glastonbury 2024

2025

I'm successful – I should be happy

For some time, I'd been noticing Helen. I was quite in awe of the way she conducted herself with real dignity among this bunch of largely marauding men.

Slowly but surely, my feelings towards her began to grow, and on the European tour that year, I decided to tell her how I felt. We went to a café in Germany for a cuppa.

I don't think she took me seriously at first – after all, she had seen me engage in all the marauding – but said she would think about it.

As the next couple of days turned into the best part of a week, it began to feel like life or death for me. Helen was hanging out with our drummer, Seb, a lot. I was so envious of him. My heart began to literally ache. I had never experienced that before. I would sometimes cry at night.

Previously, I had longed for the day Dexys would finally play Paris. Since my first time in that city, I have respected the Parisian people. They were stylish, sophisticated, and they seemed to understand what was important in life. It meant so much to me that we might be accepted there, and after Alain Weiss's rave review of *Searching for the Young Soul Rebels* in *Le Monde*, it looked possible.

That night, the audience were showering us with love. They seemed to know the words to both albums. But I couldn't embrace their enthusiasm. I was preoccupied with Helen. She was all I could think about.

After the show, as I lay in bed, I heard a couple in the next hotel room, having sex. I was convinced it was Helen and Seb. I found out the next day that it wasn't.

I was sure that I wanted to die if I couldn't have her. I didn't think I could stand the pain.

Finally, she agreed to go out with me. I couldn't believe my luck. I was elated but still nervous.

I felt very inferior to Helen in terms of upbringing and education. Not just her musical education, but also the fact that she had O levels and A levels and had gone to college. I was uneducated and felt out of my depth around her and her middle-class friends. They seemed to have a different way of relating to each other. There was a lot of teasing involved, which I felt uncomfortable with, being aware that if it was applied in the circles I was used to, it might well mean a fight.

Helen was taking our relationship much more in her stride than I was. I became obsessed with her. I couldn't see how she could be interested in me. I didn't feel I had anything to offer her. Every other man became a threat: Seb, other band members, Paul Burton, even the record company guys.

The more intense I became, the less she seemed to want to be with me. She wanted to have fun, understandably, but I was often downright miserable.

· · ·

The novelty of the pop success was over. It had become a machine, built around me. It was work, work, work. This was far bigger success than with the first album, maybe a hundred times bigger – we were getting popular all over the world, whereas the first album had only really sold in Britain.

No one around me knew how to handle what was happening. Certainly not Paul Burton. Meanwhile the record company had an attitude of, 'Just keep it going, lads.'

It was again a question of, 'Take it, it's yours.' But all I could see were the negatives. I wasn't happy with the band. We now had 11 musicians onstage and there didn't seem to be any real commitment from the seasoned session players, yet they started imposing their big personalities both during the day and onstage.

One or two of the session players were so out of synch with what we were doing, it was embarrassing. For example, during the more introspective, personal passages, one player in particular would subtly deride the moment by sniggering or doing a stupid little dance. I got the impression he thought I took the music too seriously. I thought he was a chancer.

Overall, the group was good but not a patch on what we had been the year before – yet ironically, we were playing to way bigger audiences. I was missing Jim and his deep understanding of our music.

When we performed below par, I took it personally and felt very low. Sometimes, in a desperate attempt to create some fire, I would pose at being intense, hoping for something to happen, instead of being natural and allowing inspiration to flow.

The core of the group – full-time members Seb and Billy – were still really committed, and the fiddle players Helen and Steve, who were new to the music business, were a positive presence, as was our session bassist John Edwards. The other session musicians, less so.

I could have been more forceful about what I needed, but I felt intimidated by these guys. They were very confident. I let too much build up inside of me and then occasionally let it all out with a bang, instead of picking up on the small points as they happened. The dominant force in a big band needs to be the one that is focused on making the music as good as possible. When the focus becomes about something else, it's always a journey downhill.

My life had changed, big time. I continued to live in Birmingham in an attempt to be normal, but there was nothing normal about my life any more. I would have been better off moving to London.

There were now far more fans coming up to me in the street than ever before. For that period in 1982–83, Dexys' UK profile was very high. We did a lot of big TV shows. And in those days, TV was much more powerful than it is now. There were only four TV channels, and pretty much everyone watched the pop shows.

All of a sudden, fans of Dexys' *music* weren't coming up to speak to me any more; people who had seen me on *TV* were coming up to me, purely because I was famous. That's a whole different thing and I wasn't cut out for it. I felt like a trophy, and I hated it.

What's wrong with me? Why am I not enjoying this? I would think. *I've got everything I've always wanted, haven't I? I'm successful. I should be happy.*

I really thought I was going mad. I felt a pressure to shine and look grateful. So I pretended.

There *was* stuff I liked about it, especially at first. Seeing my picture in magazines, if it was a good shot. I liked the fact that we had records in the charts, and they sounded good – I've never got tired of finishing a good record and wondering at it, thinking, *How the fuck did that happen?* Or making a good video or doing a good photo shoot. The creative stuff, I loved. And in that way, on many occasions, I felt blessed. Travelling, I also enjoyed, especially to New York.

Overall, though, I had no idea how to handle what was happening. It seemed everyone was staring at me. I felt on permanent show. I thought that I needed to act a certain way, but I didn't quite know what that way was: grateful if I met fans or record company execs; arrogant onstage and with the media. It was exhausting.

For about six months, every time I walked down the street in Birmingham, it caused a scene. I would get the bus – probably a stupid thing to do, but I didn't have a car at the time and I guess I was trying to be normal. I'd end up signing autographs for everybody on board, and the driver would stop the bus and come into the passenger deck to talk to me. I would try getting a taxi, and drivers would say, 'Please let me take you back to our cab office and meet the girls.'

It was taking me ages to get anywhere, but I found it very hard to refuse these requests, even if I was rushing for a train. If I did refuse, I'd feel incredibly guilty. I didn't have any life skills, as people call them nowadays.

If I walked into a pub, the conversation would stop and the place would go silent. It was at this point that I realised how much of an observer I am. I had always watched people's idiosyncrasies, their clothes, the way they walk, talk. But now I couldn't observe any more. I was the observed.

When I met old friends, all they wanted to talk about was what I was doing. It sounded so exciting to them. But I wanted to know what *they* were doing. I craved normality. I didn't know anyone else whose life was anything like mine. In truth, the people I would have most identified with would have been other recording artists, other singers, in London, in clubs. But I had cut myself off in Birmingham. I didn't even know any of them.

It was pretty much the same with family. And I see now that on some deep level I felt guilty because I was more successful and had more money than my dad and others in the family. That was very scary. It wasn't supposed to be that way. I was the fuck-up in the family. They were all so excited and happy for me, but I didn't feel that way.

As I write, I'm aware that this might sound like some ungrateful pop singer complaining about being in a privileged position. And to some extent that is true – I *was* ungrateful. But I agree with what Jim Carrey said: 'I wish everyone could be rich and famous … so that they could find out that it's not the answer.' That's certainly true in my case. In fact, it brought with it a whole raft of other problems that I was ill-equipped to deal with.

Fame intensifies your feelings. If you were prone to the habit of worrying what people were thinking about you before you got famous, believe me, it's going to increase tenfold if you put some fame on top of it.

I thought being well known would make me more confident. The opposite happened. You can't switch fame off. The only alternative is to stay in. And from the end of that touring cycle, that's pretty much what I did.

On one particularly tough day, I took the unusual step of opening up to my dad. 'So many people are coming up to me, I'm finding it hard.'

He said, 'You want to start worrying when they are not coming upon you.' He obviously couldn't understand.

I tried to ignore my troubled feelings but sometimes they would spill out.

When in London, we stayed in the big Tara Hotel in Kensington. After a long journey, I went to make a call from my room. I lifted up the receiver to dial, but instead of the dialling tone I heard a woman's voice. It was the hotel operator: 'Remember you promised to get me some signed pictures. Where are they? You didn't get them, did you?'

I didn't have any pictures. I had tried.

I didn't know what to say to her. I hated disappointing people.

Paul Burton was no help with that stuff. He was having a great time, partying. I was working all hours and so many people were asking me for photos to sign. I had asked Paul repeatedly, but nothing came.

When I was a kid, I'd seen Ken Dodd walking into the London Palladium, just before I bunked into his show. I asked for an autograph and he pulled out a handful of photographs and signed them. That meant a lot. And it instilled in me a sense of responsibility to my own fans.

When a fan or service person or whatever came to my home, I would end up giving away Dexys records because I didn't have any photos to sign; consequently, I only have one Dexys single left.

I'd be angry at Paul for not getting me the pictures, angry at someone like the phone operator at the Tara for driving me mad, but I would do my utmost not to show it, because that would make me look ungrateful.

I also started to resent the fact that I was making money for people whose views I didn't like. I can remember overhearing Paul Burton chatting with a couple of the *Too Rye Ay* session players and they were all talking about how they liked Margaret Thatcher. I couldn't believe it. I hated her. I think it was the fact that they felt safe enough to talk loudly about it, within earshot of me, that annoyed me most. I guess I should have spoken up.

· · ·

Sometimes at night, as I tried to get off to sleep, my body would feel as if it was being propelled skywards by an invisible but very powerful fountain beneath me. I was going higher and higher. It was very scary – I couldn't stop myself going up. I thought I was getting too successful. That it was really out of control and I needed to come down.

Whatever it was, it scared the shit out of me and, during a particularly intense episode in New York, I called a doctor out and told him what was happening. He didn't say much but prescribed me some sleeping pills. They were very strong – to the extent that even after having a good night's sleep, I would still feel drowsy the next day, and often quite grumpy and not give a fuck about what I said or did.

For example, we went to Rome to record a TV show. I had taken a sleeping pill the night before. As we got ready to do the show, I kept thinking about a popular saying: *When in Rome, do as the Romans do.*

I also recalled, from when I was a kid, one of my aunties saying that Roman men always pinched women's bums. Of course, being only seven at the time, it didn't make much sense to me. But I decided to link the two clichés.

For the TV show's opening, I was asked to stand next to the pretty female presenter. After the opening credits, the camera would cut to her face. She would say a few words, then the camera would slowly pan out to include my face and shoulders, then the shot would keep expanding until both of our bodies were in full shot.

I made sure there was a six-inch gap between her and myself. As the camera panned out to reveal my face, I adopted a Benny Hill-type leering grin. By the time the shot had widened and lengthened enough to reveal our hips, my arm could be clearly seen behind her bum, giving the impression that I was fondling her buttocks. I wasn't, of course. My hand was about six inches behind her bum, but from the front, it looked absolutely like I was touching her.

The band, the female presenter, the cameramen and even the director all roared with laughter.

They prepared to retake the clip. I promised this time I would do it properly. And I intended to, but when it came to it, I just couldn't help myself. The camera pulled away, once again revealing my very happy gurning smile, with my arm at a right angle to her bum – this time I added some circular movements for good measure.

I kept saying to the crew: 'When in Rome, do as the Romans do! I'm in Rome. What can I do? It's not my fault!'

'OK, that was funny, but now we must do it properly,' they said.

'Of course,' I said.

I pledged solemnly that I would indeed do it properly this time, and absolutely meant to. But I just couldn't resist. On would come the happy smile with the mad eyes, and out would go my wandering, swirling hand. Everybody laughed, but the crew and the presenter said, 'OK. It's funny, but we must do it properly now.'

I apologised and promised faithfully that this time I would not mess around and would give this thing the proper respect it deserved.

But I didn't. I couldn't.

They tried another couple of times after that, and still I kept doing it. Finally, they just shot our faces.

The sleeping pills gave me a 'don't give a fuck' attitude and sometimes released a lot of anger in me.

In June 1983, we were in Paris, in a taxi on our way to the first of two gigs supporting David Bowie at a big outdoor venue. I'd taken a sleeping pill the night before and angrily ignored the taxi driver's 'No Smoking' signs and protestations about my cigarette smoke.

'I'm opening a fucking window, all right?' I shouted at him from the back seat.

It was the Serious Moonlight tour. Bowie had a different support act for each city. Before the show I did an interview with a Parisian TV presenter, during which she asked me about a rumour she'd heard that we had paid to get the support slot. I told her that was nonsense. We were actually being paid £25,000 for the two nights. A lot of money in those days.

The gig itself was going well. We were about five songs in, and I could feel the set building nicely, as it usually did. We were getting a good response from the crowd, many of whom were familiar with us – we had a good loyal following in Paris.

I was heartened to hear the applause coming at the end of every song, even from way back in the 15,000-strong crowd. I usually enjoyed gigs with big audiences and often rose to the occasion. Strangely, I found massive gigs much easier than intimate shows.

There were about 200 guys down at the front of the crowd who were mostly shirtless. They were moshing about in the mud and chanting something that was indecipherable to me. I thought it was in French, and it seemed to be something positive. Not being able to speak French, and wanting to understand what they were saying, so I could maybe pay them some respect by replying in French, I walked over to Seb, our drummer, who *did* speak French, and asked him to translate.

Quietly, he said, 'They're shouting "Bowie, Bowie".'

I was shocked. We were going down well and were *playing* well. Clearly, it was only this bunch of mud freaks at the front, but I was incensed.

What about us? I thought. *What about what we're doing? This is good music!*

Maybe I should have ignored the chanting and given my attention to the vast majority of people there who were enjoying the show. But I was severely riled.

I walked back to my microphone and addressed the 200 at the front. 'You silly cunts have paid good money to sit in a filthy, muddy field, waiting all day, just to see David Bowie? You're fucking stupid, because he's nothing but a pale imitation of Bryan Ferry.'

I felt completely justified. *Fuck 'em!*

We started the next song. After about a minute, the sound went dead. I thought the PA had broken down, but no, Bowie's people had pulled the plug. Bouncers and roadies angrily beckoned us from the side of the stage.

The gig was over. I'm told Bowie had been watching from the back of the stage and had heard what I'd said, but I don't know if that's true.

Our manager and agent were freaked. The blood had drained from their faces, but it didn't even faze me. I felt justified. Some of the others in our party were nervous that some rough stuff might take place, but nothing did. A few big bouncers and roadies were puffing their chests out, and some were clenching their fists, but I didn't take it seriously. I just saw it as posturing and walked confidently past them. We were paid in full for the two nights and of course not required to return the following evening.

Of course I shouldn't have insulted Bowie. I thought he was a great talent. I'd been a fan, especially of *Young Americans*. In fact, the vocal arrangement on the *Too Rye Ay* version of 'Liars A to E' was inspired by that album.

Many years later, I wrote Bowie a letter of apology. I was glad to have it confirmed by a mutual acquaintance that he'd received the letter. I didn't get a reply.

Any figures sounded like abstract fortunes

With Helen, things weren't moving forward. We would disagree and bicker over just about anything.

Finally, in a last-ditch attempt to get close to her, I plucked up the courage to ask her to go on holiday with me for a few days. We had been working so hard and hadn't had a break in ages. There was a five-day gap in our schedule. To my surprise, she agreed.

It was my dad's 65th birthday a few days before we left and my family were throwing a surprise party for him in Coventry. I invited Helen and she agreed to come. As I walked in, wearing my newly purchased Ivy League clothes, my sister-in-law Margaret said, 'You look like an extra from *The Graduate*.'

I was thrilled! I had recently developed a passion for US collegiate clothes, and for Brooks Brothers in particular. On a promotional trip to New York, I walked past a Brooks Brothers window display and was delighted to see a jacket with patch pockets and raised edging on all the seams. It was of course so similar to the really cool clothes that were around in late-sixties London. This was the start of my second Ivy League obsession, and led to the look we wore around what would become the *Don't Stand Me Down* album.

That night, I started to notice a real softening between Helen and me. Previously, if we went to a social gathering, she would often be talking to other people and I would hardly see her. But at this party, as I was chatting to some relatives in the kitchen, I glanced over at Helen and noticed that she was giving me intermittent long warm looks.

A couple of days later, we went to Tenerife. It was a new resort at the time. We sunbathed for a day or two, but couldn't really agree on what else to do. As we lay on sunbeds, I made the suggestion that the next day we might get a packed lunch from the hotel and take a taxi out into the hills, spend a few hours there, and then be picked up at a prearranged time by the cabbie.

Helen said firmly, 'I'm not going out into the middle of nowhere with no clear way of getting back.'

I took her refusal as a personal rejection. My plan had been to get us up in the hills in a romantic setting, to try and get close to her. I lay there, feeling resentful, for about half an hour.

Is this ever going to work? I wondered. *It's been such a struggle. Maybe I should just give up?*

Finally, I decided I would have one last try. 'Helen.'

She looked up from her sun haze. She had a sultry glow about her and seemed much more relaxed now.

'Yeah?'

(Pause.)

'Do you love me?'

Almost instantly she said, 'Yes,' with a half-smile on her face. I was shocked.

'What? Really?'

'Yes,' she said.

She was smiling broadly now, and seemed pleased that I was so happy.

The words 'Will you marry me?' just flew out of my mouth. I hadn't planned to say it.

'Marry you?' she repeated in shock.

(Pause.)

'Blimey! Er … Yeah, all right then.' She smiled again.

I couldn't believe it. 'Are you sure?' I said.

'Yeah, if you are.'

'Oh yeah. I'm sure!'

All those months of turmoil and struggling just melted away. We were now totally at ease with each other, happy, and so close.

· · ·

Clearly, a lot of money would be coming in soon. Manager Paul Burton, together with my solicitor, was doing recording royalty deals with Seb and Billy – the two remaining band members who had originally signed to the label. The others, who had all left, including Jim, had received lump sums in buyout deals, precluding them from any future recording royalties. The remainder of the money was due to me.

Paul Burton had previously told me that his mother helped with the accounts in his hairdressing business – basically, looking after the money. I thought: *That's a good idea. I'll get my dad to look after my accounts.*

Whatever else about my relationship with Dad, I knew that he was meticulous with money, and if he was involved in the bookkeeping, I wouldn't have to worry about it. He had recently retired from his building firm.

I told Paul Burton that I was going to have my dad keep my books. 'OK,' he said.

Meanwhile, I was planning to move into a new flat with Helen. My high profile was making it hard for me to continue living in the house I'd bought in Bearwood. I would be sitting in the front room on a summer evening, watching TV, and I'd see a bunch of young faces peering in the window at me. I decided I would get a nice flat on an upper level.

My finances were obviously looking good so, as a gesture, I made the decision to sell my house to my dad for a knock-down price of £25,000 (it was worth £35,000). He liked the idea and wanted to rent it out as flats. I told Paul Burton what I was doing.

He said, 'You don't wanna do that. You're gonna need that money when you get married.'

I didn't respond or think anything more of it.

One morning about a week later, I was woken by Paul Burton knocking on my front door. He had an older, prim-looking lady with him. They bowled into my place, all bubbly and friendly. Paul said something along the lines of: 'Kev, you've got to meet this lady, she's absolutely lovely. She'll take care of the house for you, no problem.'

The lady had a big smile on her face. She said, 'Don't worry. Leave it to me. Oh, this is a lovely big house. I'll sell this in no time.'

Paul left almost immediately. He was all smiles.

The woman said, 'He mentioned that you were nervous about it. But don't worry, I'll take care of everything.' And with that, she started measuring up.

It seemed odd, but I didn't think much of it at the time.

I phoned my mum a few days later from Europe. Dad came on the phone, sounding angry. While I was away, the estate agents had put up a 'For Sale' sign outside the house. Dad had driven past and seen it. He opened the conversation with: 'It's funny how the more money people get, the more mean they get.'

I didn't even know they were going to put the sign up. I suspect now Paul had asked them to.

Obviously, I was in the wrong, but I'm sure that if Dad had approached me softly, saying he was disappointed, I'd have reacted differently. As it was, Dad's anger triggered me and I went on the defensive. A part of me enjoyed having a reason to stand up to him. In any event, the situation caused a rift between us.

I don't know if this was Paul's way of putting some distance between Dad and me, to keep Dad away from the books.

It does seem strange that Paul and the estate agent turned up together, first thing in the morning. He would have had to make an appointment. He didn't tell me about it, and he went to a lot of trouble about something that wasn't even within his remit. That was more than unusual for him. Also, he left almost immediately after ushering her in, making me think he was uncomfortable, and leaving no time for questions.

· · ·

I had barely seen Jim since he'd left Dexys. He was now living in London. I popped round to his place one day, unannounced. I was nervous because I didn't know if Jim and his wife Sandra would want to see me. They were both friendly, however, though I still felt a distance.

I wanted to start writing with Jim again but was too nervous to ask him. At the very least, I wanted Jim to play on the next album.

We made arrangements for him and Sandra to come up for a social visit to Helen and me, in the new flat. I was really happy to see them, and we started to chat but Jim kept popping out to the toilet. After a while, I said, 'Are you all right, Jim?'

'Sorry I keep going to the loo,' he said. 'Rather than hide it, I'll just tell ya that I went in there to sniff some coke.'

'Oh, OK,' I said.

'Do you mind if I do it here?'

'Sure. No problem, Jim. Have you got any more?'

A couple of years earlier, as a band, we'd all had some coke in Amsterdam. I had liked it, though found it very moreish.

'I've got a little bit left,' Jim said.

'Can I have some, Jim?'

'Yeah. Sure.'

'Here y'are, Jim. Do it on the table.'

Jim put out a few small lines.

'Helen, do you want a line of cocaine?'

'No, thank you.'

We sniffed them up.

'Ah that's good,' I said. 'Got any more, Jim?'

'Nah, that's the last of it.'

'Bugger!'

Helen went back into the kitchen to finish cooking the meal. A few minutes later, the nice feeling started to subside, and the idea of having another line of cocaine seemed more and more important.

'Shit! I'd love some more coke,' I said. 'Hang on! I know a guy, Harry, in the town who sells it. He usually serves up at the Rum Runner. Fancy a little wander up there, Jim?'

'Yeah, OK,' Jim said.

'Helen, just gonna pop up the Rum Runner with Jim to get some more coke.'

'What? What are you doing? The meal's ready!'

'Won't be long, Hel.'

We went to the Rum Runner. No Harry!

'Do you know where he lives?' I said to the bouncer.

'Yeah, he lives on top of the Post Office in Harborne. You have to go round the back to get in.'

'Thanks.'

We trawled around Harborne, trying to find Harry, but no joy.

Finally, we went back to the flat. Helen was annoyed and somewhat freaked out. Aside from the fact that the dinner was ruined, she couldn't understand what had come over me.

It would be four years before I touched cocaine again.

. . .

In spring 1983, Seb, our drummer, contacted me and asked if we could meet to talk about his financial deal. I had presumed he would just get an even split of the royalties, as he was signed to the label. I didn't understand the need for another deal, but didn't question it, as I remembered a conversation a few months earlier with Paul, when I said to him, 'Surely we should all get the same, right?'

'No. In my experience, that never works,' Paul had told me. 'Those that are doing less feel guilty. And those who are doing more often get resentful for doing all the work.'

I hadn't given it any more thought, but if Seb and Paul were agreed that this was what should happen, it was fine by me. There was clearly plenty of money coming in anyway, and any figures sounded like abstract fortunes – we had been broke for years.

Seb and I met at Covent Garden station and went for a cup of tea. He seemed really troubled and vulnerable. I'd never seen him that way. He told me that he had been speaking to Paul about his deal – a percentage of the royalties from *Too Rye Ay*. I hadn't even known that any conversations of that nature had been taking place.

He said that during the talks, which were solely handled by Paul and the lawyer, he was being given the runaround. They had agreed on a royalty figure that all parties were happy with, but when Seb went to the lawyer's office to sign the papers, he found the figure to be lower than what had been agreed. He was told that the contract would need to be redrawn, and that he would have to return on another day to sign it.

'I'm being messed around, Kev,' he said.

I felt for the guy. I phoned Paul and asked him what had happened.

He said, 'Oh, sorry. I hold my hands up on that one. It was totally my mistake!'

Somehow, it didn't ring true. If they had agreed on a figure, why should it be less when the papers were drawn up? And why couldn't it be amended immediately, so that Seb could sign on the day as planned?

This was one of the few occasions that I stood up to Paul. 'Come on, man! Seb deserves to be treated properly!'

With hindsight, I see that even prior to this, Paul had become quite anti-Seb in his conversations with me, dropping in subtle put-downs. Was Paul trying to drive a wedge between Seb and me? I don't know. But I *do* know that Seb would've been the one person in the band who wouldn't have been shy about raising questions over money.

To be fair, I didn't need too much encouragement with Paul's campaign against Seb. Helen and Seb were very close, particularly in the early days of our relationship, and I saw him as a threat. But in no way did I want to see the man get ripped off. I was angry with Paul, and I'm glad Seb finally got the deal he wanted.

Seb *did* seem to be moving away from Dexys and didn't want to leave his home in London to be in Birmingham, where we always rehearsed. Previously, he would stay at my place and go home on weekends.

Historically, he would always make positive comments when I showed the band a new song, but when we presented him with the pieces for *Don't Stand Me Down*, he was quiet and non-committal. He was going more into himself and seemed very different to the guy I'd known a few years earlier. He had married Helen's sister, Kate, so it's understandable that he didn't want to be away from his wife. But I've heard through the grapevine, as well as in an interview he did, that he subsequently blames me for the shenanigans that went on around his deal. I had absolutely nothing to do with it, apart from stepping in and helping him when Paul was messing him around. I didn't even take any interest in my *own* finances, never mind anyone else's.

Also, when I went to visit Seb some years later, in the nineties, to make amends for any harm I'd caused him, as I did with all band members, he mentioned a couple of other things but nothing financial.

I liked Seb. He was an incredible drummer. His musical hero was Al Jackson, who drummed on all the great Al Green stuff. Al Jackson was my favourite drummer too. I was sad that Seb left before we started recording *Don't Stand Me Down*.

I knew at the completion of *Too Rye Aye* that much of it didn't sound as good as it should have, and I felt embarrassed about that. 'Eileen' and one or two others came out really well, but largely I felt the mixing could have been much better. I asked the label for more funds to fix some of the tracks, but they refused. I put my misgivings to the back of my mind and got carried along with the success, like everyone else.

But by 1983, I was coming down. Much of the album sounded tinny. The songs were good and the performances were too, which meant it was never going to fall below a certain standard, but I knew it could have been a lot better than it was. I felt duplicitous that I had been promoting a product that I knew was under par. Also, because of the success of 'Eileen', I felt that I was now being seen as Mr Pop and I wasn't comfortable with that.

I had thought I wanted some of the Adam Ant type of success. Now I didn't feel good enough about my looks, for one thing. But more than that, it seemed shallow, and by this time I was learning that being famous is like a separate job in itself.

People close to me seemed to enjoy our success much more than I did. I can't blame them for that. What's wrong with enjoying success? I wish I had learned how to relax and have a good time.

When we got the news that 'Jackie Wilson' had gone down to number 12 – having peaked at number five – Paul, Helen and I were sitting at breakfast in our hotel a couple of days after the 1982 London show. I was disappointed and said: 'I never wanted that song released anyway!'

Paul angrily shut me down, saying, 'Don't start that, 'cos it serves no purpose.'

My honeymoon period with pop was over. I'd enjoyed the chart success up to that point. But now I yearned to do something with more depth and to be respected for it.

A year later I read an interview with Sting where he said, 'All of last year's heroes have blown it.' I felt sure he was talking about me.

'Endearing Young Charms'

In our new apartment complex, Helen and I were not surrounded by creative people. We were surrounded by bores, bragging about what they'd got (I would end up mentioning them in our song 'This Is What She's Like').

I didn't know it then, but when I moved into that flat, in summer '83, I was retreating from life and from all competition. This period lasted four or five months. All I wanted to do was watch TV, drink tea and smoke cigarettes.

Helen later said that she felt frustrated that I wasn't doing any music. But I absolutely hated the idea of it. I was trying to find some sense of meaning or normality. Basically, I was burned out from all the promotion.

I started to buy left-wing and Irish republican books and newspapers. I also attended public meetings about political action, in particular getting the British troops out of Ireland. I joined the Troops Out movement. I'd always believed they shouldn't be there and that the British border in Ireland was a disaster, but I'd only ever previously expressed it privately.

As Helen and I would arrive at the Troops Out meetings, we would face angry 'greeting committees' of local British Movement or National Front members – this was still only a few years after the horrendous Birmingham pub bombings.

Many of these BM/NF boys were skinheads, and I suspected some may have been 'Geno'-period Dexys fans. I felt vaguely embarrassed at being recognised by them as we ran the gauntlet of their insults.

1981, had been a pivotal time in Ireland. No one could help but notice the astonishing bravery of Bobby Sands and the nine other Irish republican prisoners who starved themselves to death on hunger strike in protest at the British government's attempt to criminalise the Irish freedom struggle.

I'd always been ambivalent about my Irish roots. I'd heard too much of the 'everything Irish is great, everything English is shit' nonsense, often from people whose personalities I wasn't attracted to. Plus, I had further confusion because I felt I didn't look Irish. That concerned me – more about what others thought than anything else.

But even when I hadn't been actively following what was happening in the Six Counties, I always knew that the republicans were being wilfully misunderstood by a hysterical British media and hence the UK public was only getting a fraction of the true story.

I knew, too, that the Northern six-county statelet was gerrymandered and rigged so that Catholics would never get to share power, and that successive British governments had failed to address the shocking injustices that were so entrenched there or give protection to those who dared to protest at the discrimination. On the contrary, the sectarian armed police force, armed militia and British Army tried to crush the protests with the likes of the Burntollet Bridge incident, Ballymurphy massacre and Bloody Sunday. I also knew that since the early seventies, Irish internees and prisoners were being tortured by British soldiers and the Crown forces in their own country.

Now I really wanted to learn more about Ireland. I'd been so consumed with Dexys for the previous five years that I had thought about little else. So much so that I barely even took it to heart when, after playing 'Come on Eileen', BRMB Radio – a big local radio station based in Birmingham – immediately apologised to anyone who might be offended by them playing a song with Irish connections (there had been an IRA bomb in London, the day before). That just felt normal. I was so used to the way things were that I even felt vaguely guilty for being Irish and having republican views. Anti-Irish feeling in Birmingham was very dominant. Anything Irish was strictly underground. For example, Dexys had played Irish clubs in Birmingham and learned that they were banned from advertising by the police for fear of reprisal.

There was no alternative view being presented in the media, and Ireland was not a topic of conversation that most people welcomed.

Nobody was interested in the injustice that was going on there. They only wanted to talk about the *results* of that injustice – the fact that some Irish people had taken up arms.

Obviously, if I'd been hanging out with left-wing British middle-class people, some of those might have been sympathetic to the Irish cause, but most working-class English people I knew in Birmingham didn't want to hear about it.

Dexys were never specifically trying to appeal to an Irish audience. We didn't go all-out Irish in our music. We had too many other influences, and I never wanted to be pinned down to any one thing, but the line-up of fiddles, accordion, banjo, tin whistle etc., paired with a basic rhythm section, plus the references in 'Eileen' and other songs on *Too Rye Ay*, were obvious to anyone of Irish extraction or any keen observer of culture and music. I'm proud of that. And I really liked it when I heard that I was popular among other second-generation Irish people, and that us putting Irish influences into our music meant a lot to them.

In the early summer of 1983, I read about a new band, Pogue Mahone (shortly after to be known as the Pogues) fronted by Shane MacGowan, another second-generation Irish guy who I knew a little from around London. His previous band, the Nips, had supported early Dexys on a couple of shows.

I read that his new outfit were using Irish influences, as well as having a similar line-up to what we had used on much of *Too Rye Ay*. I was delighted and I felt we could be allies.

It was announced that the band would be playing a small pub venue, the Hope and Anchor in Islington. I excitedly made plans to attend. A week before the gig, their first interview appeared in the *NME*. The journalist was enthusiastic, but at one stage asked them a question: Hang on: you've got a fiddle, an accordion, a banjo, a tin whistle and you're putting Irish influences into your music. Surely this is ground already covered by Dexys Midnight Runners? Shane replied that, while he liked our first album a lot, what we were doing now was lightweight, and the fact that we had used a fiddle riff on 'Eileen' from the Irish poet Thomas Moore's song 'Endearing Young Charms' meant that we weren't authentic, given that Moore's music was popular with British high society in the 19th century.

Many years later, the interviewer in question, Gavin Martin, told me that he felt Shane's comment was pre-rehearsed and that he had said it with a smile on his face. He believed that Shane felt he *had* to slag Dexys off, to justify the Pogues' existence.

Whatever the motivation, it intensely triggered my feelings of inferiority. Instead of seeing the situation as a rival musician feeling he had to slag me off, as Gavin Martin believed, I took it to heart.

All through the making of *Don't Stand Me Down* and beyond, the Pogues were living in my head and I felt usurped by them. It would be many years before I could begin to appreciate their music and, even now, ambivalent feelings remain.

When *Don't Stand Me Down* came out, I was asked about them in a magazine interview and I slagged them. Then in 1987, I was in the bar of the Limelight club and Shane walked up to me and asked me how I was doing. I couldn't bear it.

'Fuck off,' I said. 'You're stage Irish.'

He said some stuff back, but not much. Like me, he was with a woman, and both of them intervened to keep us apart.

Some years later, when I got into recovery, I attempted to make amends to Shane. I made an appointment to see him, but he didn't show up.

As I look at it now, I know that *Too Rye Ay* was far from lightweight and I don't need to try and prove my point, but I will say that songs like 'Until I Believe in My Soul' and 'The Waltz' (during which I sang a little in the Irish language) had way more depth than on our first album. And more than that, my parents and aunts and uncles didn't have the luxury of time to check who wrote a song to see if it was credible before singing it.

As for the accusation that we shouldn't have quoted from 'Endearing Young Charms', that's ridiculous. Singing that song and many like it was a great comfort to my family and wider relatives who were working their arses off, exiled in England and missing home – Connaught, the poorest part of Ireland. I too benefited from hearing the beauty in those songs and the emotion that came across when my family sang them. Saying that working-class Irish people like my family shouldn't enjoy something because Thomas Moore wrote it is akin to saying Irish people shouldn't read Shakespeare. My parents were working-class Irish people. Not Bohemians or academics.

Of course, the Pogues took the whole Irish thing much further than us and created something totally unique. I didn't have the knowledge of Irish history or traditional music that Shane had. But I am proud of the fact that I was the first of my era of second-generation Irish musicians to put some Irish influence into their music. Our song 'The Celtic Soul Brothers' was written in 1981 and came out in March 1982, followed by 'Come on Eileen' in early summer '82. Both songs, especially 'Eileen', flaunted my Irishness. The Pogues did their first gig in October 1982.

But now, I was going deeper into my Irishness. It was a real calling.

I started to read books about the Irish situation and its history. Kevin Kelley's *The Longest War* was brilliant and thorough, as was Eamonn McCann's *War and an Irish Town*. Also, I started to meet a few republicans in Birmingham and eventually Belfast and Derry.

Going to the Six Counties and seeing people with very little resources doing their best to live with dignity, while under constant harassment, was inspiring. In fact, it was daunting, to the point of making me feel that what I was doing – making pop music – was shallow and meaningless.

Even through my considerable pop-singer arrogance, I couldn't fail to be right-sized from talking to these people. They were living under constant fear of attack and death, enduring the most challenging circumstances on a daily basis. I found their courage way beyond my sphere of understanding. It was only later, when processing it, I realised they were not only unsung heroes, they were also being constantly denigrated and abused for their efforts. I don't know how they stood it.

The UK tabloid rags, and even the broadsheets, portrayed almost anybody who believed in Irish unity as terrorist supporters, while being completely blind to the terror being waged on Irish people by the British forces.

Republicans and nationalists existed in the North in enclaves, with virtually no outside support. They had to do everything for themselves. In the early days of the conflict, whenever there were street protests, the authorities would withdraw public transport from working-class nationalist areas for days on end. In response, the local people bought a load of old London taxis and created their own transport system. The state refused to recognise the Gaelic language or grant aid to schools teaching it, so Gaelic speakers started their own Irish-speaking schools. Local government ignored their requests to name their streets in Irish, so at night they would replace the British street names with Irish ones. Local and UK media couldn't be relied upon to truthfully report what was happening, so people produced their own newspapers.

The British Army were not there as peace-makers but to uphold British rule by defending the status quo and helping loyalism in all its forms, from the Royal Ulster Constabulary to the Ulster Defence Regiment – both of which were armed and sectarian and almost exclusively Protestant. Many of their members were also in loyalist paramilitary groups, to whom the state forces would feed names of Irish republicans to execute. No one now doubts the extent of collusion between the state and loyalist paramilitary surrogates, many of whose victims were not in the IRA. For example, the lawyer Pat Finucane, who came to prominence after his successful challenge of the British government in several important human rights cases and was killed by loyalist paramilitaries from the Ulster Defence Association, all agents of British Intelligence.

The war in Ireland was not between Catholics and Protestants. That was just the spin the British put on it so they could look like Honest Joe, trying to keep these 'uncivilised' Irish from killing each other. The truth is, the Northern Ireland statelet was set up by the British to support the loyalists, who were charged with keeping the 'disloyal Catholics' in their place. This they did with relish. A unionist prime minister boasted in 1934: 'We are a Protestant parliament and a Protestant state.'

Many people in the UK don't know about the discrimination in voting, housing and employment that made Catholics very much second-class citizens.

I also imagine that few people in the UK know that it was illegal to raise the Irish national flag, the Tricolour, in the Six Counties until 1987. Those who did were often dealt with forcibly and sometimes violently by the armed Royal Ulster Constabulary. That's why the RUC in full riot gear often stormed republican funerals – to remove the Tricolour from the coffin. The Irish weren't allowed to raise an Irish flag in their own country!

This latest bout of the centuries-old conflict kicked off in the late sixties when, inspired by the civil rights movement in the US, which was all over the TV, Catholics and some progressive Protestants started to protest and march for equal rights for Catholics. One of their most popular chants was, 'One Man, One Vote'.

In the case of the January 1969 march led by students from Belfast to Derry, the Royal Ulster Constabulary rerouted the marchers straight into a trap at Burntollet Bridge, where they were attacked by a mob of 300 loyalists, a hundred of whom were off-duty police officers. The unarmed marchers were beaten with stones transported from a nearby quarry, as well as iron bars and sticks spiked with nails. It was bloody.

Clearly, the Catholic/nationalist people couldn't trust the sectarian police force. Before long, some of them took up arms to protect themselves, especially after many were burned out and evicted from their homes by mobs, supported by the police who opened fire into Catholic homes from armoured cars.

Of course, the IRA made some horrific mistakes, but certainly no more than the British, and that, very sadly, is war.

On returning to England, I couldn't help but be staggered at how little people knew about what was actually going on in a part of the 'United Kingdom'.

Even many on the left were unaware about Ireland. A good example is when Helen and I were walking through the West End of London one day and came across thousands of people returning from a

CND march. Nuclear disarmament is something I would of course support, then as now, but I felt frustrated to the point of anger that these people were protesting about a disaster that may or may not happen. Meanwhile, just over the Irish Sea, there were state-sponsored killings, curfews and military restrictions that wouldn't be out of place in a South American dictatorship.

Those CND marchers were almost exclusively middle-class, professional-looking people, so there was little excuse for their ignorance. Their careers and lifestyles afforded time for investigation as well as access to information.

It was the same thing when I spoke to many socialists. For example, the local Communist Party in Birmingham, where I attended a few meetings, were well versed in socialist struggles the world over. But, aside from a few notable exceptions, they were completely ignoring a socialist revolution that was happening on their own doorstep! I believed then, and do now, that it was due to a deep-rooted racism towards Irish people.

• • •

Meanwhile, the wedding preparations were in full swing, and I was having doubts.

Helen had been the only woman I had wanted, despite having been in situations where women were literally throwing themselves at me.

But now I was starting to look at other women and fancy them. That shocked me. I thought it would always only be Helen. I wondered, *How can this be real love if I'm looking around? Maybe it isn't love after all?* Of course, I didn't voice these thoughts to anyone. I kept them all inside.

The *Birmingham Mail* had printed a story about Helen and me getting married and there seemed to be a build-up of media interest. I hated that, as did Helen. We talked it through and postponed the wedding for that reason.

A part of me was also relieved. We didn't set a new date, and I didn't talk to Helen about the doubts I was having. Instead, I let it drift. That must have been so hard for her.

I buried my head in the sand, and basically shut Helen out while I tried to figure out what to do. She didn't say anything about it, but of course noticed the change. I went way more into myself and was much less communicative than I had been previously. I was trying to keep busy. We were writing and demoing new songs, and most of my time outside that was taken up with my political obsessions.

This limbo went on for months. Then, finally, two days before we were going to Montreux to begin recording *Don't Stand Me Down*, I said: 'Helen.' She looked up (she told me later that she knew what I was going to say, before I said it). 'I want to break up.'

She was so upset. Why wouldn't she be? This guy had pursued her like crazy, swept her off her feet and promised marriage. Then after moving in together, he'd gone completely cold. Now, a year later, he's ending it.

Of course, she had known something was up for a long time. How could she not?

I remember one night, we smoked some weed and, as we sat there on the sofa, I had a painful insight into what was really happening – what I'd been running from. I looked at Helen and saw an expression that I couldn't fail to be moved by; it seemed to be a mixture of bewilderment and love. She didn't know what was going on. I felt sad and guilty for what I was putting her through, then pushed the thought out of my mind.

Telling her when I did made things all the harder for her – having to spend the next four weeks together in Montreux in close proximity. The kinder thing to do would have been to have waited until after Montreux. I had thought telling her before the recording would give her the choice to opt out of the album if she wanted to. But that thinking was way off: firstly, she was committed to the music, and secondly, she was totally professional.

All I had left was the music

Before we started recording *Don't Stand Me Down*, Paul Burton and I got together for a conference with my lawyers to discuss his management contract. I had initially said that I wanted to pay his commission of 20 per cent based on net earnings (meaning he would get 20 per cent of the profit). He said that was a non-starter for him – he wanted to take his cut from the gross (i.e. 20 per cent of everything that came in, *regardless* of profit).

Scandalously, that was pretty much standard practice in those days. This was summer 1983 and I had not seen any books or accounts from Paul Burton.

I knew instinctively I was being ripped off, but deep down I felt the situation too big to face. Paul was close to the lawyers and accountants. I wasn't. 'Give it here. I'll sign it,' I said, keen to impress them. On some warped level, I thought, *If I'm nice to them, they might not rip me off as much.* Of course, it was a spineless strategy, but to say I was overwhelmed was an understatement.

I felt I was surrounded by people who only wanted what they could get from me (other than Helen and Bill, who were good people). Paul Burton would talk about my 'career' and I just pretended I knew what he was talking about. And although I might use the word career now – it's really only talking about a time frame. I didn't think of it in those terms, and I still don't. For me it's just about trying to get the next miracle (song or creation of some sort) to happen.

. . .

In the spring of 1983, we had recorded a new song, 'Reminisce, Pt.1'. I called it 'Part One' because I knew it was an idea I would expand upon. It was for a B-side on the soon-to-be reissued 'Celtic Soul Brothers'. I was really excited about it because I felt it was a new direction for us. Not only was it mainly spoken word, but it was basically a conversation over music, with some singing at the end. That may have been done before, but I certainly hadn't heard anything like it. It was engineered very well by Colin Fairley. He got a great sound and the band had grooved well in his presence. I made a mental note that Colin would be good for the next album, but with all the stress that ensued, it didn't happen.

Recording in Montreux was a month-long, very expensive experiment, with Tom Dowd producing. It didn't work, but we got one song out of it, 'Listen to This'.

Back in London, we tried a few other producers, including Jimmy Miller, who had previously worked with the Stones. We tried to record 'This Is What She's Like' and 'The Waltz' with him. Nothing was working, but that was mainly because the combination of players in the band wasn't right.

One thing we did do with Jimmy Miller was run through a version of the standard 'The Way You Look Tonight' (a song I used to do in my brother Pat's band, New Blood). It turned out great. The record company and management heard it and said it was a number-one hit and wanted to release it immediately. I refused. I wasn't planning for it to be on the album, and I believed that releasing another cover version halfway through the recording process might dilute from the end product. But more than that I couldn't bear the idea of jumping back into the pop world.

In one conversation with Roger (our A&R man), I asked, 'Do you think Trevor Horn would be interested in producing us?' ('Relax' by Frankie Goes to Hollywood, produced by him, had recently been released and I thought it was brilliant.)

Roger said, 'He might be, shall I ask him?'

Then I said, 'Nah.'

Although I thought Trevor Horn was great, I guess I was nervous about losing control. Experience had made me wary of producers. But looking at it now, he probably would have *got* it. 'This Is What She's Like' was originally intended to be a 'Bohemian Rhapsody' for the eighties.

I imagine he would have been into that idea. The original demo was just under seven minutes long. I knew it was a great song and reasoned that there had been many previous hit singles of five minutes or more – and if we left off the conversation at the front of the song, it would be down to six minutes.

We were wondering if we'd *ever* find someone to help us make the album when Paul Burton said, 'What about the devil you know? Alan Winstanley. If you work with him, you can do what you want.'

So at that point, we decided to basically produce *Don't Stand Me Down* ourselves, with the help of Alan Winstanley, who had co-produced *Too Rye Ay*.

Most musicians we tried couldn't get near the groove we wanted. The biggest problem was the drums. We tried a few 'name' drummers, and we might get maybe one song that was workable. Finally, Helen reminded me of an Al Green concert we'd been to a few months earlier at the Albert Hall and how we'd both remarked on the amazing drummer. She said, 'Why don't we just get him over?' It was a great idea.

Tim Dancy came over and, after a brief rehearsal, nailed 'This Is What She's Like', 'Knowledge of Beauty' and 'The Occasional Flicker' in a morning! Later that day, we did 'One of Those Things'.

We couldn't believe it. We'd been trying for a year to get grooves like that effortless, back-of-the-beat feel that the best UK drummers couldn't get near. Timmy nailed them immediately.

After finishing the drum tracks, the next issue was trying to get the rest of the players' performances good enough to fit in with Timmy's grooves. That wasn't easy. He had laid down ridiculously good rhythms. If whatever we tried to lay over them wasn't completely in the pocket, it stood out like a sore thumb.

The process was very time-consuming. I was obsessed. I felt all I had left was the music and nobody was going to take that away from me. I was disillusioned with *everything* else. As I write, I get a sense of those days. Heavy, tired, unsexy, and experiencing enormous pressure about the record. It was the most important thing in the world.

The Helen thing was haunting me. *Was I mad for breaking up with her?* She was such a great girl. Why did I change my mind?

We didn't compromise on the record. No *one* of us could have produced the album alone and got it to the standard that it ended up. It was my vision, but Helen and Billy were very committed to achieving it.

At the time, there was total unity between Helen, Billy and me, which is why I was surprised and disappointed to read in recent years that both Helen and Billy said they often didn't understand what I was looking for when we were recording and, in Billy's case, he was quoted as saying that the sessions 'were somewhere between intense and batshit crazy'.

There was never any discussion of that at the time, or even in the years that followed. On the contrary, even though I know that we all found it a strain at times, we all trusted each other's judgement, and all of us were united in our agreement that media rumours at the time – about us getting confused in the studio and spending days looking for appropriate tapes to work on, or going over and over the same part obsessively – were rubbish. I know that was how Helen and Billy felt at the time. They both said so then, and since, and would have spoken up strongly if they felt otherwise. The truth is, we were never lost or confused, despite the enormity of the task and the very high standard we were going for.

The album was costing a fortune, and the label and manager were pulling their hair out and wondering if it would ever be finished. But we were determined to get this 100 per cent right, unlike with *Too Rye Ay*.

. . .

During the recording, I would often spend the later part of my evenings kerb-crawling around Paddington. I rarely picked anyone up, but I spent a lot of time there, driving around. Initially I found it quite exciting but after a while it became an addiction and I was doing it against my will. I'd resolve to stop going there, but I'd pretty much always weaken.

It was secret, lonely and I hated myself for it. I would drive around, wearing dodgy old worn-out tracksuits. I had lots of lovely Ivy League clothes in my wardrobe. Old tracksuits felt appropriate. The original idea for the clothes had been to hide the Ivy League stuff (Dexys' next look) lest anyone saw them and stole the idea.

I could easily have been arrested by the police. They were often patrolling the area in squad cars and nicking kerb-crawlers. If I'd have been caught, I don't doubt that the story would have received significant coverage in the likes of the *Sun*. I was dicing with destruction and humiliation, and I knew it, but I couldn't resist.

Of course, if I'd gone out to nightclubs, I probably could have met women, but I felt too uptight and intense, and I wasn't ready to face the sight of the New Romantics – they were now the dominant force in the London club scene.

. . .

To say I had been the black sheep of my family would be a big understatement. Now, however, I was the golden boy. And I rinsed that status for all it was worth, visiting my parents far more than I had done in years. I wanted to bathe in the glory.

My brother Pat had managed bands in his spare time and was now building a small studio in his back garden in Coventry to develop new artists and groups, along with his friend Mick. They had been speaking to EMI Music (the publishing company that I was signed to) about their project. EMI had agreed to advance Pat and Mick £5,000 towards getting the venture off the ground. I didn't feel good about it; deep down, I guess I was still holding on to resentment towards Pat over the Jackie situation. On the day they were due to get the £5,000 advance, I broke off from recording and phoned the relevant guy at EMI Music and said: 'This deal you're doing with Pat. Is it anything to do with me being on EMI?'

'Well, it *is* a very unusual situation,' he said.

'Well, listen, don't feel obliged to do it on my behalf,' I said.

EMI pulled out of the deal.

That was a downright mean thing to do. I told myself it was because

I didn't want to compromise my relationship with them, and I'm sure I even believed it at the time. I said the same thing when Pat phoned me later that day, but that was bullshit. Almost immediately, I felt really bad about it. But I didn't have the awareness to see my motives and reverse the situation.

Some years later, in an argument, Pat said, 'You were enjoying being the golden boy of the family, and you didn't want to take even the smallest risk of losing that.' He was right.

That being said, the considerable success that Dexys achieved at that time did rock and reshuffle the dynamics of my family. I had been the one who was always in trouble – prison material – and was often criticised for my interests. Now everything had been turned on its head. I hadn't gone down the path that Dad had told me was the correct one. I had gone in the opposite direction and become way more successful than any of them!

A big part of me found that hard to deal with. On some level, I was shocked that I'd done well and felt undeserving of it. They call it imposter syndrome these days. The more successful we became, the less sure I was of myself. And the less sure I was of myself, the more I wanted to please my parents and get their approval.

Dad would even sometimes ask my opinion about things now – something he previously wouldn't have dreamt of doing. And I was desperate to have this 'good relationship' continue, to the extent that I became a lot more conservative in my outlook, to fit in with my parents. To be clear, the music and clothes for *Don't Stand Me Down* were great and I totally stand by them, but there was nothing on that album or its surrounds that would offend my parents. My dad was a staunch Irish republican, and my own feelings and frustrations about Ireland and the UK class system as expressed on the album were genuine, but I was also very happy that my stance was pleasing Mum and Dad.

That, of course, wasn't healthy. It was a big step backwards – after breaking away and forming the original Dexys, I now crumbled in some way, and the world became too scary to navigate under my own steam.

Plus, there was so much happening that I wasn't dealing with honestly. My internal life was untenable.

. . .

I'd visited New York for a few days' break in late 1984 and got the feeling it would be a good place to mix the record.

We anticipated a time when we would be ready and booked the trip. However, when the date arrived, we still hadn't finished recording. We reasoned that a lot of the outstanding work could be done in New York and went anyway. Helen and Billy stayed a few weeks. Alan Winstanley (our engineer and producer) returned home shortly afterwards.

I stayed on, working with another engineer. In total I was probably there about two months. During that time, I never went out to socialise. Instead, I would go out on my own in the evenings, to strip clubs and hostess bars. I stayed in uptown hotels with middle-aged businessmen, as opposed to downtown where the musicians, artists and young people hung out.

If anyone talked about clubs or the like, I'd say something like, 'Fuck that, I'm not interested,' but deep down I longed to be out social-ising with people of my own age. I had backed myself into a corner and I felt unable to get out of it.

One day when Alan Winstanley and I were in the studio, we got a call from a UK record-company guy we both knew. He was in town, asking Alan would he like to go out with him in New York that night. I wasn't invited. I'm sure Alan was aware of how I felt about going out, and just presumed I wouldn't want to.

Alan and I were both staying at the same hotel, and that night I ran into him in the lobby. He was on his way to meet the record-company guy.

For a split second, I had the awareness that I would love to go out with them. As we talked in the lobby for a moment, Alan said, 'I'd better go, he's waiting for me.'

I really wanted to say, 'Can I come?' But I just couldn't.

Meanwhile, in the hostess bars, when it became obvious that money was all the strippers or hostesses wanted, I'd sometimes get resentful at them, which was of course crazy – this was a *hostess bar*! They were there for money.

. . .

Finally, the album recording was finished, but it still needed mixing. I returned to London and asked the advice of my trusted friend, ace mastering engineer, and later producer, Arun Chakraverty. Arun had done a lot of work on *Too Rye Ay* when I brought it to him. I was unhappy with much of the mixing. He agreed that it could be better, and helped it along a lot with his mastering skills.

Dexys worked with Arun again later when he produced 'Because of You'. We should have worked with him more. He was a great guy and an excellent producer.

Arun suggested Pete Schwier for mixing the record. Pete turned out to be absolutely masterful. We even re-recorded the vocal on one of the songs, 'Occasional Flicker', and it worked way better than the previous version.

Suddenly, all the hard, intense work was starting to bear fruit. The album was sounding great, perhaps even better than we had envisaged. I was delighted, as were Helen and Billy.

Swimming against the tide

Just before *Don't Stand Me Down* was to be released, Paul Burton asked me to come round to his place in London for a chat. At that meeting, he resigned. Then he said to me: 'The good news is you've got £40,000 in the bank. The bad news is you've got a tax bill for £80,000.'

I was shocked, and just mumbled something about the accountant not having shown me any books. Other than that, I didn't say anything. I didn't want to show him my true feelings. I wasn't stupid, and I realised that, at the bare minimum, many hundreds of thousands of pounds had been paid into the account, but I needed to go home and process this.

In the three years that we had been working with our accountant, I hadn't been shown any books, any accounts, or any financial records by either him or Paul. In fact, Paul, who had been working with us for five years, hadn't shown me any financial records in all that time.

Admittedly, for Paul's first two years, it was a case of making ends meet. The first band had broken up, and there were times when there wasn't enough money to pay the wages. Paul had put his hand in his own pocket, so no way was I going to ask him about financial records at that stage. I was grateful that he was helping to keep things going.

But when the big money came in from *Too Rye Ay* in 1983 and '84, I was busy working and I presumed the finances were being looked after, though over time I started to realise that they weren't.

I had been introduced to our accountant in late '82, by my lawyer after a gig in Dublin. He was recommended to me as someone who well understood taxation, particularly Irish taxation. I was told that because my parents were Irish, I would benefit from Irish tax law – as an artist, I would pay either zero or very little income tax. I found out later that this information was incorrect. At that first meeting, I didn't feel comfortable with the accountant. Once again, I ignored my instincts.

With regard to the other guys in the band, I later learned that Billy Adams received a buyout (a one-off payment, for all recording royalties) via Paul Burton and the lawyer, during the recording of *Don't Stand Me Down*.

The deal Billy did meant that at least he got *something*, which is good, because *Don't Stand Me Down* ended up being massively expensive, and as its costs were cross-collateralised against *Too Rye Ay*, it meant that Dexys' royalties account with Mercury didn't go into profit until 2014, almost 30 years later, when the recording debt was finally paid off.

That year, 2014, we received our first royalties from the label in 30 years! Prior to that date, we didn't get a penny.

That's how large record companies work, for many deals. They are a bit like a bank. They lend you the money to make the album and don't pay you anything until that debt is paid off, which is fair enough. What wasn't fair enough, on our deal at least, was that if that record sold extremely well, as ours had, and recouped its original recording costs many times over, as ours had, we never owned it, no matter how many times it paid for itself. The label own the record forever. Modern deals are usually much better in that ownership reverts to the artist after five or ten years.

Seb was the only exception, as regards recoupment. When doing his deal, he wisely made sure that any future recording costs would *not* affect his *Too Rye Ay* royalty payments. Good move. Jim and the other guys who had been originally signed to the label, but left in 1982, also received royalty 'buyouts' at the time.

A deal wasn't done for Helen, I guess because she joined well after the band signed to Mercury and hence wasn't contracted to the label. I don't know if she spoke to Paul Burton about a deal when the money started coming in. She was on wages when she joined in 1982, and continued to receive them until the money ran out. Thankfully, some years later I was able to pay Helen a lump sum. And now that the Mercury Records account is in the black, Jim, Helen, Billy and others also get a cut of the *Too Rye Ay* twice-yearly recording royalties. That will continue.

. . .

We decided to *not* release a single from *Don't Stand Me Down* – we wanted to be seen as an album band in the way that the seventies progressive bands like Pink Floyd and Led Zeppelin had operated. I wanted the record to be seen as a proper serious album. We didn't, however, clearly communicate that to the record label or the media, and it ended up being misunderstood.

Ironically, the 'no single' idea didn't come from me, but from our manager, Paul Burton, before he resigned. I was originally planning to release 'This Is What She's Like' as some kind of 12-inch or extended single. I mentioned the idea to Paul. He said, 'Or not release a single at all!'

I liked the idea and immediately felt it would take all the pressure off me. We could make music and promote it without being on the pop treadmill. It was a brave and bold move and if the album had come out in 1983 or even '84, when we still had a reasonably high profile, and if we had communicated our idea properly, it could have worked.

But in dealing with the record company, now managerless, I clashed with a couple of hard-nosed bosses who had replaced the more sympathetic guys during the recording of *Don't Stand Me Down* and had no understanding of what I was trying to achieve. I'd actually told the previous label MD, Brian Shepherd, about the idea of a more credible album release without a single, and he got it and was up for it. But these new guys were seeing it as nothing but me being awkward. It became a point of principle.

Roger, our A&R man, had left the company to head up London Records, so I was on my own. The idea was that Roger would still work with us, even though he wasn't in the building. But I got the clear impression from these new guys that they didn't like that arrangement and wanted to stamp their authority on the situation.

I'm no manager, but I didn't have any choice but to take the reins myself at that point. I didn't even know any other managers to approach. But I was too emotionally invested in the work to not get triggered by people who were being hard-nosed about it. Any hint of criticism would rile me. One example was when I asked the MD what he thought of the album. He said: 'I don't like the coughing,' referring to a cough I left in during the talking in 'This Is What She's Like'.

I felt we'd made a masterpiece. *Why couldn't they see that?*

In the end, we lost the support of most of the label. Even the everyday label workers and promotion people seemed baffled as to why we weren't releasing a single. The whole thing was a failure in communication.

When all is said and done, these bosses were trying to do their jobs. I do think they could have handled it more sensitively. If they *had*, I think I would have been open to a 12-inch single, which was their wish. ('This Is What She's Like' finally came in at 12 minutes long.) But one certain way to get my back up in those days was to give me orders.

Plus, a big factor in this was that I was still angry at myself for going along with releasing 'Jackie Wilson Said' as a follow-up to 'Eileen' a couple of years previously. I was now staunchly resisting record-company suggestions that I felt were wrong.

In commercial terms, it had been three years since the release of *Too Rye Ay*. In those days, that was a hell of a gap. We had lost our pop audience – they had moved on to other things – and I guess the followers who had seen us as more credible in 1980 and '81 had judged us to have gone pop in '82, because of the success of 'Eileen', and weren't really interested by '85. That's my reading of it, anyway.

Personally, I never saw what we did as one thing or the other – pop or credible. I just saw it as music. Roxy Music had chart hits, but their music was full of depth. I saw us like that.

If we had been able to work properly with the label I think our idea could have been a good and intriguing marketing strategy. In the end, it ended up as a stand-off between us and the label bosses while we desperately but unsuccessfully tried to get our message over to their staff (the radio and TV pluggers, etc.). There was so much misinformation and confusion. I had envisaged radio stations would just choose a track they liked and play it. They didn't.

Another factor was that we felt out of synch. The music business had changed. Live Aid had just happened six weeks previously, and everything was different now. Feeding starving people of course dwarfed the importance of pop music. And a knock-on effect of the whole Band Aid / Live Aid period was that it made the UK music *industry* (as they were by then calling it) seem bigger, more professional and more mainstream. The label seemed to be full of young professionals who might once have gone into the likes of estate agenting, but instead chose music. It seemed less quirky and we didn't fit.

We did a few shows at the release of the album. They were good, but I think a fair percentage of the audience were puzzled by us acting out the songs. Even the road crew didn't get it and there were technical problems galore. Billy and I were trying to use small radio mics pinned to our lapels, so we could walk around during the talking bits. Nowadays, it would be no problem, but at the time, certainly with the crew we were using, it was impossible.

We seemed to be swimming against the tide and being misunderstood at every turn. We had some great ideas, but we didn't have the infrastructure around us to pull them off. The result was mainly confusion. Meanwhile this album, which felt in a different class to the previous two, was slipping away. We couldn't believe how something we felt was so good was being ignored.

To this day, some people still think it's uncommercial. That is rubbish and part of the miscommunication that was going on. Some said we didn't release a single because there wasn't a good enough single on it! That was ridiculous. The album was anything but uncommercial. There were some infinitely great pop tracks on there. 'This Is What She's Like' was bursting with hooks and, if we'd edited it properly, it could have done well, and 'Listen to This' would have been a surefire choice for a single.

Robert Elms, always a supporter of Dexys, described it in his *Face* column as 'the famous album without a single'. I don't know if he meant there wasn't a song on the album that would be suitable for a single, but that's what I took it to mean. It *was* commercial – all commercial means is that people like it. Commercial isn't a type of music. Yet the issue was that we *chose* not to release a single. We overshot our luck.

A month after its release, and with airplay and sales not doing what we'd hoped, the label convinced us to go with an edit of 'This Is What She's Like' as a single. Except this time, they were taking control. The radio plugger, Julian, decided what the edit should be. It even chopped off the sung intro. It was three minutes long and a travesty. But the label were holding the cards. If we didn't go along with what they wanted, they would have an excuse to not try to get airplay. In the end, no radio stations played it anyway.

. . .

And now it's September 1985, I'm onstage at the Manchester Apollo. I feel very awkward and stiff and I'm going through the motions, trying to make some excitement happen. I look out into the audience and see my brother Pat. I feel guilty. I had treated him badly.

A couple of days later, on that same tour, I was sitting behind Tim Dancy (drummer) and Jerod Minnies (guitarist) on the bus. They didn't know I was behind them. I listened to them talking to each other. I was struck by how relaxed they were, and how the conversation flowed between them. There was no competing, just a genuine relaxed vibe. I felt that I hadn't conversed like that in an age. Everything felt like a struggle for me. I wished I could be like them.

. . .

We filmed the video for 'Knowledge of Beauty' in County Mayo. At the suggestion of director Jack Hazan, I had my parents in the film. Jack ended up doing a fantastic job on the three videos for the album ('This Is What She's Like', 'Listen to This' and 'Knowledge of Beauty').

He really understood what we were doing musically, and reflected that in his films.

My younger sister Grainne and her husband happened to be over in Mayo at the time. On the day of the shoot, I asked them not to attend the filming, saying it would make me too nervous. But the real truth was, I wanted to continue my time in the sun with my parents, alone. As I look at it now, it was pathetic.

• • •

Ten days after *Don't Stand Me Down* came out, I arrived at BBC TV studios to do an interview to promote the album on *The Old Grey Whistle Test*, a big music-based TV programme.

As the show's opening credits ended, a video of 'Come on Eileen' came on the monitor screen. That puzzled me. Then Richard Skinner spoke some opening words direct to camera: 'Dexys Midnight Runners, who did so well earlier in the decade, have just released their new album. It went into the charts at number 22, then went straight out again.'

Then he turned to me.

'Kevin Rowland, why do you think people are not buying your music any more?'

Shit! It was an ambush. I felt like hitting him. I had been given no advance warning that I was going to be challenged about record sales. I thought I was there to talk about the music, but all they wanted to discuss was how badly it was doing. It might have been paranoia, but it seemed that plenty of people were enjoying our lack of success.

It was also an indication of how the music business and media had changed. Even a credible music show like *The Old Grey Whistle Test* was now talking about record sales. I don't think that would have happened a few years earlier. In response to Richard's questioning, I mumbled something about the album being a success as soon as we'd left the studio.

I had always liked Richard Skinner and I don't hold resentment towards him now. He'd previously been a big supporter of Dexys.

And there it was – *Don't Stand Me Down*, gone. When the dust had settled, I actually felt a strong sense of relief. I was off the pop-music merry-go-round. The feeling of failure felt comfortable and familiar.

PART FOUR

What the fuck happened?

In the couple of years that followed the release of *Don't Stand Me Down*, 1986 and '87, I felt like I was waking up to a bad dream. Not *from* a bad dream, but *to* a bad dream – and that dream was reality.

What the fuck happened? What was all that about? Where have I been for the last five years?

It was like I had missed the whole thing. I'd been in my head and in a state of high anxiety throughout. I'd been driven, uptight, and I hadn't allowed myself to relax in years. And I had barely enjoyed any of it.

I'd been a fucking pop star! The thing I'd dreamt about when I was a kid, and I'd missed it! I'd missed the whole fucking thing. I felt like I hadn't really experienced any of it.

Now the fantasy world was over. This was reality. I now had no success – nor possibility of success – to shield me from my own thoughts and feelings.

I was depressed when I woke up every morning. But did I mention any of this to anyone? Of course not!

I thought about all the opportunities I'd missed. How I should have made sure that we'd got the money that we were due. Instead, it was as if I'd been in a trance and let the money slip through my fingers, while others close to me were struggling. What a cunt! *What the fuck happened?*

To top it off, I was broke, and there were Dexys bills coming at me from all directions. Invoices for equipment, fees from a dodgy management company I hired that were supposed to be looking after us in '85. Session player fees, tour expenses (the *Don't Stand Me Down* tour had incurred a massive loss), a bill for unsold merchandise, and on and on. Dexys' debts were gigantic, and *all* of them were landing at my door.

More than that, there were some very big official bills: income tax, VAT and many others. I had to sell the flat in Birmingham. I rented a place in London. Helen moved to London too, and for a while we rented flats in the same block.

I found out some time later that well over £1 million had gone through the bank account (over £4 million at today's value). The accountant set up some companies in the Isle of Man, which were supposed to mean I would pay very little tax. The idea was presented to me as a great way to save money. It turned out, he had the wrong information. It didn't save any tax. There were three people who had access to the account: Paul Burton, the accountant and me. I have never seen any records, bank statements or accounts of Dexys income or spending for that period, from either the accountant or Paul Burton. Joe O'Sullivan, a decent London accountant who took over the financial situation in 1986, told me that a friend of his had heard Paul Burton boast, laughingly, at a party, 'They'll never get to the bottom of that mess' (meaning Dexys' finances).

Five years later in 1991, bankrupted by the government and completely broke, I angrily challenged Paul Burton in a phone call about what had happened to the money. He said it had gone on my staying in fancy hotels in New York, during the making of *Don't Stand Me Down*.

That was, of course, rubbish – my New York period was a maximum of two months, and it was at an average cost of $100 per night, say $6,000 in total. And besides, an artist's accommodation is supposed come out of the recording budget, paid for by the record label, not out of their personal bank account.

I have calculated my spending for the period from mid-1983 to mid-1985. I splashed out £9,000 on a new car. I bought a flat in Birmingham for £37,000. I spent a maximum of £15,000 on clothes, and I received my living expenses for two years – maybe £50,000 (and that's being generous). All this makes a total of £111,000. If you want to know where the balance went (over one million pounds) you would have to ask Paul Burton, or the accountant, who I would like to name but for legal reasons can't. And Paul Burton died of lung cancer in 2004.

Why did I do so little about this in 1986–87, when it was obvious what had happened? I think it was because I was in shock and, on some level, afraid to face it. I'd allowed myself to be robbed. I felt like such a fool. And I was confused about it, too. People don't tell you that they've ripped you off. They blame *you*! But over time, and plenty of turmoil, little things that I hadn't fully picked up on started to slot into place.

Ah – maybe that's why Paul Burton brought that estate agent round to my house, out of the blue, and got her to put a 'For Sale' sign up – so that he could put some distance between me and my dad, so that Dad wouldn't be involved in the bookkeeping?

And was that why Paul wanted Seb out of the way? Seb, above everyone else in the band, would have been sure to have kept a proper check on the money.

And was that why Paul did a buyout deal with Billy: easier to rob one than two?

If that was the case, fucking hell, Paul! You were clever!

Reeling from all of this, in 1987 I went to the music publishers and got a £50,000 advance. I said, 'If you believe in me, you will give me this money.' They gave it to me.

I put a £5,000 deposit down on a flat in Cricklewood. I also passed some money on to a few people that were close to me – perhaps a desperate attempt to make amends for not helping when I supposedly had money. I also made financial amends to my brother Pat, paying him £5,000 to compensate for blocking him getting that money from the music publishers.

Joe O'Sullivan (my new accountant) suggested that I start looking at paying off the bigger bills that were staring me in the face – the £80,000 tax bill that Paul Burton had presented me with, plus a large VAT bill and many others that had subsequently come in.

Instead, I started to act like I was a wealthy pop singer, shopping in expensive West End clothes shops, even though I couldn't afford it. I was living way above my means, but appearances were all that counted.

Joe negotiated a stay of execution with the large government bills. I paid tax on whatever new money came in, but he told me even at that point it looked like I would have to go bankrupt as my income wasn't going to be sufficient to pay off the debts. I didn't pay much attention to the warning.

I did, however, eventually go and see a lawyer to make a start on pursuing Dexys' money through legal means. But, for a reason I still don't understand, the solicitor lost interest and just stopped working on the case. I should have pushed him or got another lawyer, but I was still like a rabbit trapped in the headlights – overwhelmed, not thinking straight, and unsure about any move I made.

Joe O'Sullivan, my brother Pat and others were telling me it would be better if I just forgot about what had happened with Paul Burton and carry on making new music. I see now that I couldn't really do any music with any passion until I'd done my best to try and deal with what had happened. It was too big to ignore, but ignore it I did.

Also, I was unsure of who I could trust and who I couldn't. I didn't know who was in on it and who wasn't. I suspected pretty much every-one. I was even suspicious of Joe initially, and he definitely turned out to be trying to help me.

Most of all, I was ashamed. Ashamed that I'd allowed it to happen, that I'd been such a mug. I did my best to hide it.

• • •

To top it off, the record label had gone cold on us. In my experience, these companies aren't truthful with you about the transition from being wanted by them to being surplus to requirements.

They don't sit you down and say: 'Kevin, Billy, Helen; it's over.'

Or, 'Kevin, you've blown it.'

Or, 'We are more interested in these new groups now. We will keep you here even though we don't think you will be successful any more. However, we can't be sure of that, and we wouldn't want you to have success with one of our competitors, so we will retain your contract, but you are no longer a priority for us.'

Instead, what happens is that you notice one day, when you walk into the label's offices, they aren't as friendly as they used to be. They maybe give you a quick smile then look away, whereas previously they would have been double-friendly. That's how it works. Or at least that's how it worked for me.

. . .

Billy, Helen and I seemed to be drifting apart musically. There wasn't much holding us together, and there seemed no point in hanging on to Dexys. I knew I couldn't go through making something like *Don't Stand Me Down* again (far too draining). Billy felt the same. And by late 1986, both Billy and Helen had left to do their own things. It felt like the right thing for all of us.

I began writing again, simpler songs, mainly on my own. I was way beyond broke, and I tried to make the songs as commercial as possible. They ended up on a solo album called *The Wanderer*.

Before I started the recording, I went to a London hotel to meet Bobby Womack. I think it was Helen who had told me he was in town (we were both massive Womack fans) and I asked my record label to track him down for me with a view to him producing the album.

I met with Bobby. The production thing didn't materialise, but while I was in the hotel room, Ronnie Wood turned up. Bobby played him, and a few other people who were there, a couple of my songs. I was feeling quite exposed, but Ronnie really liked one song in particular, 'Tonight'. He had his acoustic guitar with him and played along with the song, adding some really nice touches. Then he said, 'I'd really like to be in the studio when it's recorded.'

I just nervously mumbled something.

Ronnie Wood *wanted* to play on one of my songs! The guy who wrote and played those incredible riffs on 'You Can Make Me Dance, Sing or Anything' and 'Stay With Me'. He was, and is, a brilliant guitarist. Now he was offering to play on my record! I should have jumped at the chance. I guess I was too nervous in the presence of a musical figure of his stature, and just froze.

After Ronnie left, Bobby Womack told me that Ronnie had said to him, 'They [I guess he meant the music media] missed his last album, man!'

Wow! Ronnie Wood was espousing the virtues of *Don't Stand Me Down* to Bobby Womack! I was shocked that Ronnie Wood had even heard it. Incredible.

Around the same time, I met Jimmy Ruffin in the street! He was with a record company guy that I knew. I'd loved Jimmy when I was a youth. I really would have liked to have spoken to him about how he made such songs as 'Tell Me What You Want', which was, and remains, one of my all-time favourite records. But I just pretended to be casual. I was acting how I *thought* I should act. I was so confused about everything and was by now distrustful of everybody.

I much preferred ecstasy

When I finished writing 'Walk Away', the single from my solo album, *The Wanderer*, I believed it could well be a hit, as did the record company. I wanted success to help my finances as much as anything.

As part of the promotion for the single's release, I was invited to be a guest on the Radio 1 *Round Table* show, the big Friday evening new-release show.

Gary Davies was hosting. The plugger from our label brought me to the BBC building, introduced me to Gary Davies, and then left me outside the studio while she took Gary into another room to play him 'Walk Away'.

I wasn't in a good mood that day and, typically of me, I projected whatever I was feeling outwards. I was thinking negatively towards Gary Davies.

When they came out of the room, Gary Davies had a massive smile on his face and was waving the single in his hand. 'Your plugger has just played me this!' he said. He was obviously waiting for me to say, 'What do you think?' And it was clear from the big smile that he was going to give me very a positive response.

I didn't ask him what he thought. I just gave him a miserable look and said, 'OK.' Basically, I blanked him.

I could tell he noticed my miserable reaction. He probably felt embarrassed – his positive response had been rejected. He didn't say anything else, but the plugger told me a week later that when his producer had programmed the song to be played on his show, it was removed at Gary's request.

. . .

I realised that, for my sanity as much as anything, I needed to start going out and socialising. I was 35 and wanted to have some fun before I was too old. I didn't find it easy. I hadn't socialised for years and it was like I'd missed a generation. I felt out of synch whenever I went out to a club or bar. But at least I was trying to come out of my isolation.

One of the things that appealed to me most about acid house was that at the very beginning at least, in the best London club on that scene, Shoom, there was a wide mixture of people: fashion designers, football hooligans, trendies, builders, pop singers, window cleaners, photographers – they were all there. It was brilliant. And the thing that was making it happen was ecstasy. It was a great drug. Like so many others, I wouldn't have been open to acid house music were it not for ecstasy. And that summer of 1988 was a very exciting time. It was a big change in London culture. And though I resisted the standard acid house outfits (surfwear, bandanas, dungarees with sock-less Converse) and wore a more casual version of my smart clothes, I was aware that it was, indeed, a powerful scene – the music was great and the opportunities for sex were everywhere! Ecstasy was new and people were throwing their inhibitions away. I loved it.

Six months previously, if you had bumped into the wrong guy in a club, it would have meant a fight or at least a confrontation. Now if you bumped into the same man, it was, 'No problem, mate. Are you OK?' I know it was chemically induced, but it was real at the time and a lot better than what had preceded it. There were stories of top boys from rival London football firms sitting down and having chats together. Previously they would have tried to kill each other.

I had taken ecstasy in 1987, before the acid house scene exploded, and I was blown away. It did me a lot of favours in that it showed me what was wrong with me: how restless and unrelaxed I was, and also what could be possible if I was able to just loosen up. Without E, I had presumed women wouldn't want to speak to me. With E, I was confident and relaxed and many women responded. It was a revelation!

E slowed me right down and gave me courage to give people a longer look and a warmer smile. Ecstasy changed my reality.

Before long I reasoned, 'If one pill makes me feel *that good*, surely more will make me feel even better,' and on one occasion I drank a cocktail of beer and ecstasy powder, and later found out it had enough powder in it to make 15 to 20 Es. I was sick for the whole weekend.

I considered diving right into ecstasy and the whole acid house scene, but I didn't have a lot of money and, of more concern sometimes at the end of the night, E made me feel very seriously vulnerable and paranoid. At those times, I had to get away quickly and be on my own.

. . .

'Do you always have it?'

That was the question I asked every new cocaine dealer. All of them said 'yes'. All of them lied.

It's surprising that I chose cocaine, given that I was already fear-driven and prone to paranoia. Heroin or another calming drug would have suited me better. But it's more the case that cocaine chose me. It wasn't even my favourite drug. I much preferred ecstasy. But there was something about cocaine. It felt familiar from the first time I tried it.

In 1978, a friend who was a hard drug taker, said to me, 'If you're a weak person, or you've got problems in your life, you shouldn't take class-A drugs.' Although he wasn't referring to anyone in particular, I knew I was in at least one of those categories.

Cocaine put me in the present. It made me feel normal. It gave me something to say, an opinion, the ability to stand straight and take my place in the world. It took away the awkwardness and discomfort that I almost permanently felt.

But even in those early days, it would sometimes make me paranoid. I didn't know if it was going to make me feel like a lion – attractive, strong, independent – or painfully insecure, weak and inferior. Later, it would pretty much always be the latter, but I would perversely grow to *favour* even that.

One night, I met a girl, whom I will call Zanna. We started an intense relationship in the summer of 1988, and by spring '89 she had moved in with me. She was a very sexy woman: independent and strong. She did what she wanted, when she wanted, which I found very attractive.

In bed she was highly charged. She held my cock in a way that felt warm, sexy, assured and different to how it had been held before. She seemed to have a knack. It wouldn't surprise me if she'd studied it; she was a girl who took her pleasure seriously.

It was ecstasy that brought us together. I don't think we would have otherwise met. She was very middle class and I didn't particularly like her dress sense. But this was an example of ecstasy opening up possibilities that wouldn't otherwise have been considered. I was standing next to her at the bar one Saturday night at Shoom, just as I was coming up on my E. I was overcome with an uncontrollable urge to stroke her bum. It looked big and round and very alluring. I touched it. She didn't object.

Later that night, I was dancing with her from behind, experiencing the warm, sensual, fiery heat of her body. I put my hand down the front of her shorts and inside her knickers. Then my friend Declan came over and joined in, putting his hands up the front of her T-shirt and playing with her tits. I wasn't so keen on Declan's involvement, but I didn't say anything, and Zanna didn't raise any objection.

But she was way more than somebody I'd met in a club and had a mess-around with. There was something about her. A part of me didn't even like her, but I was certainly intrigued by her.

On our first proper date, we went out for a meal to a fancy restaurant then did some club-hopping. I was careful to take her to a couple of clubs where I was known by the bouncers and would have easy entry. For a few moments, I felt like Ray Liotta in *Goodfellas*, as we passed the front of the queue to the sound of: 'Hello, Kevin. Come in.'

Through the Dexys and immediate post-Dexys years, I had socially stagnated. Now I was trying to make up for lost time, and with Zanna on my arm, I felt all right! I was living beyond my means, sure, acting as if I had a lot of money in the bank, but I didn't have to face that reality just yet.

One Sunday, quite early on in the relationship, we'd been doing drugs since the previous evening and were round at Declan's place. He had already made a point of coming on to her in front of me at another party we'd all been at. I was freaked out but remained quiet. On some level, I didn't think I was as good as Declan, and I let him get away with small things that I didn't feel OK with.

God knows why I took Zanna around to Declan's place. I had only quite recently become friends with him and I really didn't know how to conduct a friendship. I was doing what I thought friends were supposed to do. I was obviously far too trusting, or stupid. But Declan had invited me round, and as Zanna was with me, she came too.

We arrived at Declan's front door and knocked, but no answer. I was relieved. I was tempted to walk away and my instinct told me to, but I knocked again. We waited a couple of minutes. A part of me was telling myself, *Go, get out, this is your chance.* Just then Declan and his mate Dave walked around the corner, holding bottles of booze. They had been to the off-licence.

We went in. I tried my best to come over as confident, but every time Zanna spoke to Declan or vice versa, I would go into a panic and, worse, I thought they could see that I was frightened. I started to think about how stupid I had been for bringing her there. I hadn't really told her that I had strong feelings for her, even though I'd only seen her a few times.

She was sitting on one side of me, Declan was sitting on the other. He had a misunderstanding/argument with his friend Dave, who was sitting on the other side of the room. Declan was upset. Zanna reached past me and put her hand on Declan's knee, I guess to console him, and kept it there, looking intently into his eyes. He responded by staring equally unflinchingly back into hers. It seemed to go on for an eternity. I felt paralysed, speechless. I wish I could have said to her, 'What are you doing?' But I was afraid to, in case the confrontation would cause her to choose. If it did, I believed she wouldn't choose me. So I did nothing, apart from feel weak and incredibly self-conscious.

After what seemed like forever, they stopped. I felt more and more uncomfortable and fidgety, afraid the situation would escalate. I was desperate to get out of there. I waited for what I hoped looked like a healthy period of time (maybe 20 minutes) before saying, 'It's time we went. I have to be up in the morning.'

I didn't have to be up in the morning at all.

I could see both Declan and Zanna grinning. I felt they both knew I was lying. It *did* seem very obviously early to be leaving. Even as I said it, I was afraid that Zanna was going to say she wanted to stay there. Thankfully, she didn't.

I was so nervous about the exit. Declan stood at his door to say goodbye to us. I was nearest the door, so went first. Zanna was behind me. I really wanted to turn around and see how she said goodbye to him. I was scared that she would give him a sexy kiss, grab his cock, or slip him her phone number. I didn't look around.

She left early the next morning, and I was convinced she went round to Declan's place.

. . .

Zanna and I continued seeing each other. Eventually, she moved in.

The next few years were absolute paranoia – thinking someone was going to take her from me. Cocaine certainly didn't help. If I was out with her, and a man talked to us, I had to be on top, the strongest one. I couldn't show any sign of weakness, otherwise she would go off with him, I thought. I was literally expecting her to go off with any friend, at any time.

I'd also look for that weakness in other men and think, *I don't want to be like him. His woman will be after his friend.*

I started to subtly discourage Zanna from going out. I see now that I'd done the same in previous relationships, except now, with cocaine, it was much more intense.

One night we were nearing the end of a coke binge, in my flat, and had run out. We tried to get some more but failed and decided to just go to bed. I was feeling paranoid. I walked past the bathroom where Zanna was getting herself ready. She noticed me and looked embarrassed. I remember thinking, *Oh! She thinks I'm somebody. She thinks I'm a person*

*who is worth feeling embarrassed for. She obviously doesn't realise yet that
I'm just a weakling.*

I loved lying in bed with Zanna. We seemed to feel so right for each
other, and there were times that I wanted to be like a baby in her arms.
I had a really strong urge to lie on her breasts and snuggle up. I even
asked her once if that would be OK. She said it would be welcome to
have that kind of softness from me as she generally experienced me as
quite the opposite: rigid.

But when the opportunity came to lie on her chest, I just couldn't
do it! I really wanted to but, despite her assurances, I was scared she
would instantly go off me and be unfaithful if I showed any weakness.

We were doing quite a lot of cocaine. Certainly *I* was. Sometimes
my fear and paranoia about her being unfaithful would spill out. Though
I tried to hide it, she seemed to be aware of my insecurity. We talked
about a mutual friend; I had the feeling she fancied him. I kept bringing
the conversation back to him, to probe. Finally, she said, 'You're fretting
about him, aren't you?' I strongly denied it. I was way too embarrassed,
but she was right.

. . .

Then something happened. One night, high on cocaine, I started to
strongly fantasise about Zanna having sex with other men. Given my
insecurity about her being unfaithful, I was shocked to the core by this
powerful feeling, but it turned me on intensely. I was confused.

Zanna had a temporary day job as a secretary for two businessmen,
close to where we lived. It was summer and she wore short skirts to
work, over her beautiful bare, brown legs, without underwear.

In my imagination, one of these men would see that she wasn't
wearing knickers, as she sat in her swivel office chair. She would be
aware that they could see and would enjoy the attention. They would
all continue working in this highly charged atmosphere, with Zanna
occasionally swivelling round to give some typed papers to one of the
men, with a beautiful, sexy smile on her face. Eventually, the tension
would be too much and they would all have sex.

To say I was in turmoil about the power of these fantasies is an understatement. But the more I tried to resist, the stronger they got. I really wanted to hear her tell me about her experiences with other men. But I didn't dare ask.

I dreamed up this crazy, cocaine-inspired idea, where I said, 'If either of us ever have the desire to be unfaithful to each other, we should talk about it first – tell each other what we are thinking.' This was my crazy, covert way of trying to get Zanna to tell me about her sexy thoughts or experiences with other guys without letting her know that it turned me on. She was understandably confused.

Sometime later, we stayed in a hotel for a night on a coke binge and there was a big, strong, good-looking, black man delivering room service to us. During the night, we called him a few times. Zanna was in bed, wearing just her black suspender belt and stockings. I was fantasising about her answering the door to him, wearing very little, and things progressing from there.

I loved to see her sexually aroused and I started to feel that I wanted to experience that fully. In other words, I wanted to watch her have sex.

That night as we lay in bed, both of us high on coke, she cradled my cock in her hand, and for the first time I plucked up the courage to ask her to tell me about any previous sexual experiences that stood out for her.

She happily told me about a summer night when she had gone to a party wearing only a white dress. She walked into the kitchen and made eye contact with a man. She walked out into the garden. He followed her. They kissed and he ended up fucking her against a garden wall. When they had finished, they went their separate ways, without ever having spoken a word to each other. I felt so close to her in that moment, and privileged that she had allowed me into her inner, intimate world.

Similarly, when we were out at parties where toilet facilities were slim, we would sometimes share the loo as we peed. I loved seeing her pee. It reminded me of being a very small boy with my mum when we were out shopping and she would take us into the toilet with her.

'You're a McDonnell'

An early sign that I was getting in over my head with cocaine came on my birthday in 1989. Zanna and I went out to a club and ran into a dealer friend. He came back to our place. After an hour or two sniffing coke and drinking, Zanna said, 'I'll go into the bedroom now and get your birthday presents ready. You'll be in soon, right?' She wanted to give me the presents she had bought, and carefully wrapped, alone.

'Of course,' I said. 'In a few minutes.'

It was more than three hours later when my dealer friend left, and I finally went into the bedroom. Zanna was crying. She tearfully confronted me. I felt genuinely sorry and apologised for my selfishness.

'I'm such a thoughtless bastard. I'm so sorry.'

'That's not our problem, Kevin,' she said.

'No? What is?' sensing and fearing what she was going to say.

'Cocaine is our problem,' she said. 'It's taking over our lives!'

A panic rose up in me. Then a thought:

'Look, it's true that we *are* doing a lot of cocaine, right now, but are we having a good time, most of the time?'

'Yes,' she said. 'Sometimes it's really fun.'

'Well, look, if we are still taking this much cocaine in three months' time, then for sure, we will have a problem, and we'll address it. OK? But for now, let's just enjoy it.'

'OK,' she said.

My panic subsided. My cocaine taking was safe for another few months.

I told Zanna, 'I will never put cocaine in front of you again.' And I meant it. But I didn't realise that I wouldn't be able to carry through with the promise.

. . .

I also started to fantasise about men. It was mostly in a setting of having sex with Zanna, but for the first time I allowed myself to feel that attraction. I had occasionally experienced previous feelings of attraction for males, often when I'd had a smoke of weed or on an ecstasy pill, but it would freak me out and I'd quickly shunned the thoughts. Now it was different; cocaine made the urges so strong and clear that they were impossible to resist.

We had a friend, Paul, a good-looking black guy. I loved the idea of Zanna flirting with him and would fantasise about us bringing him back to our place. Paul, who was athletically built, would be standing against the door and bulging in his dark-brown tight leather jeans. Zanna, looking sexy in black lingerie, would be kneeling at his groin, smiling at me, before taking out his cock.

She would caress it, then kiss it, then writhe up his body, the palms of her hands working their way up his stomach to his strong chest. She would unbutton his shirt, and then kiss him on the lips. I would come over and suck his cock, as she stood kissing him. Then we would both suck his cock together, smiling at each other.

I eventually *did* tell Zanna about my fantasies, and once she was over the shock we actually experimented with something like the above, but by that time I was so cocaine crazy that there was far too much paranoia for it to be properly enjoyable for anyone.

· · ·

While cocaine and other drugs initially helped to open me up and show me what was possible, cocaine *addiction* caused myself and others a lot of pain and problems: extreme paranoia, more and more intense mood swings, rows and mounting debts that were now reaching a completely unmanageable level.

Zanna and I had quickly gone from going out and socialising in clubs to sitting up in bed, both in our white towelling dressing gowns, on coke binges. I would often think, *What am I doing to this girl? She must*

surely see what a pathetic wreck I am now. I hope she's not looking at me –
she'll see that the facade is over.

Occasionally, I would risk a peek and usually be relieved to find
that she wasn't staring at me or seeming to have a realisation about my
uselessness. In the end, though, she did come to comprehend how weak
I was for cocaine.

For example, one night we were at my dealer Phil's place, to pick
up a couple of grams. Money was tight for me now and Phil would
often give me extra coke or be very generous with his own stash. He'd
just moved into a new place and didn't have a music system. I brought
round an old cassette player for him and began setting it up. He stood
at one end of the room, about 12 feet from me. Zanna was in between
us, sitting on the sofa.

I'd finished rigging up the music system and needed a cassette to
try it out. I said to Phil, 'Chuck us a cassette, Phil?'

He looked at me, took a cassette from the top of the desk where he
was standing, held it up to about eye height, and made only the feeblest
effort to throw it towards me. Basically, he pretty much dropped the
cassette in front of him, meaning that I would have to walk over from
the other side of the room, like a little boy, to pick it up. This I did.

As I bent over to get it, I looked up at Phil and saw that he was
looking straight at Zanna and smiling, as if to say, 'He's in my pocket.'

I could only risk the slightest of glances at Zanna. She was watching, taking it in.

People could treat me any way they wanted if they were giving
me cocaine.

I made efforts to stop taking it and would sometimes last weeks
at a time, going to the gym or running for miles daily. Zanna would
cook healthy meals and encourage me, but I would always eventually
go back to it.

I went to see a hypnotherapist. We talked about my cocaine problem, among other issues. He would hypnotise me to help me stay clean.

He also made a tape for me that I would listen to every morning, telling me, 'Cocaine is no longer a part of my life. I have moved on …'

· · ·

At one point, I was sure I'd beaten cocaine. I was six weeks clean, and Zanna and I were in one of our many break-ups.

Through the hypnotherapy I had been directed to think about my relationships with my family. Incredibly, I had given those issues barely any conscious thought in my adult life.

I had done some therapy briefly, in 1987, just before I got into cocaine. The issue of Dad and our relationship came up, and as a result I took him out for a drink and said: 'Dad, when I was a kid, it seemed like you didn't love me.'

He replied, 'All this talk of love is a new thing. When I was a kid, if you had enough to eat you were doing OK.'

Old Irish songs like 'The Wild Colonial Boy', written in 1880, disprove that, for example in the line: *And dearly did his parents love the Wild Colonial Boy.'*

Now I was facing the fact that there was turmoil in my relationship with my dad and my family. I had been unconsciously terrified to admit that, because deep down I thought everything was my fault.

The hypnotherapy was bringing up so much confusion in my mind. *Why was Dad like that with me when I was a kid? Why did he single me out from the others, telling them not to be like me?* Talking it through, we decided that I needed to sit Dad down and calmly ask him about it.

Before I did, I phoned my brother Pat and said, 'I want to ask you something really important, Pat, and I want you to be completely honest with me. Is that OK?'

'OK,' he said.

'Pat, when I was a kid, before I started getting into any trouble, *was* Dad down on me, more than the other kids in the family?' There was a long pause. 'Please tell me the truth, Pat.'

'OK. He *was*, Kev.'

'Definitely, Pat?'

'Yes.'

Strangely, it was a relief. I *wasn't* mad. I *hadn't* imagined it, which is what I got told as a child if I went anywhere near that subject.

In the hypnotherapy sessions, we talked at length about how Dad used to say I was like Mum's side of the family, the McDonnells/Brownes, and not in a positive way. The hypnotherapist suggested it might be good to ask Dad about *his* relationship with the McDonnells. He suspected there may have been some difficulties. It was an astute observation.

We made a plan. I would go up to my parents' house and ask Mum if I could speak to Dad alone. Mum agreed.

'Dad, can I ask you a few questions?' I said. 'And please be completely honest, Dad. It's important to me.'

'All right.'

'First of all, I want to ask you, do you think I'm like you?'

As quick as a flash, he answered, 'No.'

'Not like you at all?'

'No.'

'Who am I like?'

'You're a McDonnell.'

'I'm like them?'

'You're *just* like them.' The way he said it didn't sound positive.

'Really?'

'Yes.'

'Dad, what was your relationship with them like, when you were young?'

'Huh! They thought they were better than everyone else, but we were *all* peasants. And they didn't think I was good enough for her [my mum].'

I don't know if that was something Dad had just picked up on, or if any of the McDonnells had said it directly to him, but while they were *all* poor, Mum's family had a café and were known in Crossmolina for putting on plays and the like. Dad's family was from a small farm in Castlehill, a couple of miles away. But whatever Dad might have thought of himself, he actually *was* a sophisticated man – he always went for quality when he was buying anything, he had style. He was astute and didn't trust what was being piped out to him in the news.

'Dad, when I was a kid, you were always putting me down and criticising me. I thought there was something wrong with me.'

'Why are you shoving this stuff down my throat now, and me an old man?' (Dad was in his seventies at this point.)

He was very keen to get Mum back in the room and, before long, he called her in. It would have been a good time for me to stop there, but this was my first serious attempt at a very real conversation with Dad. I carried on.

'Dad, when I was eight, you told me that I'd be married by the time I was 17, as in, I'd get a girl pregnant.'

'Well, I wasn't far wrong, was I?' he retorted aggressively.

This made my blood boil. Rage soared up in me. *Fuck this shit*, I thought. I stormed out of the house in anger. As I did, I shouted: 'And I won't be at your funeral.'

That was a rotten thing to say. And I would later rightly apologise to him for it.

Pat and Joe were waiting for me in the pub around the corner, as pre-arranged. When I walked in, Joe was sitting alone. I walked over to him, hugged him and started crying uncontrollably. Years of emotion came flooding out of me. Pat came over and it was like we were kids again. The three brothers. I felt very close to them and I think they felt the same. We talked about our childhood and happy days causing mischief around Wolverhampton.

I told Pat what I'd said about Dad's funeral. Pat looked concerned.

I felt that all of the progress I'd made was invalidated because of that last statement. I also knew it would become the main 'takeaway' from the conversation. The family would get to hear that Kevin said he wouldn't be at Dad's funeral. Ironically, those words would turn out to be prophetic, but for completely different reasons.

That night, Pat, Joe and I went to another pub, where I met a girl. She came back to stay with me at Joe's house, just around the corner from Mum and Dad's. She was still there in the morning when I was alarmed to see Mum walking up the path towards the house. I felt panic rise up in me. It was obvious that the girl and I had spent the night together. I felt overpoweringly awkward in front of Mum; I'd always hidden anything sexual from her. Now I'd been caught red-handed.

Again, I felt that any power I had taken back through talking honestly with Dad was completely diminished from being seen to have spent the night with a woman. I see now that it was only a feeling, and I was a grown man in his late thirties, but at the time it devastated me. I was still a guilt-tripped Catholic boy.

The girl sensed the uncomfortable atmosphere, quickly made her excuses and left. After which, Mum didn't waste time in chastising me.

'He was like a wounded animal when I walked into that room last night! And you said you wouldn't be at his funeral!'

I couldn't answer.

That conversation with Dad had been too much, too soon. Though I did briefly reflect that seeing me as a McDonnell was maybe why Dad put me down so much, perhaps thinking I would grow up to look down on him. But it was only a fleeting thought.

During the next few months, I made a few more attempts at getting clean, and would sometimes last weeks. But each time the old anger and extreme discomfort would come up in me and I would relapse.

· · ·

In the end, Zanna was as sensible as she was sexy, and left.

Over the three-plus years we were together, I had treated her abysmally. First, she was subjected to my wooing – incredibly charming, big, bold, dramatic gestures of 'love' – and then ultimately to every black mood, whim, paranoid thought and prejudiced bitter idea that came into my head. There were many.

I would fly off the handle at the slightest thing. I went into a very dark place and I took a lot of it out on Zanna. There were many, many arguments. Incredibly, I really believed that *she* was the problem.

I encouraged her to get rid of pretty much all her friends. I felt intimidated by them and I'd say things like, 'I'm not sure about so-and-so. I don't know if they really respect you.' She stopped seeing her friends, one by one, until it was just her and me.

I was outraged when she first made it clear that she'd had enough of me. I truly believed she was dependent on me. She had cried and cried and cried so many tears over the time we were together. I thought that meant she couldn't live without me. But I was wrong. The tears were her grieving process, until finally it was over. And when it's over for a woman, it's over. She had moved on.

I'm amazed that she stuck with me so long, but she loved me and was hoping that I'd change.

The deepest truth is that I was intimidated by her, frightened of her power, her sexuality and everything about her. I thought she was stronger, better, more free, more balanced, more educated, more honest, more rounded, more confident than me. And she was.

But instead of being honest about that, and either leaving her alone, realising she was out of my league, or being truthful with her about my insecurities, I tried to control her and diminish her. It was disgusting behaviour. But if anyone had pointed out to me what I was doing at the time, I'd have been outraged. I was in total denial.

As well as being sorry for being such a bully, I also wish I'd been able to make more of my time with Zanna. She was an incredible girl.

I was living only for cocaine

Now it's 1991 and I'm standing in the Strand at the High Court, about to lose my flat. I'd been saddled with an old merchandising debt from the *Don't Stand Me Down* tour. Some guys I barely knew had offered to do the merchandising for the shows. No money or financial deal was discussed.

They were inexperienced and ordered way more merchandise than was needed. When it didn't sell, they dropped it all off at my brother Pat's place in Coventry (his wife Margaret was then running the Dexys fan club) and sent me the bill for the goods. It was many thousands of pounds, and I didn't have it.

Eventually, they took me to court and won. The original ruling was in 1988. But instead of paying the debt (which I was loath to do), I buried my head in the sand.

They got an order on my flat for £20,000, which meant that if I should sell it, they would get their £20,000. The flat was worth about £50,000 at that point. After a few months, when I still hadn't paid anything to them, they took me back to court and got an order from the judge, allowing them to sell the flat over my head while I was still living in it. The arrangement was that they would take their £20,000, plus legal costs, out of the sale, and after the mortgage was paid off, I would get whatever was left.

However, shortly after that ruling, I was declared bankrupt by Her Majesty's Government with debts totalling £180,000, mainly to the Inland Revenue (I still hadn't paid that £80,000 tax bill, which had now increased because of interest), plus Customs and Excise, as well as Barclays Bank, from whom I had secured a £20,000 loan to finance my cocaine-taking lifestyle.

The government appointed a 'trustee in bankruptcy'. As I sat before him, he asked me to hand him my credit cards. He then took out a large pair of scissors, cut them up and told me that I would be bankrupt for three years. During that time I wouldn't be able to hold a bank account or credit cards. I would be allowed a living wage but, as I wasn't earning anything, that would just mean my dole money (I had been signed on, for two years, since being without a record deal in 1989). They would take everything else – the balance from the forthcoming sale of the flat, my songwriting royalties etc.

Furthermore, a couple of weeks into the bankruptcy, which had been reported in the tabloids, the trustee called me back into his office and told me that someone who knew me (he didn't say who) had made them an offer to buy the rights to all of my royalties. The trustee said his office were considering the offer.

I didn't hear any more about it, so finally deduced that they had declined. I'm very glad. It would have meant that I would never again earn a penny from the Dexys songs I wrote or recorded in the eighties. To this day, I still don't know who it was that attempted to buy my music rights from the trustee.

Over the next few years, apart from unemployment benefit cheques, I would also receive the occasional small payment from EMI Records for sales of the first album. For some reason the trustee in bankruptcy missed that one. But since *Searching for the Young Soul Rebels* sold very little when compared to *Too Rye Ay*, the cheques amounted to only a few hundred pounds a year.

Estate agents started turning up and showing people around my flat. I didn't like it and did my best to make them feel unwelcome, being awkward, uncooperative and abrasive with any potential buyers.

The guys who had taken me to court soon realised they weren't going to be able to sell it while I was living there and brought me back before the judge for a third time. This time the judge gave me 29 days to vacate the property. As I left the court that day, bizarrely I felt relieved and much lighter.

By spring 1991 I had been declared bankrupt and turfed out of my home by the courts, all within the space of five weeks.

I looked around at bedsits and flats, but I didn't have enough money for a deposit, and was relieved to learn that the Social Security would help with that. Finally, I found a flat in Willesden and, after the first month, stopped paying the rent. Cocaine was my priority. I was now squatting. Soon afterwards, my electricity was cut off for non-payment of bills. A friend rewired it, bypassing the meter.

. . .

Maybe if I could get a record deal, things would be better. Jim Paterson and I had been writing some good songs in between my binges. We were managed by an ex-Mercury employee and friend, Bill Judd, who started to look around for a record deal. Two significant companies showed interest in signing us.

One, Go Discs, loved the demos we presented to them and enthusiastically agreed to sign us. All seemed to be going well until I scuppered it. Fresh off a coke binge, I phoned someone at the company and started ranting at them because things weren't moving fast enough for me.

The second opportunity didn't go much better. Sitting in a meeting at Virgin Records in another dark coke comedown, I asked the A&R man, whom I was finding irritating: 'Do you actually like music?'

That was the end of that one.

I was living only for cocaine. My budget was, of course, severely limited. Sometimes, I would spend all my dole money on cocaine and in the following days I'd be trying to find pennies around the flat to get myself some fish fingers or pasta. Sometimes, I couldn't find anything.

'Cocaine is a different drug the way you do it,' a dealer friend had said to me.

He was right. I did it in big fat lines, then just sat or lay there for five minutes or more, in silence, with my eyes closed, drifting off into peace. My relationship with it was more like the way people use heroin.

In my early cocaine days, I liked to chat with people, hang out and have fun. Now I just wanted solo oblivion. I didn't want to talk to *anyone*. Initially, cocaine gave me energy. Now it made me feel tired, but still with an overactive brain.

I became much more paranoid and totally believed any negative comments or thoughts about myself. Those thoughts had always been there, but now had much more power. If I was out socially (and that was becoming rare), I'd be talking to someone and simultaneously there would be another powerful dialogue going on in my mind. I'd be thinking, *I wonder if this person knows I'm a no-talent fake.*

. . .

During a few days clean in the summer of 1991, I met my daughter for the first time.

I had received her letter only two days earlier. It said: 'My mother has just told me that you're my natural father.'

There was a little photo of her inside. She looked very much like some of my relatives in Ireland. She was 17. In the letter, she told me all about herself – that she was good at drama and music. It was almost as if she felt she needed to sell herself to me. Of course she didn't. I was dying to see her.

She concluded the letter by saying the sweetest thing: 'I know that you tried to see me and were turned away. I just hope you don't turn me away.'

That night, I phoned the number at the top of the page and spoke to her Aunty Janet in Scarborough. I'd met Janet when I was going out with Sophia, my daughter's mother. She said she would accompany my daughter down to London, two days hence.

I started to panic. I was living in a dump. The place was dirty and a mess, and there were cardboard boxes everywhere. Jim's lovely wife Sandra helped me clean it up. She also lent me some money to take my daughter and her aunty for lunch.

We arranged to meet outside WHSmith at King's Cross station. I waited nervously. Finally, a woman of about my age appeared; she had a teenage girl with her who was wearing a red dress. I was wearing a red T-shirt. I said hello, shook my daughter's hand, and gave her a peck on the cheek.

I couldn't believe this lovely girl could be my offspring. Her hair was brown and curly but bleached by the sun. Did she look like me? I wasn't sure. Then she put her hair up. The shape of the back of her head was a dead giveaway. It was my family all over. And when I saw her from the side, I knew she was a McDonnell.

We had a lovely day together – a meal and then I took them both to meet Jim and Sandra. In the evening, we went to the Wag club. She loved it there.

We spent some time together the next day, and then she went back up north. I cried for the rest of that day and the following day. My tears were for all I'd missed – the life of this person, who was a part of me. For the first time, I understood a deep truth – the profound connection between father and child. Something I'd previously had no comprehension of.

I don't need cocaine any more, not now that I've found my daughter, I thought. I was wrong. Cocaine addiction was way more powerful than me or my love for anyone.

. . .

On cocaine, I'd become way too paranoid to interact with other people, and didn't want to share my gear anyway.

I'd sniff a big line as I lay in bed alone in my scruffy apartment, then pull the blankets high over my chin, making sure I was nice and warm. I'd then put my palms down onto my thighs. I would begin to feel a warm glow in the rest of my body. My cock and balls would be feeling electrified and calling out to be touched. I would cup my hands over them and enjoy that warmth. It was a kind of bliss, and the only time I would feel at peace. But it didn't last long and would soon be followed by ever-increasing paranoia and longer and longer comedowns, where I would feel some combination of complete despair and anxiety. The downs were by far outweighing the brief enjoyment I experienced at the start of my binges. But I couldn't stop.

If it had only been about that nice feeling that I got for the first few minutes of the binge, I might still be doing cocaine. But there were so many negative consequences. In between binges, I no longer wanted to live. Almost all my energy, vitality and optimism had gone, and I couldn't see a way out.

Each time I got a few days clean, denial would trigger me to believe, *This time it's going to be different. I will be able to control and enjoy my cocaine, like other people do, and like I did in the early days.*

My daughter moved in with me, and after a few weeks realised that her father had a real problem. She would hear me walking about during the night as she tried to sleep. We had an honest conversation about it, where she told me that she knew I was addicted. I had a moment of real clarity and lucid sanity. I saw what I'd become.

I was living in a squat, while my beautiful, talented daughter was wanting to go to drama school, and I couldn't even help her because I was blowing anything I had on cocaine.

I felt a conviction and strength rise up in me that I'd never experienced before. I made a firm decision there and then: it was over.

I swore to my daughter with all of my heart that I would never touch cocaine again, and I knew in that moment that I had the strength to stay away from it forever. If you had put me on a lie-detector test, I would have passed it because in that moment I was telling the truth.

During the following days, I felt empowered. I couldn't believe how stupid I had been. *Why had I been so weak to allow cocaine to get a hold of me?* And what about all the money I'd wasted? But now I had beaten it. Finally! As each day passed, my conviction grew and I *knew* I would never take cocaine again. I was two weeks clean and feeling great.

I went out to a gig. A friend said to me, 'Kev, do you want a little one?'

'No, thanks,' I said firmly.

He started to turn towards the toilets.

As he walked away, these words came out of my mouth: 'Yeah. Go on then.'

All of the determination of the previous couple of weeks had completely disappeared. I was off again. Once I'd had the first line, the *only* important thing for me was to get more. I was on another binge. I was with people who could do it socially, but I was completely different to them. I needed to get away, be in my room, alone with my cocaine. My daughter had moved out by this point.

I felt I was going insane, and feared insanity way more than death. Death would have been a relief.

I would lie in bed, high, trying to sleep after a coke binge, attempting to banish the thought from my head that I had fucked up again and would have no money for food this week.

Then I'd hear a sound. Maybe the police were coming in the windows or were already in the flat?

Shit! Panic.

I'd better check.

I'd get up as slowly and quietly as I could, naked, dripping with sweat. I'd pick up the carving knife that lay next to my bed. Trying to avoid making the floorboards creak, I'd walk towards the front room, kick the door open, knife outstretched, convinced I was going find the police in there.

Phew. Nobody there.

I'd better check the other rooms. Maybe they're in the wardrobe. Or in the fridge.

I would actually look.

I'd get back into bed, safe in the knowledge that there was nobody there. I'd close my eyes and try to sleep.

Then: a sound! *I'd better have another check around.*

This would go on and on.

When the paranoia would lessen, it was still impossible to sleep. My mind would be racing with deeply negative thoughts, and the bedclothes would be literally soaking from my sweat. I would instead lie on the other side of the bed, but 30 minutes later, that section too would be soaked. I'd put a bath towel down over the mattress. Soon that would be soaking wet too.

Despite the tiredness, I would feel sexually possessed. My body was exhausted but my sexual urges were far more powerful and I would have to wank until I came. As soon as I had ejaculated, the overpowering urge to come again would be right back on me. This would go on for hours. I would come eight, nine or ten times, and feel my arm was going to drop off from pumping.

My insides were starting to weaken. There were occasions when I didn't make it to the toilet in time for a bowel movement.

Even when I was off coke, my anxiety was now off the scale. Any noise, the slamming of a door, for example, would make me jump. Cocaine had shot me to pieces. I was tired, weak and dead inside. I hated myself and everyone else. I didn't want to live, but I didn't have the guts, or whatever it takes, to kill myself.

An old friend, Chris, told me some years later he had spotted me from his car as I walked through Willesden, and how shocked he was at the change in me. I'd looked paranoid and crazy, talking to myself.

Sometimes I would find it hard to get the strength to walk down the street to the supermarket. I felt like a very old man. On one such walk, I saw some people putting up posters for a meditation organisation. I was curious and went along. They were called the Brahma Kumaris and operated locally in a building that looked clean and pure. The polar opposite to how I felt. They offered stress-management courses for free. That puzzled me. But I was desperate and took one.

Next, I did what they called 'The Course'. They taught me that we were all part of a never-ending cycle. That we had all been here before, approximately 5,000 years ago, and we would keep repeating the process infinitely, and that we are now living in the Iron Age (Hell on earth). I didn't need convincing on that one.

They said the world would soon end, and shortly afterwards we would once again ascend into a Golden Age (bliss on earth). Those of us who had this knowledge were the advance party, the chosen ones, tasked with the responsibility of leading the world into this new era. It was attractive and I liked what these people had, peace and serenity. They looked clean, I felt dirty.

Their blissful meditations convinced me that there really was something powerful going on here. I began to do what they suggested: wake at four every morning, meditate, then join them at the centre for more meditation at 7am. Much of the focus was on what I now know to be the third eye (the point just above and in between the eyes). Whatever it was, it was certainly working on me. During those meditations, I not only felt more peaceful, but often as high as a kite. Absolutely buzzing with a spiritual connection. I felt that I had found God. God had been talked about in my childhood, and was something I believed but never really felt. Now I had a connection!

Then they told me that in order to be a member, I was expected to be celibate. I was not only required to abstain from alcohol, drugs, cigarettes, meat, fish (I was happy to sign up to that), also onions and garlic (which were said to induce horniness), but I also needed to be 100 per cent celibate. No masturbation, nothing. If sexual thoughts came, I was to hand them up to God.

That was a shock. I spoke to the guy who had been my main teacher.

'Why didn't someone tell me about the celibacy earlier?' I asked. I was now a few months in and completely hooked.

'It wasn't the right time to tell you,' he said.

I was in turmoil. This felt like the best thing I'd ever found. When I would wake at 4am to meditate, I would sometimes howl with laughter in happiness. I felt privileged that at last I knew God, and I was so excited that I told almost everyone I knew. But celibacy was *some* commitment. They explained that, because we had been sexual beings throughout the Silver, Bronze and Iron Ages, it was now time to get ready to be spiritual beings as we approached the Golden Age, and that meant purity.

I decided to go all out and do it.

Cocaine, alcohol, cigarettes, meat – all seemed to fall away, quite easily. Sex was more troublesome. Sometimes I would last a month, sometimes a couple of weeks, before succumbing to masturbation or sex, after which I would feel terrible, as if I had betrayed God. I was already a guilt-ridden Catholic, but this was on a whole other level.

. . .

Just as I was getting into the Brahma Kumaris, an old friend, Olly, told me about a programme of recovery for cocaine addicts. He was a former cokehead himself but now completely clean.

I really didn't think I needed it. The BKs would be enough, I believed, but I decided to go along to a couple of meetings, as I always enjoyed hanging out with Olly.

At first it seemed to be just a load of people struggling. I couldn't see how this could be more effective than the Brahma Kumaris. In fact, I enticed a couple of people from the meetings down to the Brahmans.

But before long I started to really struggle with the BKs. I was finding it very hard to do the celibacy thing. I tried to talk to one or two of the people there about it, including one of the elders, but didn't get much understanding, just a 'get on with it' attitude. I started to wonder why I couldn't do celibacy like the other BKs.

Cigarette smoking was the first thing to return. Then, one day, sitting in a cocaine addicts' meeting, I made the decision to start taking drugs again. I was listening to a guy talking about how he had just relapsed on heroin and crack and how miserable he felt. I thought, *Really? That sounds fucking great to me!*

I reasoned that I hadn't taken enough heroin. I'd tried it a couple of times, but that was all. I decided that if I took a little bit of heroin here and there, I'd be able to handle the cocaine paranoia. It made perfect sense.

I knew there was some money due in from EMI Records. I planned my relapse, down to the day. I decided I would only drink alcohol on the first night and not take any cocaine. I believed that as I had not enjoyed my drug-taking in the last couple of years, this was a chance to approach it in a different, more rational way – to savour it, enjoy it.

Simultaneously, I decided to leave the Brahma Kumaris. In doing so, I felt I'd turned my back on God. That guilt would haunt me for years.

Just before my relapse, I bumped into Zanna in a supermarket. I mentioned that I was about six months clean by this time. She said, 'You look so well!' I thanked her and told her that I was planning a few binges. She said warmly, 'Kev, please don't.'

I was touched by her concern, and perhaps some very small part of me knew she was right. But my mind was already made up. I was excited.

On the night in question, I got dressed up and went out to my favourite bar.

I will just drink alcohol. No cocaine or other drugs tonight. I'll go slow and enjoy it.

I bought a bottle of Becks and took a small sip. It tasted odd, just like the first time I'd tried beer when I was a kid. I was able to take another couple of small sips, until finally I could control myself no longer. I gulped the rest of the beer down and finished it in a few seconds. I looked around, *Where's the dealer?*

I found one.

Again, I was determined to be like a normal person taking cocaine, not an addict, so I invited an acquaintance to have a line with me.

Once inside the toilet, as I was unwrapping the coke, I told him, 'This is my first in seven months.'

'Oh, so it's a big thing?' he said.

'Nah. No big deal,' I lied.

If I remember correctly, I didn't fully lose control that night. I think it was about 24 hours before I was once again intensely paranoid and in despair.

The experiment of combining heroin with coke to take the edge off might have worked if I hadn't kept taking more and more cocaine, rendering the calming effects of the heroin useless.

I did the same with sleeping tablets. I would take them, thinking I would get some sleep, enabling me to save a little cocaine for the morning. But I would continue sniffing after taking the pills, so that the cocaine completely overrode them.

Finally, I decided buying heroin was a waste of money. I only wanted to go one way. Up! Not down. Whatever money I had would go on cocaine only. Of course, that just made the comedowns far longer and more intense.

I wasn't enjoying the binges. And when you are taking drugs compulsively and they aren't working, it's very dark. There was no buzz any more. It was just me in bed with my cocaine.

I tried to stop several times but couldn't. I wondered if this was the end for me: death or insanity.

I thought about the guys in the recovery meetings and wished I was with them. I also thought about the Brahma Kumaris. I would imagine them all wearing white and peacefully meditating, like I used to. Once or twice I thought I saw one of them in my wardrobe.

How could I get out of this and back into some kind of recovery? Cocaine was making all my decisions.

I had heard someone in the meetings saying, 'When you can't stop, pray for the willingness to stop.' I did that. I got down on my knees and begged. Nothing changed for a few weeks. Then right out of the blue, on a day that was by no means the worst, a very strong feeling came over me: *I just can't do this any more. I can't live like this any more.*

I knew there was a meeting the next day at noon. It was a question of hanging on till then. I counted the minutes and hours until, finally, I was so happy to arrive at the meeting.

They had a section reserved for newcomers. I said, 'I'm back and this time I'm staying. Day one!' I meant it.

They gave newcomers a white plastic chip, which signifies surrender, and that's what I was happily doing – admitting I was beaten. That was 28 August 1993.

I grabbed every piece of literature they would give me, and stuck much of it on the wall of the bedsit in Harlesden where I now resided (I had been turfed out of the Willesden squat). I would repeat the slogans aloud over and over as I sat in my room. I would also write insights and positive thoughts on Post-Its and put those on the wall too.

Since that first meeting in 1993, I've never had to take cocaine or any mind-altering substance. The powerful obsession that had me in its grip has been removed, thanks to the programme, for which I'm immensely grateful.

PART FIVE

Big man with the cufflinks

In those days, a lot of people in the recovery meetings went to rehabs, so I thought I'd do the same. I'd heard about a 'daycare' place and decided to try it. It was free to those who were broke and on the dole (people like Eric Clapton raised money for this and other treatment centres). It was a five-day-a-week, nine-to-five set-up, and we were expected to attend regular evening recovery meetings of the fellowship where I'd got my newcomer chip.

On my third day, as I sat in a group therapy session with more than 20 addicts, about to tell my life story to the whole of the room, the counsellor loudly asked me if I was nervous.

'No,' I said.

'You look it,' he said.

'I'm not,' I said.

I thought he was digging me out and trying to make me look bad in front of everyone.

'Are you *sure* you're not nervous?'

'I'm absolutely sure!'

I was actually terrified, but I had never admitted to anyone that I was frightened in any way. That would be way more terrifying than the fear itself. I strongly believed it would be used against me.

I was all charm initially in the groups, and then found myself getting annoyed at a couple of the other clients who employed that 'therapy' way of speaking all the time. One of them confronted me in a group session over a joke I'd made during the break. This guy had clearly been living in a therapeutic community for some time and knew all the lingo. I was coming straight from living alone, paranoid and in one room. This way of speaking was like a foreign language to me.

I had thought the idea in rehabs was to show how strong you were. I did my best to shut this guy up, as the counsellors looked on. It turned out that being tough wasn't what they were looking for, far from it. They wanted us to get vulnerable. That didn't make any sense to me.

The counsellors got annoyed at me for what I perceived at the time was just standing up for myself. I felt as though they were ganging up on me. It seemed unfair and I told them so.

The main counsellor, in front of the whole rehab group, asked me if the way I was feeling in that moment was familiar. It was actually *frighteningly* familiar and exactly how I felt in my family.

'No,' I said, 'not at all,' and continued my defence. All I knew to do was fight.

In the next group therapy session, I took on everyone who was there, including the counsellors. I told them they had treated me unjustly. The counsellors mostly sighed with exasperation. I had no idea what they meant, and continued to be disruptive.

Three weeks later, in another group session, a girl was saying how happy she was that she had made so many good friends there. I abruptly interjected, 'I feel like I want to spoil your nice fucking party!' The therapist (who happened to be the family counsellor), just looked on and didn't say much, but over the next few weeks I got the strong feeling she was observing me closely. I was a bit nervous around her – vaguely uncomfortable about my rudeness.

Not long before I left, it came to be my turn in the family session, led by the same counsellor.

As the rest of the group looked on, she asked me about my grand-parents, aunts, uncles and extended family, and she wrote their names on a big display board in the form of a family tree. She asked me to speak a little bit about each of them. She would add notes as I spoke, putting a big 'A' over their name if I said they were alcoholic. She then asked more about my immediate family and we looked at the various roles we'd all taken or been assigned.

She asked a lot about my dad. 'Did he say this?' 'Did he say that?' 'Did you feel like this?' 'And how did your siblings respond?'

I was shocked that what she was saying was so spot on. It was unnerving! Finally, in all seriousness, I said, 'Do you *know* my dad?' She just smiled.

She continued asking questions and making observations with uncanny accuracy. Then, finally, over my name, she wrote the word, 'SCAPEGOAT'. It was a shock, but it *wasn't* a shock. I knew that it was the truth. What *was* definitely a shock was that she was so right about everything. But it felt great to be understood.

I was the scapegoat in the family!

Yes, I played up to it and got in all kinds of trouble, but I was the scapegoat before that, too. In that role I soaked up the negative energy that was flying around.

The trouble I'd gotten into with the police was explained when she told me I had a 'classic criminal upbringing'. She didn't mean that I was from a criminal family. She knew that I wasn't. She was talking about the pressure that had been piled on me, and how much unexpressed anger was stored up in me as a result, and how such an upbringing very often leads to a life of crime and anti-social bitterness. I could totally see that.

Growing up, and in adult life, I was so angry that I did not give a fuck! I would have been quite happy to go to prison. It's a miracle that apart from a few days in police cells, I've never spent a day in jail. In my teens and later, I would have done *anything*. I didn't care. It was only breaking Mum's heart that stopped me from exploding with anger. Rage and guilt were one hell of a toxic mix.

Around the time of the first Dexys album, I had suggested in all seriousness to Jim and Kevin Archer that we should follow the album with a film, then, as a third and final act, blow up the Houses of Parliament and go to prison for a long time.

It was probably only the first Dexys wanting to kick me out that gave me the impetus and renewed vigour to carry on in music. If Kevin and Jim had been interested in the film and Houses of Parliament idea, I would have been up for going through with it. Obviously the grand drama of the artistic and political statement appealed, but I also see how little regard I had for my own life.

Music had kept me so busy and obsessed that it saved me from acting out in other ways, which surely would have landed me in jail. In that way, music saved me. Yet even with the help of music, I came very close to prison. When I was on the suspended sentence for violence in 1981, it didn't even occur to me not to hit audience members at the front who were heckling. My manager would say, 'Kev, for fuck's sake! You're on a suspended sentence, man!' But the rage was always there.

Earlier in that revelatory family session, I had told the counsellor about one of Dad's typical criticisms: 'Look at him. Big man with the cufflinks.'

At the end of the session, I said, 'Well, all of this makes so much sense, but what do I do now?'

She just smiled and said, 'Get yourself a great big pair of cufflinks!'

I felt like a weight had been lifted off my shoulders.

I'd love to say that session was a significant turning point with permanent effectiveness, and certainly there were other major break-throughs, not least when I cried genuine, heartfelt tears in the group therapy. They'd asked me to write a letter to my eight-year-old self and read it out in front of everyone. At their suggestion I'd also brought in a photo of myself from that time. I'd hesitated before reading the letter and kept making excuses.

'I can't see the point of this. This is just method acting.'

The counsellor finally said, 'Why don't you just read it?'

I held up the picture in front of myself and started to read. Instantly, I burst into tears and sobbed uncontrollably for the next five minutes, to the extent that I could barely read what I'd written.

However, sadly, for the remainder of my time in the rehab, I went back into debilitating anxiety. The backlog of emotion was just too big. When I had an intense feeling, I'd hide it.

For example, on one occasion I was chatting with a girl in the social area, and her counsellor approached, saying, 'I'm thinking we should extend your stay here as it's coming up to Christmas and it's a vulnerable time.' The girl agreed. *I* had started at the same time as her and was due to leave at the same time too. No one had suggested *I* stay on. I immediately started to convince myself it was because I was disliked. And instead of expressing those ugly feelings in a group, or even to my counsellor, I kept it all inside.

That was only one example of many, with the result that I started acting as this gentle, sensitive man, because I thought that's what was required. I winged my way through the rest of my time there and felt bitter at those who completed their stay with more authenticity than I had.

. . .

I was still living in my bedsit in Harlesden and money was short. If I didn't manage my benefit money carefully, I wouldn't have enough for rolling tobacco or even food. One day, when my old friend Chris, who was also now in recovery, came round, we found a £10 note in one of my jacket pockets. We were so delighted, we almost danced around the room.

I was going to my programme meetings, but I wasn't doing much more and spent a lot of time alone. I didn't get a sponsor (mentor), which was recommended in the programme, and I began to feel more and more confused and despondent. I was clean but that was all.

After about seven months off drugs, I could stand it no more and went to see a psychologist at Central Middlesex Hospital. I was planning to 'nut myself off' (i.e. volunteer to be sectioned). They said they would take me in for observation. It felt like a relief.

Coincidentally, on the same day, I had an appointment at Brent Council to organise a free bus pass to enable me to get to recovery meetings. I went from Middlesex Hospital straight to the council office. The caseworker I saw there was a friendly guy from the North of Ireland.

While processing my travel pass, he asked me how I was doing. I don't know why, but I opened up to him. I said, 'I'm really struggling, man. I'm looking at going into a mental hospital.'

He said, 'There *are* other options, you know.'

'Like what?' I said.

'Secondary rehab treatment?'

He offered me the opportunity of six-month secondary care at a live-in, all-male rehab in Clapham. I'd heard about the place and I agreed to try it.

I'd been quite isolated in the last few years, and being in close proximity with 20-plus other men was going to be difficult, but I needed to do something drastic, and I knew in my heart that it was a better option than going into a mental hospital and being pumped full of drugs.

I ended up sharing a room with two other guys in a big old house. It was a shock to the system but, overall, positive. The three meals a day, alone, was grounding and nourishing, and I actually found myself starting to adopt all the therapy-speak.

I met a kind female counsellor there, Blom. She showed me incredible patience and warmth, and counselled me for some time after I left.

I would sometimes snap when a fellow resident asked me about Dexys Midnight Runners. I no longer wanted to be the guy from Dexys. I wished I had no history in that respect. I just wanted to be the same as everyone else.

Another reason I hated being asked about Dexys was because on some level I knew how seductive praise had been for me. I had succumbed to it before and it had damaged me. I didn't want that to happen again. Not to mention that I didn't feel ready to face the fact that I'd made such a hash of things. Plus, Dexys was only one facet of my personality. I hated, and still do, when I'm seen only as the guy from Dexys. That feels so limiting and stifling.

Much to my surprise, the other residents foolishly and naïvely voted me in as house leader. It was a month-long gig that meant I would need to organise the cleaning rota for the rest of the guys and make sure everything was being done properly.

I did the job with relish. I was bossy and perfectionistic, and even encountered rebellion from one or two, which I took personally, of course. In the end, I was actually relieved when the month was over, as I think some of the residents were!

One of the tenets of the recovery programme was prayer. On a day when I felt particularly down and doubtful that I would ever feel better, I prayed, 'If there is anything out there, please give me a sign. Show me that I'm on the right path.'

About two weeks later, some money, £80,000, that I had been chasing for years came through.

In the late eighties, London Records made it clear that if I left Mercury, they would sign me to their label. After I did, London Records changed their minds, and went cold. It took me about a year to realise that they weren't going to sign me. On the advice of my accountant, Joe O'Sullivan, I contacted a lawyer, Richard Southern, who pursued them for compensation.

I had dreamt of getting my hands on that money when I was in active cocaine addiction. Of course, the bulk of it would have gone up my nose. And if it had arrived during my bankruptcy period, I've no doubt the trustee would have taken it. Fortunately, by this time, my bankruptcy period had just ended.

Now I would be able to do some positive things – maybe put a deposit down on a flat, help my daughter a little. I knew it was a blessing.

In touch with my femininity

While in rehab, popular songs from my childhood and early teens had started to jump into my memory like beacons of light. They connected with me on a deeper level than any of the group therapy I was taking. They seemed to reveal profound truths. I was so emotionally raw that I cried as I remembered pretty much each one. These songs seemed to be guiding me. I *knew* that my next musical step had to be to record them. Easier said than done.

I'd been used to singing my own lyrics that held obvious meaning for me, but with these songs I hadn't written the words. Then I saw a quote from Levi Stubbs of the Four Tops saying that just because you hadn't written a song didn't mean you couldn't find a way to get inside it, and more than that, it was crucial that you *did* if you wanted the song to connect with other people. I thought a lot about that, and with the help of singing coach Mark Meylan I managed to bring my own meaning to each of the songs.

After significant interest from a couple of other big companies, I signed with Creation Records as they were the happening label of the time. The album was produced mostly by Big Jim Paterson and the masterful Pete Schwier and, apart from a few ups and downs, the recordings went well. Some of my best singing up to that point is on there.

The record was called *My Beauty* and came out in 1999.

. . .

Not long after leaving the treatment centre and way before recording the album, completely organically, I started to get in touch with my femininity. At first I painted my finger and toenails, started wearing sarongs, and later dresses and a little make-up. It felt nourishing and great.

That was the look I wore for the *My Beauty* album.

I'd love to say that the media reaction to the album was mixed, but it wasn't. With one or two notable exceptions, they lambasted me. Not for the music – that was barely mentioned – but for the look. I wore a dress on the cover, pulled up to reveal stockings and men's lingerie. I guess it must have disturbed something deep in them to have triggered such vitriol.

With regard to the record label, when I first showed Alan McGee (the company boss) the cover for the record, he absolutely loved it and said: 'This is great! It places you in Radio 1 land. I love it!' That's a direct quote. He felt that the clothes I was wearing made the whole campaign much more contemporary, and gave us a serious chance at getting Radio 1 airplay, whereas without it, Radio 2 would have been our only port of call. But when the media started lambasting me, I felt I was on my own with it, as if I was someone perceived to be very vulnerable and damaged, who had been taken off the scrap heap and signed as an act of benevolence.

Also, for some reason, he would tell me the negative comments that some of his staff were making about me. I would think, *Why on earth is he telling me that? How could that possibly help anything?* I was already struggling with the onslaught from the media, all this did was upset me further.

Admittedly, the first full-length image people saw was extreme and with hindsight, it may have been advisable to start the visual campaign with something less shocking. But together, we had devised the idea of massive full-length posters, and I was up for it.

It had been 11 years since I'd released a record. During which time, the media had heard virtually nothing from me – and now I was back as virtually a different person, and that was exactly how I felt. I wished at that point that I didn't have a musical past. I felt it was dragging me down.

Alan says retrospectively that the clothes I wore on the cover rendered the album non-commercial. That's not the impression I got at the time. If that had been how he saw it, I'm sure he would have suggested we secure some radio play for the album first (he had told me how good he thought the music was), *before* revealing the visuals, which was in fact an idea we discussed. At the time, it was my clear perception that Alan initially very much liked the shock value of the look. For me it wasn't a gimmick. It was a lifestyle.

People were saying I was crazy. *Maybe I was*, I thought. It seems incredible now that wearing a dress could evoke such vitriol and, even worse, the most patronising 'well-meaning, caring' attitude towards this guy who was so vulnerable, he had lost his marbles'. It was such bullshit.

And there were so many double standards going on. For example, I did an interview with Billy Bragg when he was guesting as the host on a Radio 2 Saturday afternoon show. During the live interview, Billy picked up the album cover. Laughing, he pointed to the picture and, in his broadest Essex accent, sneered, 'Look! You can practically see your cream crackers there, mate.' That old feeling of shame engulfed me. The blood went up to my head. I was overwhelmed and unable to defend myself.

He had turned all blokey. It was only later, when I could compose myself, that I realised the absurdity of somebody who presents themselves as politically 'right on' demonstrating such double standards. If he'd picked up a picture of a woman and made the same comments – 'Look, I can practically see your minge there, babe' – he would rightly be lambasted. And he *himself* would probably lambast other men for doing the same thing.

But it was open season on me. And what he was saying wasn't out of the ordinary.

Billy Bragg was somebody whose politics I would mostly agree with, apart from what I felt to be his ridiculous position on the Six Counties in the north of Ireland. He said publicly, in the eighties, that he believed the British troops should remain there. Now I can understand how any young working-class man or woman could be seduced into joining the British Army without knowing what they were really fighting for, but I find it much harder to understand how anyone who publicly supports freedom and socialist struggles the world over could support the British Army's occupying presence in the north of Ireland. Socialism could never happen in Britain while Irish people were being denied their basic rights.

When I did that radio interview in 1999, I didn't know about Billy Bragg's views on the Six Counties. To me, he just appeared to be a reasonable bloke, and when a seemingly reasonable bloke starts to criticise you, it can be very crazy-making.

Some years later, I was really pleased to read a comment on YouTube from Junior Campbell, who co-wrote 'Reflections Of My Life', about my version of the song, which was on the album: 'Brilliant heartfelt version of my song, personalised by Kevin. I frigging love it.'

Unable to live in the world

The longer I was off cocaine, the more uncontrollable anger came up. I realised that if I didn't deal with it, I was going to go backwards and start taking drugs again.

I decided to properly launch myself into the programme of recovery. I got myself a great mentor, Paddy, who was a lovely human-rights lawyer from the north of Ireland. He really helped me.

I learned that in cocaine addicts, the will is useless when it comes to cocaine. Any *real* cocaine addict cannot stay away from it on their own power for any length of time. I've heard other people say that they stopped on their own power, and hence be critical of people like me who need help. What they don't understand is that *they* are not *real* addicts. The very *definition* of an addict or alcoholic is that they *can't* stop on their own power. Willpower is useless for real addicts, no matter how strong it may be in other areas.

The only hope for a *real* addict is spiritual help.

I also learned that when cocaine enters the system of an addict, they lose all control. It isn't a question of choice. The craving is far more powerful than any desire or reason to stop.

I learned that I didn't start off as a cocaine addict. I had at least a modicum of control and enjoyed good times when I started, otherwise I wouldn't have continued. I became an addict as a result of taking cocaine. It damaged my brain and body.

The delusion that I would ever be able to control cocaine was smashed. Prior to that, I'd always fallen prey to the belief that a period away from coke would enable me to enjoy it again. But now I saw that was a lie. I looked at my cocaine-taking history and realised that each time I'd relapsed, believing it would be different this time, I immediately went back to my old paranoid and crazy addicted state, willing to do anything to get more cocaine.

I learned that cocaine addiction is an illness and that I desperately needed to work the rest of the programme or I wouldn't stay clean.

It is a prerequisite of the process to believe in some kind of power greater than yourself, a god of your own understanding. That was difficult for me, because although I initially chose a more friendly concept of God than the one I grew up with, just the mention of the word brought up the old Irish Catholic guilt, complete with all its punishing, vengeful associations. I say 'Irish Catholic guilt' because Catholic guilt is one thing, and Irish Catholic guilt is a whole other. Certainly that was my experience, and it was, and is, very difficult to break free from.

Through the programme, I started to see that I wasn't the person I thought I was. I saw that at times I had behaved despicably. I had always seen myself as socialist and egalitarian – and in my heart, I believed in those principles – but my actions said something different.

And I had been incapable of being honest, even with myself: I had spent my life trying to act like a tough guy so that I wouldn't be bullied. It hadn't worked.

I saw that although I had worked hard at presenting an independent image, I had been a chronic people pleaser. I'd said yes to things I wasn't sure about, and would then get resentful at the other parties later when things didn't go the way I wanted, often leading to a bigger confrontation than if I'd been clear in the first place. Yes, in childhood, I had needed to act, to get by at home and at school, but I'd carried on with this massive dishonesty in adult life, all driven by fear.

I began to see that I was afraid of being alone, I was afraid to be around people, I was afraid of being a failure, yet I was also afraid of being successful, because that meant people would be jealous and take shots at me.

Basically, I was unable to live in the world. Playing a part had become the only self I knew, hence I had no idea that I'd been living in such fear. It was unthinkable to try to be my real self in front of people. I simply couldn't. After many years in the programme, that's still a work in progress but massively improved.

I had been a sole enterprise since I was about ten years old. That was the age I stopped trusting other people and started pretending.

In romantic affairs, fear of being alone meant I would rush in before I was even sure I was ready, then have doubts later. What I really meant when I said 'I love you' was: 'I want you to commit to me and no one else.'

I knew all about obsession, but nothing about *real* love or how to be honest in difficult times. I didn't know how to deal with a partner when I was in one of my down moods. I thought everything was supposed to be rosy, all the time, if I was in a happy relationship. So I would just pretend, until I couldn't pretend any more, and then I would leave.

And I saw what a bully I'd been, to girlfriends, band members and others.

I also discovered that I suffered bouts of low-grade depression. I was officially diagnosed by one of the best psychiatrists in the country and, while I accepted the diagnosis, I'm happy that I declined drug-based treatment, preferring to find natural ways to treat it.

With the help of another sponsor, Mick, I saw that I had a self-centred tendency to be massively over-responsible and blame myself for everything bad that happened. He told me, 'You think you're to blame for everything. If someone said, "Where was Rowland in 1939?" you would take that on.' And as ludicrous as it sounds, as he spoke, I started to feel as though I could be responsible for the war. Not logically, but in the way I felt. Obviously, that was ridiculous.

I had to make amends to everyone I'd harmed. Jackie and Zanna were high on the list. I'm happy to say that both have forgiven me and we are now good friends.

I also discovered that many of my old pals from my younger days were also either in recovery from alcohol or drug addiction, or had died from one of these illnesses. It's as if we had gravitated towards each other before any of us even got properly into substances.

'The worst mess I've ever seen'

After a day trip down to Brighton in 1995, I decided to move there. The air felt fresher than in London, and the general vibe much lighter. I'd always seen it as a cool town.

After getting a mortgage and buying a one-bedroom flat, I excitedly did it up with more feminine edges than I would have previously. Purple and pink fabric adorned the walls.

But within six months of moving, I got some news from the trustee in bankruptcy.

Although my official bankruptcy term had finished in 1994 and I had started to receive songwriting royalties again, the bankruptcy debts were still not fully paid off, so they'd decided to seize all my songwriting royalties once more until every penny was paid up. The problem was, I had just taken out a mortgage and had no other way of making the repayments.

I signed back on the dole and spoke to the Social Security about help with my mortgage. I found out that a new law had been introduced the previous year, where the government would only pay 25 per cent of the interest on mortgages for the first two years of the term. Apparently, some people had been buying expensive properties, then signing on the dole and getting the government to cover the mortgage repayments.

I started to really panic. There was nothing for it but to sell the flat and move back into a bedsit. It didn't bother me much. I just wanted rid of the stress hanging over my head.

But just as I was about to put the flat on the market, I opened a letter from the Performing Rights Society, the non-profit agency that collects TV and radio broadcasting royalties on behalf of songwriters. Obviously I wasn't receiving any royalties from them, so I was surprised that they were sending me mail.

It was a circular letter, asking for donations to help songwriters who had fallen on hard times. It talked about PRS's 'Members Fund' and its long tradition of helping songwriters who were down on their luck.

Hang on, I thought. *That's me!*

I phoned PRS and told them of my situation. One of the staff came down to my place in Brighton about a week later, and looked at all the paperwork that proved my situation was genuine. Shortly afterwards, a cheque arrived from PRS that would pay my mortgage for the next 12 months! I was so grateful to them, and still am.

However, at the same time some large, old and disputed Dexys bills that had come to light since the bankruptcy resurfaced, meaning that I found myself once again in the High Court.

Richard Southern, who had previously been my lawyer but no longer had a licence, was helping me, even though he wasn't allowed to speak in the court. I had to defend myself. I lost. The debts were piling up and it was looking like bankruptcy again.

I'd heard people in the recovery programme say, 'When you're in trouble, reach out to someone and share what's going on for you.' It was something I'd pretty much never done, but after much deliberation I reached out and told a beautiful, very humble man named David Enthoven. He had managed Roxy Music from their early days and was just starting out looking after Robbie Williams. Obviously, with him being in the music business, he might understand.

I told him straight: 'I'm screwed, I've got a court ruling and debts up to my eyeballs, with more coming in all the time. My royalties are frozen and I don't have the money to pay the debts.'

'You need Ronnie Harris,' he said.

'Who?' I asked.

'Ronnie Harris.'

'Why? How?'

He went on to tell me that Ronnie Harris, an accountant from the company Harris and Trotter, manages the business affairs of people and companies, particularly those in music, entertainment and sports.

I wasn't hopeful. Why would Ronnie want to help me? I had no money, and besides, I'd met other accountants and lawyers in the past, and most only seemed interested in themselves or, at the very least, working with more successful artists. Moreover, I didn't know how *anyone* would be able to sort out the absolute chaos that was my financial situation.

Nevertheless, I phoned him up. He told me that he was due to be at Gatwick Airport a few days hence, and suggested we meet there. 'Bring all the papers you have,' he said.

We sat in a hotel lobby as he looked over what I'd brought. 'It looks a *real* mess,' he said. 'Let me take a proper look at it and I'll get back to you in a week.'

A few days later he said, 'This is the worst mess I've ever seen. I'm probably never going to earn anything from you, but I've made a lot of money from the music business, so I don't mind putting something back.'

He decided he was going to take on the whole mess. Even then, I couldn't see how it could be cleaned up. It seemed too big. But over the next six years, that's exactly what Ronnie Harris did – sorted *everything* out.

He started by finding broadcasting royalties from countries where they hadn't been collected. He then meticulously went through all the debts; there was another big tax bill from the London Records settlement, and all manner of other bills.

He even went to the Isle of Man, to work out what had happened with those useless companies that had been set up as part of the eighties deal that was supposed to save tax. Whatever little money he found, he would allocate to the various creditors, in order of priority – all at no cost to me.

Until finally, about six years later, I was completely free of debt, as in *completely* free of debt! As in, I didn't owe *anybody, anything!* It felt amazing. All thanks to Ronnie Harris. Not only that, simultaneously he had negotiated with the trustee in bankruptcy and got my royalties coming back to me. Incredible.

By 2002, I was not only free of debt, but had an income. It wasn't a massive income, but it was an income.

Ronnie Harris is one of the kindest men I've ever met. Getting to know him over the years, I discovered that he is a socialist. Many people talk about how society should be fairer; Ronnie actually *works* to make it happen. He is always raising money for the needy, particularly children's charities by way of sponsored walks, climbs, bike rides and the like, which he undertakes himself. His efforts in helping less fortunate people are on another level. He is Jewish, and I understand that what he did for me is called a mitzvah – a very good turn for another human being. But that mitzvah didn't stop me from selfishly letting him, and myself, down. I will talk about that later.

As part of my amends process, I paid back all of the debts I was aware of on a personal level. That took time. A few years later, I decided I'd check with the bankruptcy people to see how much the seizing of my songwriting royalties had impacted my debts. When I finally got the figures, I was delighted to learn that *all* of the creditors had been paid in full: 100 per cent. The only reason that the bankruptcy remains on public record is because, although they've received all the money they were owed, they weren't paid interest.

'Pat, Pat, Pat'

I'm on the phone to my dad, bragging about how far I'd swum in the sea that morning. He immediately becomes grumpy, telling me I need to be careful or I could drown.

There goes Dad, treating me like a fucking idiot again. Fucking hell! I thought.

Then it occurred to me: *Hold on. He's concerned that I might actually drown.*

The man had already lost one son.

. . .

I told Pat that I loved him before the end. He was diagnosed with cancer of the oesophagus in May 2005. He would pass on 11 November of that year.

I went to the hospital in Coventry. It was awful to see my brother in such suffering; unable to speak, hooked up to a ventilator, and with so many tubes and wires coming out of him. At first, he was visibly afraid and desperate to get out of there. But in his last week or so, a real peace and acceptance came over him. He couldn't speak, but by pointing to the letters on an alphabet, he spelled out the words, 'I'm a lucky man.'

I was so desperate to be with him at the end, and my biggest fear was that I wouldn't be. But on that early morning, *all* his family were around his bed. The nurse could tell from the machine that he was slipping away. When the time came, she said, 'He's gone.'

And that's exactly what had happened. Pat had gone. I felt so much love for him as I looked at his body, lying there so still.

'Pat, Pat, Pat,' I said, over and over again. Even though I knew he was going, I was still shocked.

I'm not a Catholic any more, but on that November morning, I was moved by the way my parents, my brother Joe, my sisters, Pat's wife and kids, all said the rosary over his body.

Later, we went back to Joe's place to try and sleep for a while. Mum was getting ready to go back to St Albans. I felt for my little old mum. As she reached up to Joe and me in an effort to hug us both, she said, 'Look after yourselves. I used to have three sons, now I've only got two.'

The next day, Pat's daughter Molly phoned and asked me to read the eulogy at the funeral. I didn't think I deserved it – we hadn't been in touch much in later years, and I told her how I felt. She said, 'It's what he would have wanted.'

Pat and I were reunited.

He had been like a father to me when I was growing up – the one I looked up to and aspired to. In later years, even when I wasn't seeing him so much, I always thought about him. Nothing can take away the real love that existed between us.

I remember when he would go away on holiday. I'd count the days until he was due back. On the day of his scheduled return, I would be restless, excited, waiting. One day when he was due back from a trip, I was playing in the park and I could see him walking towards me. He was like a vision. I ran to him.

I didn't think Mum and Dad would survive Pat's passing, but they did. A couple of years later, I said to my mum, 'I was concerned that you wouldn't be able to carry on after Pat's going, Mum.'

She said: 'Ah, well, I've got to be here for the rest of ya.'

I could sense the suffering

Working the programme was helping a lot, but I had picked up the notion that I had to be perfect. I thought that if I behaved 100 per cent correctly, everything would be great and no one would upset me.

I would be puzzled when, for example, my dad would come out with a comment that I would find insensitive. I would blame myself, thinking I mustn't be working the programme properly, otherwise he wouldn't have said it. If people didn't respond to me positively, I thought it meant *I* needed to apologise.

It took me a long time to find some balance. Finally, I started to learn that the programme is teaching me to live in an imperfect world, not in some kind of spiritual haze where I would get on well with everybody and float around on a cloud.

As the result of talking about my family with my counsellor, Blom, I decided to speak with a relative from my dad's generation. We talked about my roots, until finally, completely unprompted by me, this relative told me that when they were parenting their young children, Dad had taken them aside and said, 'Most of your kids are all right, but watch out for *that* one.'

My relative's spouse was furious on hearing about this, and said that if they'd been around, they would have given my dad a piece of their mind.

While not pleasant for this family, it was comforting for me to know that Dad had been that way with someone else as well as me – negatively singling out a member of a family who was in no way worse than the others, nor to blame for anything.

. . .

It's 2009, I'm in County Mayo, Ireland, close to where my parents grew up.

Before leaving London, I googled 'vegetarian accommodation, Crossmolina'. The first name on the list that came up was Enniscoe House, Castlehill.

I visited my parents that Sunday before leaving.

'Mum, Dad, do you know Enniscoe House?'

'Enniscoe House? Of course we do,' Mum said.

'It's not even a mile from Crossmolina!'

It was the same distance in the other direction to the little farm where Dad grew up.

'What are you going there for? It's a big house!'

'Oh, they let rooms out,' I said.

'Do they?' Mum said, surprised. When she and Dad were in Mayo, it was purely a landed gentry's house.

Mum and Dad told me that the Enniscoe House family had been decent to the local people, in that they had paid their workers a better wage than other gentry in the area.

As I drove from Knock Airport to Crossmolina, past all the barren, rocky fields, it struck me that Mayo is almost deserted – still decimated from the potato blight of 1845 to 1850. And it is *haunted*. There is no other word for it. I looked over the deserted fields where villages once were, and I could feel spirits crying out to be heard. I could sense the suffering.

Enniscoe House is a massive country home that was built in the 18th century and has been in the same family of English gentry ever since. It has one of those huge quarter-of-a-mile drives up to the house, like you see in films.

Once inside, I was immediately overcome with sadness that people here had been living in such splendour while my dad was growing up in a family of eight in a tiny stables a mile away.

I decided to phone my mum to let her know I'd arrived. I knew she'd be curious.

She was delighted. 'Hullo, Keven,' she said in her soft Mayo tones. And with almost childlike enthusiasm, she said: 'Where are you?'

'I'm in Enniscoe House, Mum,' I said.

'Are you?' she said, enthusiastically. 'Is it nice?' not being able to contain her excitement.

My voice broke into a cry, as I said, 'I'm sad that dad was living in stables just up the road, while the ancestors of these people were living in such splendour, Mum.'

Mum could hear the tears in my voice.

'Ah well. At least they were nice people, love.'

I really felt for my dad and got a sense of just how hard it was for him and his family. I pictured them during those dark, miserable evenings with not enough to eat, undernourished and ravaged by TB. His mum died of it when he was 13, as did his sister Theresa, leaving his young sister May, a girl of 12, to do the cooking for the family.

Mum's childhood circumstances were similar, in that she had grown up in a big family, in a very small home, with virtually no money.

Later that night, as I sat in the massive sitting room, I looked around and saw the paintings of the previous family members, dressed in their British Army officer uniforms, some from 1925, when my dad would have been a seven-year-old boy. I couldn't help but feel angry.

My dad's father, Peter Rowland, was a coachman. The use of his family's home – the two-roomed outhouse that later became a stable – came with his job. It stood at the foot of a big house (Castlehill House) where a family of gentry lived. These were *Irish* gentry – quite unusual at the time.

When he wasn't doing manual work for them, he would chauffeur them in their horse-drawn coach. Dad and the other children were required to salute the occupants as they passed!

I must say that the family that ran Enniscoe House treated me with pure grace – lovely people.

. . .

During a previous trip to Crossmolina, Mayo, a decade earlier, I was directed to an old boy of 99 years of age. He had an amazing knowledge of the local people, much of it passed down from those who had gone before him.

I was particularly interested in the 'famine' of 1845 to 1850, the worst years being 1846 and 1847, when over a million died. But it wasn't a famine. It was a potato blight. Many other foods were grown and exported, but because the poor lived pretty much only on potatoes (many of them having been turfed off their land by gangs of thugs employed by absentee British landlords), they starved to death.

The old man told me that the police would guard the food as it was being transported for export. Starving people would be trying to get at it, but the police would beat them off.

He said that the Rowlands weren't so badly affected because they had tilled land and were able to grow other things. He didn't know anything about the McDonnells or Brownes (Mum's side) or the Conways (my paternal grandmother's side). But County Mayo was one of the worst-hit areas. No one knows how many died, as so many deaths went unrecorded. Some people were buried in shallow graves or in ditches, and some were just left to decompose and were eaten by rats or dogs.

There were officials who were motivated to misrepresent the numbers of deaths. In some workhouses, deaths from diseases, like cholera, were drastically under-reported lest the full extent of the horror be known. But the population of Ireland had halved by the end of the 19th century and it's estimated that 1.25 million starved to death between 1845 and 1851, while another two million emigrated. That shrinking population trend continued, mainly due to emigration, until the 1960s. Up to that point, it was the only country in the world whose population was getting smaller every year.

While I'm not into blind patriotism, I am proud of the massive contribution second-generation Irish Catholics have made to British culture – music in particular. From Boy George, Cathal Smyth (Chas Smash in Madness), John Lydon, Elvis Costello, Siobhan Fahey in Bananarama and Shakespears Sister, Shane MacGowan, all of the Smiths, and all of Oasis.

There is something unique about second-generation Irish Catholics in England. It's almost a social class in itself, completely different to first- and third-generation Irish. Most of our dads were working on building sites and judged as scruffy Paddies, while we were obsessed with being at the front of British culture.

I didn't like their vibe

I mentioned previously that I let down Ronnie Harris who, for a period of over five years, worked tirelessly, without pay, to get me out of financial trouble.

In 2012, after a 26-year break, I was at last ready to do a Dexys album. I told my fantastic manager of the time, Tim Vigon, that the time was right, and we set about looking for the right label.

Tim had come into my life in 2004 and waited patiently until I felt ready to do something. He never pushed.

The first company we met was a small label called 100% Records owned by Toby Harris, who also happened to be Ronnie's son. I liked his energy and positivity. Everything seemed right and, after a couple of meetings, I felt ready to sign for him there and then.

Bizarrely, I had a sort of premonition that a bigger label with more money but less passion would come in for us, and we'd be tempted but it would be the wrong move.

And that's exactly what happened. BMG Records registered interest and Tim and I went to see them. I didn't like their vibe. However, whereas 100% Records were a small label and unable pay an advance, BMG offered a fair-sized down payment, which we needed to finance a tour.

Tim, who had previously given me pretty much only great advice, was saying to me, 'It has to be BMG. You'll need the money for the shows.'

I got completely stressed out and overwhelmed. A small part of me wondered if I should talk to Ronnie and say, 'I want to sign for Toby, but we need to raise some money to tour. Is there a way we can do that?' But instead, I went into panic mode, buried my head in the sand and, in a sort of trance of denial, signed to BMG. It wasn't a good relationship. They were way less than proactive.

Despite *One Day I'm Going to Soar* being, I think, Dexys' best album up to that point and getting great reviews, they did the bare minimum. That was a bitter pill to swallow.

I can't blame Tim. It was only me who fully understood my deep relationship with Ronnie and it was only me who felt in my gut that Toby's plan and energy were much better than that of BMG's. But after all Ronnie had done for me, it was a disgraceful decision.

Anyway, fortunately, this episode has a happy ending. I got the chance to sign Dexys to Toby's 100% Records label for the 2023 album, *The Feminine Divine*. It turned out to be a real blessing. They loved the album and worked their arses off to make it Dexys' biggest chart success since 1982.

Once a man, twice a child

And now it's 17 August 2010, my birthday, and I get a phone call from my mum and dad. They sing happy birthday to me down the phone, which is unusual in itself. At the end of it, I chat with my mum for a couple of minutes. Then she says, 'I'll pass you over to your dad.'

'Happy birthday, Kevin,' Dad says in his usual clipped tone.

I say, 'Thanks, Dad.'

Then he says, 'Well, I can't think of anything else to say.' And passes the phone back to Mum.

I thought, *Typical bloody Dad. Doesn't want to talk to me. If it was someone else in the family, I bet he wouldn't be so quick off the phone.*

He put Mum back on. She paused for a second, and then said, 'He's crying.'

What? I was really shocked and touched.

I can't say that my relationship with Dad changed from that point on, but it was a welcome interval. I continued to be sensitive and easily triggered when I felt he was being critical and sometimes I would snap at him. I felt bad each time and had to make many apologies. I hated hurting Dad. But the truth is, if I didn't stand up to him, he would have completely dominated me. It was a tricky balance, which I often got wrong. I eventually saw that my lifelong mistake had been trying to impress him. It was never going to work, and nor should it. For an adult of my age to be still trying to impress his father was childish. I also resigned myself to the idea that things would never be great between us and that there would always be a distance.

Then something happened. In 2016, Dad had a mild stroke. Initially I couldn't see much difference in him, but I did wonder if he was a little more laid-back. Then I found out for sure.

My poor little mum was on her last legs from a load of ailments, but mainly lung disease, and often resident at their local hospital, Watford

General. I stayed with Dad at their home in St Albans one night during this period.

I woke early and went out to get something from my car. I heard the front door of the house slam behind me and realised I didn't have a key. I was locked out.

Shit! I would have to wake Dad up. That thought frightened me. He's going to be annoyed and ask me how the hell I managed to lock myself out. I could feel myself going into the old panic mode.

I knocked on the door. Dad answered, but there was no criticism or ill temper. He just let me in without any fuss. He had changed.

My beautiful mother passed on New Year's Eve 2016. She had a lonely passing in 'Bloody Watford', as she called the hospital. She hated that place.

Mum's favourite song was 'When I Leave the World Behind'. She sang it with such grace.

I leave the moon above to those in love
When I leave the world behind

. . .

Whenever I visited my parents in Mum's final few years, I would usually bring my laptop and a speaker. They would request their favourite old (usually Irish) songs, and Mum, Dad, my brother Joe and myself would sit and listen to them together. It was a great way to communicate. There would be no misunderstandings, no bickering. All of us would connect spiritually through the music.

If the version played wasn't performed well, it would *literally* hurt Mum. She was so familiar with the songs that she would find it painful if the tempo or performance didn't do the piece justice. But whenever I found a good version, a great big smile would light up her face.

Unbeknown to her at the time, she helped me find the right rhythm and tempo for one or two of the songs I was working on for Dexys' 2016 album, *Let the Record Show: Dexys Do Irish and Country.*

She was the same with clothes. It really affected her if an outfit wasn't right. I could immediately tell if she felt something I was wearing didn't flatter me. She wasn't rude about it, but she would start with a subtle question, like: 'Is that a new shirt?' I would answer and her indifferent response would give the game away. If the subject of the shirt came up later, she might say something like, 'That colour's not good on ya, love.'

The fact that I could see how it actually hurt her to see colours that she thought didn't complement each other, coupled with the fact that she was now an old lady and did it in such a sweet way, meant that I wasn't offended. She was a lovely thing.

. . .

And now it's five years later: 6 January 2021. Other immediate family members had been sitting with Dad through the previous nights, but his last night on earth turned out to be my first full night with him of those final few days.

He slept peacefully, as I lay on the sofa opposite his bed. At about 6.30 that morning, he opened his eyes to see me doing my Qigong exercises and greeted me with a warm, peaceful smile.

As I'm writing this, I once again remember what I wrote about him in 'All in All (This One Last Wild Waltz)'.

All in all, I'd say things have turned out good.
You still don't smile at me, but then I never thought you would.

But he *did* smile at me that day, and I'm so glad.

He passed later that afternoon. I was holding his hand. He was 102 years and nine months old.

And there had been many other smiles in the previous three or four years, post-stroke.

I would occasionally have him to stay over at my place for a night or two in those last few years. I enjoyed it so much, though he could be high maintenance. I particularly liked putting him to bed, seeing him get comfortable. His pillows had to be just right; he liked *everything* to be just so. A lot like his youngest son!

I would kiss his forehead and tell him I loved him. He would give me a smile and say the same. These were my happiest times with Dad.

I loved holding his hand when we would go out walking, or helping him get dressed. He was like a little boy. He needed me, and I felt grateful for that. His way of asking for help if, for example, he couldn't do up his shoelaces was so sweet. He'd say something like, 'Are you any good on these?'

'Yeah, I'm pretty good on shoelaces, Dad.' I would smile.

Surprisingly, none of my siblings wanted to do Dad's eulogy and it was to fall to me. It seemed ironic – out of all his children, I'd had by far the worst relationship with him. I didn't want to do it, but I agreed, with a couple of provisos.

I told my sisters that as well as eulogising Dad, to give the speech the weight and gravitas it deserved I would need to open with: 'Dad and I clashed a lot, and it's surprising and ironic that it has fallen to me to do this eulogy. It's also an honour. He was an incredible guy.' From then on, it would be all about his achievements, including his meeting and falling in love with Mum, raising a family, his incredible rise in the building trade, and lots of positive and loving recollections from all of us, as per Mum's eulogy. I also planned to explain that Dad was born into and raised in poverty, and that his mother and sister died young from TB. My plan was to end the eulogy with something along the lines of, 'It would be impossible to capture the essence or the impact of John Rowland in a eulogy, no matter how long it went on. He was a phenomenon,' and 'Dad, you were some man. We will never see your like again.'

Or something along those lines that the family might decide on together. I also wanted to add a paragraph saying, 'The expression "once a man, twice a child" was so true for Dad' and had allowed me to get closer to him in a way that I had never been able to do before.

I ran these ideas past my sisters, who had a very different relationship with Dad. They strongly disliked them. I also ran them past my brother Joe. He liked them, but my sisters' voices were loudest. They felt that, because Dad was a proud man, the 'once a man, twice a child' passage denigrated him.

They also disliked the idea of me saying he was born and raised in poverty, saying that he wouldn't have wanted that to be said. My experience was completely different: when we were kids, and in adult life, Dad *often* talked about how poor and desperate his family had been. He spoke of these things with no sense of shame. And to me, the fact that he came from such poverty made his achievements in England all the more remarkable.

It was obvious I wouldn't be able to tell Dad's story truthfully in the eulogy and after much soul-searching, and discussion with one or two close friends, ten days before the funeral, I decided, 'OK, it's best someone else does it.'

As Mum's eulogy had been made up of positive experiences from all of us, I had no reason to think this one would be any different, so I also said, regardless of who does the eulogy, those last years of Dad's life were my only real happy experiences with him, so I want the following passage included:

> Kevin said recently, 'The expression "once a man, twice a child" was particularly true for Dad.' He became such a sweet man in his final, vulnerable years that he was a lot like a little boy – holding his hands out for his wrist shirt buttons to be done up, unsteady on his feet, or holding his leg out so that his shoelaces could be tied. Kevin is very grateful to have spent time with him during this period, where he was able to get close to his dad in a way that he had never been able to before.

Whereas up to that point, my sisters and I had discussed every detail of the funeral arrangements together, I wasn't privy to any discussions after that, about who should say the eulogy or how they should be briefed or not.

In short, after running around trying to find out what was happening, I learned at 10.30pm the night before the funeral that the passage

I wanted in was not going to be included. What most hurt me was not that the passage I wanted in was going to be excluded, it was that I felt I had been given the runaround.

I realised that I couldn't attend.

I know that my dad would have liked us all to be together on that day, but the way I saw it was Dad was at peace now. What was important to me was that I act with dignity. And I wouldn't have had any if I'd gone to the funeral. I don't regret that decision.

Instead, just before the cemetery workers filled in my dad's grave, I sang 'Danny Boy' – as was his wish – in a beautiful close little gathering, made up of my daughter and my three grandchildren. We all hugged as I sang.

> Oh, Danny boy,
> The pipes, the pipes are calling
> From glen to glen and down the mountain side.
> The summer's gone and all the flowers are dying,
> 'Tis you, 'tis you must go and I must bide.
> But come ye back when summer's in the meadow
> Or when the valley's hushed and white with snow,
> 'Tis I'll be here in sunshine or in shadow,
> Oh, Danny boy, oh, Danny boy,
> I love you so.

I couldn't sing properly because my voice was full of tears, but I did my best.

I'm going somewhere better

Now it's February 2024. I'm in a Thailand hospital and my kidney function levels are failing at an alarming rate. The doctor can find no reason for the fall. It's scary.

After some treatment, the levels start to rise, just a little, and the hospital says that as long as I commit to doing certain things, they can discharge me to a nearby retreat centre. I'm glad. I do as they suggest. On my next visit to the hospital, the levels have risen a little more. The kidney specialist is pleased.

A couple of weeks later, I return, feeling optimistic, only to find the kidney function levels have severely dropped. They are now lower than ever. If they go down by another five percentage points, my only options are a kidney transplant or being kept alive on a dialysis machine. Both are non-starters for me. I'd rather bow out. I'm scared and I feel very down for a couple of days while I process what's happening.

After a discussion with Walter, one of the senior instructors at the retreat centre, comes the faith that if I'm to leave my body, I will be OK. I feel the certainty that I'm going somewhere better.

I start to think about my daughter and grandchildren, and I am comforted that they will get regular money from my royalties, which will hopefully continue. My main concern now is making sure all my affairs are sorted out, as well as the realisation that I need to make a funeral guest list for my daughter. I have many friends that she's never met.

I feel grateful for all I've been through and survived and mostly grown from. I'm grateful to all the people who have helped me. I'm glad that I won't have to face the difficulty and pain of living for much longer. I start to understand how the musician Wilko Johnson felt when he was told he had only months to live – relief. I feel the same.

I start to tell a few friends. I can hear the panic in their voices and even their text messages. But that's not how I feel. I start to get irritated by their over-positive messages (denial) designed to buck me up, or suggestions on what I need to do to recover (advice). They don't realise that I'm doing everything I can. Plus, as I learned recently, when someone gives me unwanted advice, it overwhelms me and cuts me off from the vital energy that allows me to make my own intuitive decisions. I feel stifled, just as I did when I was a kid.

I know that I want to be cremated in Ireland. That's where I've always felt most at home. I think about all the friends that I want to attend my funeral – many of them British, and who have never experienced the beauty and magic of rural, small-town Ireland.

I start to feel a little better. Then I get an avalanche of messages from various friends, asking me what function level my kidneys are at. When I write back, telling them the admittedly worryingly low figure (20), I realise that recounting this number brings my mood *right* down. I'm lying in bed all day and night, worrying about my health, and death, apart from when I'm at the hospital for tests, which is equally anxiety-inducing. It's always: *will my levels be up or down?*

I see that talking about what's wrong with me isn't helping. In fact, it's harming me. I text my friends and tell them: 'With the best will in the world, please don't ask me about my kidneys. Thinking about them makes me fall into negativity and everything gets worse. I appreciate your concern, and I will for sure advise you of any significant change, but right now, I need to *not* focus on my kidney levels.'

I talk to the kidney specialist. I have some serious questions. 'Will my passing be painful if I don't accept the treatment?' She assures me it won't. I will just slip into a 'nice dream', she says – a coma – and then pass away. That's reassuring. I speak again to Walter. He gives me some good advice: 'Whenever you start to worry about your health, just say to yourself, "I'm happy, healthy and wealthy." Just keep repeating that. You will feel better. Worrying will make everything worse.'

I also speak to my homeopath and friend, Trevor. He says the same thing: 'Your body is incredible; trust that it can heal.'

I take this on and start to feel a little more positive.

I force myself to do Qigong every morning, sometimes sitting on a chair when I feel too weak to move, and sometimes only for a few minutes. A couple of people at the retreat centre comment that I am looking less ill. Previously, they were concerned. One guy, well meaningly but bluntly, had suggested that I make my peace with anyone I had unfinished business with.

I start to put on a little weight (I had been down to nine stone). My kidney levels go up – just a little, but they are going up. The doctors tell me I'm well enough to travel home to London without danger. I keep up this positive thinking; sometimes I forget, but it's definitely working.

It's at that point I realise the depth of my negative thinking generally, and how it's so easy for me to slip back into the darkness. I start to apply the same positive affirmations in other areas of my life.

There are many times, when I'm already swamped in negativity and/or worrying about health before I can catch it. But I am definitely seeing the benefits of thinking positively.

. . .

I start rehearsing with the band, and we play at Glastonbury to rave reviews. My anxiety leading up to it is off the scale. The *Guardian* newspaper asks all the artists performing what they have learned from their Glastonbury experience. I say, 'I see clearly now that anxiety has always been by far the biggest problem in my life.' From the moment the show was confirmed, I was worrying about it. I've always been the same way.

But we *did* the show! And there were plenty of significant moments when I felt happy to be singing, and I know that I generally sang well.

It's July 2024. I get my kidney levels tested again. They are moving in the right direction. There is still a long way to go, but I am determined to keep positive and not slip into victim / self-pity mode.

It's up to me now: positive or negative.

· · ·

Dexys' US manager Brad Misell tells me that the world's currently most successful songwriter and producer Jack Antonoff (who has written and produced for Taylor Swift and Lana Del Rey among others) has said in an interview that Dexys are his favourite songwriters. I read the article and think he must mean another Dexys. But no, he means us. I then get the message that he is playing in London with his band, Bleachers, and would love me to come to their show. Mike from Dexys and I go along. We go backstage. Jack says, pointing at me, 'I owe this guy royalties.'

I go, 'What?'

'Come on, man. You are a massive influence. We have a saying, when we're in the studio, "Play it like Dexys".'

'Really?'

'Yeah, man.'

Wow.

'Is it the old stuff you like?' I ask.

'All of it, man. I love all your stuff.'

It feels a bit like a dream. It's so amazing to be appreciated by someone so talented.

'Would you like to have a mess around in the studio?' Jack says.

'What?'

I'm floored. Jack notices this and thinks I'm being falsely modest and says, 'Come on, man. Are you kidding me?'

'No – I'm shocked.'

Jack shouts out to his manager, 'Jamie, fix it up for Kevin and me to get together in the studio.'

'Sure,' Jamie says.

The recording session doesn't materialise, but it doesn't matter. I don't care. I've had the genuine affirmation. It feels so good.

· · ·

Soon afterwards, I finish writing a new song with Sean Read, called 'Once A Man, Twice A Child'. I think it's one of the best things I've ever written and decide to send the demo to renowned music producer and film-score composer David Holmes, who mentioned a while ago that he'd like to do something with me.

A couple of days later, I get a message back: 'Holy shit! This is incredible! We could turn it into a spiritual classic! So moving, so hopeful! Brilliant song.'

We speak on the phone and make plans to record it. In the same conversation, David tells me how much Dexys means to him.

'I have Dexys days, when I listen to Dexys all day,' he says.

I can't help but feel positive about Dexys' past and future.

State of grace

One of best things about singing and performing is that, as I said previously, I can reach what I think of as a state of grace – an unsurpassable feeling where everything just flows. I'm no longer *doing* it. It's all just happening. Anxiety is gone, the audience are captivated, and I know I can take them in any direction I want. That feeling is priceless.

From the start of Dexys in 1978 to now, I've really tried to make great music. Occasionally that hasn't worked out but, whenever I've been active, I've pretty much always given it my all. Which is why I find it difficult when I hear people enthuse about a gig they saw in 1981 or '82 while ignoring the subsequent journey we've been on. It's natural to reminisce about something that happened all those years ago, but albums like *One Day I'm Going to Soar* and *The Feminine Divine* are right up there with what we did in the eighties, as tracks like 'Nowhere is Home' and 'My Submission' attest. Similarly, the live performances of recent years are on another level compared to our shows back then. Of course, Dexys had the urgency of youth in those days, and it worked really well, but it would be ridiculous to try and recreate that now.

In the same way that I feel I am much more myself now as a person, the Dexys of recent years are realising their true creative potential. I always had theatrical ideas in the eighties, but I didn't have the wherewithal or confidence to realise them. Now nothing is holding me back. I have the courage to really shine, and that's what our live performances and records are all about. In Dexys now, I write about things I couldn't possibly have contemplated in the eighties. I didn't have the experience. Our old stuff is relevant, I know it turned out well, and I often enjoy performing it, adding new interpretations, but our new stuff is where I'm really at.

A music journalist recently made a big deal about so many musicians having passed through Dexys. That was missing the point. Yes, if you compare Dexys to a traditional band, it looks as though we have failed to retain a constant line-up. But Dexys wasn't a traditional band. In fact, it wasn't really a band at all. It was always about the music and ideas, not the personnel.

And while I'm not a solo artist, since the demise of the first incarnation, I've had total control, over everything. And even in the first line-up, I made sure I got my vision across. We've had a different line-up for virtually every album and I'm the common dominator. Many great musicians have come along and contributed to the whole, and pretty much all of the comings and goings were to the betterment of the music. If I'd had to stick with the same musicians, I would feel incredibly trapped and stifled. I don't know what Dexys was, or is, but it wasn't, or isn't, a band.

As well as inspiring me, working with others gives me discipline. If I know someone is coming round to work on a song, I will be ready and will probably have done extra work in advance. But if no one is coming round, I probably won't bother doing anything.

I can still have a love/hate relationship with doing music, which stems from the feeling that I have to keep proving myself by writing and performing, otherwise I feel like I'm not good enough as a person. This pisses me off and makes me down tools, which explains my periods of inactivity. But I always feel better when I'm singing and working on music.

Recently, when my literary agent, Matthew, read the first draft of this book, he said, 'It's great, but you don't acknowledge your talent anywhere in it.'

I told him, 'I don't think I have any talent: each time I write a good song, it's like I don't know how it happened. It's a miracle, and I've no idea how the next one will come about.'

I *will* say that I think my singing of late is at least as good as it's ever been, much helped by my great vocal coach, Kim Chandler.

I feel grateful that I've been involved in the process of making music. It's something I could only dream about when I was a kid. And there is no way that would have happened without my gifted song-writing partners: the talent and vision of Kevin Archer, the depth of Celtic soul brother Big Jimmy Paterson, the belief and honesty of Billy Adams, the discipline and talent of Helen O'Hara, and the musicality, commitment and connection of Sean Read and Mike Timothy.

I'm grateful that I get a decent living out of songs that I co-wrote/wrote and recorded, and that the main core of the Dexys are OK and still alive.

I'm particularly grateful for the love of my lifelong friends Jim and Sandra Paterson. They are the most incredible people and have always been there when I've needed them. Similarly, the warmth of the mighty Kevin Archer.

These days, I'm even grateful for being a cocaine addict. Cocainism smashed me to pieces and recovery from it forced me to confront the facade that was me. It brought me into a new way of living that is the best I've ever known. People don't change unless they have to. I had to.

I'm still very much a work in progress, but I can say that I'm a much better person than I ever was. I feel much less need to try and be someone else. And I'm making a point of standing more upright to combat the old feeling that I had to apologise for my existence with my posture.

Right now, creativity is flowing, and I'm grateful for that, but peace of mind comes first. Without that, life isn't worth living. Previously, I didn't know what peace was. I hadn't experienced it, except briefly on drugs. Now I am familiar with it and I have more happiness than I've ever had.

In earlier life I picked up the notion that everyone should get married and settle down, but it's never really felt right. I'm probably less close to settling down now than ever. And deep down I don't really care. My problem was that I thought I had to be like everyone else.

Also, I thought I had to think long term. I tried to do that, but it doesn't work for me. I find it suffocating and reductive. My life seems better when I just let it happen. I have no idea where I'll be or what I'll be doing in five years' time, and I'm good with that.

My life has been one hell of a trip, and I wouldn't want to repeat it. But I guess, to the best of my ability, I did what Elvis suggested, I *followed that dream, wherever that dream may lead*.

And I'm glad I did.

Acknowledgements

Lorna Russell and Michelle Warner at Ebury, you have been really great. I so much appreciate it. The book has gone to another level. Also, to Patsy O' Neill, Shelise Robertson, Vanessa Milton and all at Ebury.

My reader friends, Máire Fahey, Paolo Hewitt, Ted Kessler, and latterly, Chris 'Cross' Keenan. Thanks for your encouragement and feeback.

Special thanks also to Máire for coming up with the title, *Bless Me Father*.

Much gratitude also to Danny Morrison, Chris Clifton, John Rowland, Nigel Templeman RIP, James Burke, Pat Mahon, Ronnie Harris, Sean Read, George Russo, Mike Timothy, Christos Tolera, Chris Sullivan, and Elvis Costello for *Allison* lyrics permission.

Much thanks also to my agent, Matthew Hamilton, especially for connecting me with Ebury.

Not forgetting, Alan Stephenson, Amy Ridler, Azeer Ariff, Brad Misell, Charlotte Harris, Chris Fowler, Christine Harkness, Claire Harper, Daniel Scott, David Holmes, Ed McDonald, Jeff Barrett, Larry Coles, Lucy Morgan, Matthew Maxey, Nick Ford, Patsy Sprice, Paul Gorman, Paul Sproston, Pete Barrett, Sarah Hodson, Sonia Tiernan, Steve Homer, Sue Humphrey, Tim Vigon and Toby Harris.

Thanks to all of my recovery guides: Paddy, Ralph, Mick, Mike, Dan, Tim, Jackie, Jamie, Phil.

Image Credits

Plate Section 1

Mike Laye (Images 12, 13, 14, 17)

David Corio (Image 16)

Brian Cooke (Image 19)

Harry Goodwin (Image 21)

Plate Section 2

Kim Knott (Images 1, 2, 3)

Kevin Cummins (Image 4)

PA Images / Alamy Stock photo (Image 8)

Andy Sheppard (Image 10)

Duncan Bryceland / Shutterstock (Image 11)

Amy T. Zielinski (Image 12)

Jake Walters (Image 13, 14)

Sandra Vijandi (Image 17)

Joe Lepper (Image 18)

Nicky Johnston (Image 19)

Illustration on page 216 by Clarkevanmeurs

Images on pages 345 and 392 by Nicky Johnston

Song Credits

'Runaway' – Del Shannon (Shannon, Crook)

'Follow That Dream' – Elvis Presley (Weisman, Wise)

'King Of The Whole World' – Elvis Presley (Roberts, Batchelor)

'Things We Said Today' – the Beatles (Lennon, McCartney)

'All My Loving' – the Beatles (Lennon, McCartney)

'Concrete And Clay' – Unit 4 + 2 (Moeller, Parker)

'Dedicated To The One I Love' – Mamas and Papas (Pauling, Bass)

'Breakin' Down The Walls Of Heartache' – Johnny Johnson and the
     Bandwagon (Randell, Linzer)

'Everybody's Talkin'' – Harry Nilsson (Neil)

'It's All In The Game' – Tommy Edwards (Sigman, Dawes)

'Sad-Eyed Lady Of The Lowlands' – Bob Dylan (Dylan)

'You Wear It Well' – Rod Stewart (Stewart, Quittenton)

'You're A Lady' – Peter Skellern (Skellern)

'Welcome Home' – Peters & Lee (Dupre, Beldone)

'Moon River' – Audrey Hepburn (Mancini, Mercer)

'I'll Be There' – Jackson 5 (Gordy Jr., West, Davis, Hutch)

'My Friend, The Sun' – Streetwalkers (Whitney, Chapman)

'Parade Of Broken Hearts' – Ned Miller (Miller)

'Madame George' – Van Morrison (Morrison)

'Caravan' – Van Morrison (Morrison)

'Alison' – Elvis Costello (Costello), published by Sideways Songs, admin-
     istered by BMG Rights Management (UK) Ltd. – BMG Gold Songs
     (ASCAP)

'Danny Boy' – Elise Griffin (Weatherly)

'When I Leave The World Behind' (Berlin)